ABOUT THE AUTHOR

When Jenny Cathcart travelled to Senegal in 1984 as a member of the BBC TV film crew that produced *The Africans*, she met with the rising star Youssou N'Dour. It was a fateful meeting which led to her abiding interest in African music and culture. When the term 'world music' was coined in London, Jenny was a producer on the pioneering TV series *Rhythms of the World*. In 1995, she proposed an African summer season on BBC Two and produced two of the programmes: the first ever African Prom and the documentary *Africa's Rock 'n' Roll Years*, a social and musical history of post-independence Africa. Ten years later, in 2005, she was series producer and director of BBC Four's six-part TV series, *The African Rock 'n' Roll Years*. While working at Youssou N'Dour's head office in Dakar, she managed the artists Cheikh Lô, Orchestra Baobab, and Pape and Cheikh.

I am pleased to dedicate this page to Ragnhild Ek, film-maker, music producer, communications expert and tireless worker for humanitarian causes who was keen to support the publication of *Notes from Africa* because of her love for African music.

NOTES

from

AFRICA

A musical journey with
YOUSSOU N'DOUR

JENNY CATHCART

unbound

This edition first published in 2019

Unbound
Level 1, Devonshire House
One Mayfair Place
London W 1 J 8 A J
www.unbound.com

ISBN 978-1-78965-048-8 (ebook)
ISBN 978-1-78965-047-1 (pbk)

Text designed and set in Minion by Tetragon, London
Printed in Great Britain by Clays Ltd, Elcograf S.p.A.

1 3 5 7 9 8 6 4 2

In Memory of Fama Sow Cama

SUPER PATRONS

CONTENTS

PART IV: A CONTINENT IN CONCERT

NOTES
from
AFRICA

1. *Youssou with the author.*

PREFACE

I first travelled to Africa in 1984 as a researcher for the BBC television series *The Africans*. In Senegal, Youssou N'Dour, the new pop idol, was already the subject of gossip, rumour and hype. Women loved him. Youngsters idolised him. '*You Do Nit*,' they would say, meaning 'Youssou is more than a human being!'

I had been brought up in Ireland on Beethoven and the Beatles but was thoroughly mesmerised by what Peter Gabriel called the 'liquid velvet voice', the scintillating *sabar* drums, the kaleidoscopic charm of Youssou's modern dance music. Furthermore, I was so taken with Senegal and the Senegalese that my BBC colleagues began to call the country 'Jenegal'!

Youssou introduced me to African music just as a new musical phenomenon, termed world music, was beginning to emerge. He and I were to become close friends and collaborators in promoting his own international career as well as those of other stars from Senegal, including Cheikh Lô and Orchestra Baobab. As one of the leading and most charismatic figures in modern African music, Youssou was the perfect guide to what was for me a thrilling musical journey.

At the dawn of the new millennium, Youssou was named 'African Artist of the Century' by *fRoots* magazine, and in 2007 *Time* listed him as one of the hundred most influential people in the world. He has appeared at high-profile concerts including Live Aid and the Free Nelson Mandela concert at Wembley. He took part in Amnesty International's *Human Rights Now!* world tour alongside Sting, Peter Gabriel, Bruce Springsteen and Tracy Chapman. With Bono and Bob Geldof, he joined the ranks of those lobbying for debt relief for African countries. His collaborations with Peter Gabriel, Alicia Keys, Deep Forest, Annie Lennox, Ryuichi Sakamoto and others raised his global profile, and in 2005 he won a Grammy award for his album *Egypt*. In 2011 he received an honorary doctorate from Yale University and two years later, following in the footsteps of Bob Dylan, Ray Charles, Quincy Jones, Miriam Makeba and other major artists, he was awarded the prestigious Polar Music Prize.

Having chosen to remain in Senegal, Youssou has succeeded as both an artist and a businessman. In 2010, when President Wade threatened to remain in power for a third term, Youssou entered politics and became a candidate in the 2012 presidential election. Though he failed in his bid, he succeeded in his aim of helping to remove President Wade and was appointed Minister of Culture, then Minister of Tourism and today retains a ministerial post as a special adviser to President Macky Sall.

As a television producer on the BBC's pioneering world music series *Rhythms of the World*, and as series producer of *The African Rock 'n' Roll Years*, I had the opportunity to work with other great African stars like Ali Farka Touré, Baaba Maal, Salif Keita and the Guinean group Bembeya Jazz National. Youssou N'Dour provided a vital link to all of them.

In this book I cover the rise of world music and the role that African musicians have played in it, most particularly those from Senegal and West Africa but also leading names from around the continent. More generally, I explain the modern musical styles that have developed in Africa since the 1960s, when many countries gained independence from colonial rule. Stars like Franco and Papa Wemba (Congo), Miriam Makeba, Hugh Masekela and Abdullah Ibrahim (South Africa), Thomas Mapfumo (Zimbabwe), Angélique Kidjo and Wally Badarou (Benin), Manu Dibango (Cameroon), King Sunny Ade (Ghana) Fela Kuti (Nigeria) and Khaled (Algeria) blazed a trail for the next generation of talented musicians whose music reflects the exuberance and confidence of their emerging continent. The journey has been enchanting and enriching, the music mesmerising and memorable.

JENNY CATHCART
March 2019

Part I

VOYAGE OF DISCOVERY

2. *Panorama, Dakar.*

3. *Seascape, Dakar.*

1
DAKAR, SENEGAL

I have heard it said that Dakar took its name from *dakhar*, the fruit of the tamarind tree that the Egyptians used to darken the faces of their mummies. In the city which I saw for the first time in 1984, I recognised Ryszard Kapuściński's description: 'A beautiful coastal city, pastel-colored, picturesque, laid out on a promontory amid beaches and terraces, slightly resembling Naples, the residential areas of Marseilles, the posh suburbs of Barcelona.'[1] The sea was limpid, the air pure, the gardens lush with billowing bougainvillea and hibiscus flowers, golden yellow and ruby red. On the seafront at sunset, lone figures, silhouetted against the skyline, sat gazing at the ocean, seeking solace or space, soothed by the rhythm of the breaking waves. The warmth of the welcome, combined with the elegance, grace and charm of the Senegalese people, made a deep and lasting impression.

In 1902, when Dakar was still only a settlement of four hundred buildings, it replaced Saint-Louis in the north as the capital of French West Africa. Following an outbreak of cholera in 1914, the French *colons* moved the indigenous population from the airy Plateau, the old neighbourhoods, down to marshy flatlands around the bay of Soumbédioune. The new quarter, called Medina, where Youssou N'Dour was born, was laid out in geometric grids, creating streets with numbers and no names. Senegalese from various ethnic groups lived in wooden houses, which would later be replaced by concrete structures. Dakar became the capital and administrative centre of Senegal in 1958.

In the years following Senegal's independence in 1960, life was for living *sénégalaisement*. On Sunday afternoons, citizens packed picnic baskets and strolled through the streets of Point E and the residences of Fann on their way to the Corniche and the beaches of Ouakam, Yoff or Ngor. Gradually, as severe drought hit the Sahel region, the economic landscape changed and more and more people migrated from the countryside to the city. In 1986 the entire population of Senegal was 6 million; by 2006 the same number of people lived in Dakar alone and the population of the country as a whole had risen to 12 million.[2]

There are currently some 16 million people in Senegal, 60 per cent of whom are aged twenty-five and under, and the once placid, airy capital city has, in the space of thirty years, become overcrowded and polluted. As the centre of Dakar known as the Plateau grew more and more congested, developers moved down the peninsula towards the Pointe des Almadies, the westernmost tip of Africa, and then further along the coast. In the name of progress, access to the seashore has been blocked by a modern dual carriageway, while luxury hotels and shopping malls interrupt the sea views. The once fashionable bungalows at SICAP Amitié, Baobab and Liberté are being razed to the ground and replaced by high-rise apartment buildings, offices and shops. Swish bars and nightclubs on and near the so-called 'millionaire's mile' on the Route des Almadies attract night revellers, including inter-national footballers and trendy young jet-setters, while the outer suburbs of Dieuppeul, Derklé, Pikine, Guédiawaye and Parcelles Assainies are already overpopulated. Back in the city centre, at Dakar's Place de l'Indépendance and close by cool ice-cream parlours and the Marquise patisserie, disabled beggars take up their positions outside the main banks. Then there are the barefoot street children, scantily clothed and underfed, who can be seen with their tin cans, waiting for customers at the petrol station in Ouakam. Sadly, the money they earn goes straight to their marabout masters.

The word 'marabout' is derived from 'El Morabbatim', which in Arabic means 'the one who lives in a monastery', and the term is mostly used to describe Senegal's religious leaders, whose followers are called *talibés*.

The topography of Medina has changed over the years as the area has become increasingly cosmopolitan. The first immigrant families moved to Senegal from French colonial territories like Syria and Lebanon. They settled in regional towns such as Kaolack or Diourbel to trade in peanuts, a cash crop introduced by the French in the 1840s, and then they came to Dakar.

Today wealthy Malian and Guinean families, who prefer to invest in Dakar rather than in their home countries, own high-rise buildings financed by the money they make working in Europe or America.

On Gorée, a small island just off the Dakar coast, where Portuguese, Dutch and English slave traders set up trading posts, the original House of Slaves, built in 1776, is preserved as a sad memorial to the millions of Africans who passed through its 'door of no return' on their way to the Americas. It is a place of

4. *Street children in Dakar.*

pilgrimage, especially for African American visitors, who feel at once the anguish of their ancestors described by Maya Angelou as 'the legions, sold by sisters, stolen by brothers, bought by strangers, enslaved by the greedy and betrayed by history.'[3]

When in January 1974 Michael Jackson travelled to Senegal to perform with the Jackson Five, he visited Gorée. The plight of those slaves, some of whom could have been his ancestors, and an appreciation of their background and bravery, made a definite impact on the young star, who later wrote, 'It was a visit to Senegal that made us realise how fortunate we were and how our African heritage had helped to make us what we were. We visited an old abandoned slave camp at Gore [sic] Island. We were so moved. The African people had given us gifts of courage and endurance that we couldn't hope to repay.'[4] Pope John Paul II and Nelson Mandela have visited the island, and in June 2013 the President of the United States, Barack Obama, was photographed with his family contemplating the ocean at the symbolic spot where slaves took their last look at Africa.

5. *Traditional house in Medina.*

8. *Gorée Island.*

The island retains vestiges of its colonial architecture, but many of the buildings have fallen into disuse. Some finely restored houses with sea views are owned by wealthy families such as the Schlumbergers, bankers and film producers from France. The island's small Catholic church was the location for the marriage of film director John Singleton (*Boyz n the Hood*) to actress Akosua Busia (*The Color Purple*), daughter of former Ghanian president Kofi Busia.

Gorée is well known for its art and textiles. It became home to the sculptor Moustapha Dimé and the painter Souleymane Keita, both of whom have now sadly passed away. Mody Kane, whose mother made the island's first commercial dolls, signs his contemporary glass paintings 'Le Nègre de Gorée'. The Cape Verdean seamstress works upstairs in her garret while women gather to gossip in Bigué's curiosity shop, and others pass their days working coloured skeins of thread on pure white cotton to produce the embroidery designs that are typical of the island. Behind burnt ochre walls draped with hibiscus fronds and bougainvillea are

7. *Bigué Ndoye in her curiosity shop.*

8. *The House of Slaves.*

secret gardens, balmy with jasmine, which open up to the public once a year during the art festival *Regards sur Cours*.

As well as the historic House of Slaves, a museum dedicated to Senegalese women is approached through a quiet alleyway. Named after Stanislas de Boufflers, French governor of Senegal from 1785 to 1787, the Chevalier de Boufflers hotel and restaurant, distinguished by its terracotta red exterior, overlooks the harbour where small boys duck and dive to retrieve coins thrown into the water by visitors arriving on the ferry from Dakar.

The overall atmosphere is one of peace and tranquillity, for there are no cars or bicycles on Gorée. At night, after the last ferry has returned to Dakar, the swish of the ocean waves is broken only by the sound of residents chatting on their verandas in the cool of the evening.

2
A NEW DAWN

Back in 1986, the late Professor Ali Mazrui noted in the nine-part BBC series *The Africans: A Triple Heritage* that Africa had absorbed several shock encounters with the Western world. First there had been slavery, then colonisation, then independence, and now democracy. What took 2,000 years to happen in Europe had taken just a couple of generations in Africa.[1]

Following years of poverty, drought and war, Africa is starting to become, in the words of George Soros, the Hungarian-born financial business magnate and philanthropist, 'one of the few bright spots on the gloomy global economic horizon.'[2] It really does seem as if clever, inventive, enterprising Africans have everything to play for, everything to gain. In March 2012, *The Times* carried optimistic reports about Africa. According to its contributors, Africa has a new generation of leaders with alternative ways of looking at their situation. In the newspaper's opinion column, former British prime minister Tony Blair noted how, in the first ten years of the new millennium, six of the world's ten fastest-growing economies were African, and that these economies were developing faster than East Asian ones. Sixty million Africans now have an income of more than $3,000 per annum, and the middle class is expanding.[3] Mobile phones have also transformed trade. Malaria rates have fallen by a fifth, and HIV infection rates have plummeted.[4] Africa is moving forward at a dizzying pace.

All the same, the rush to make money has led to corruption, and in many African countries the gap grows dangerously between the haves and the have-nots. In May 2014, Bob Geldof told TV journalist Jon Snow that he believed it was the inequalities within

Nigerian society which had contributed to the rise of the terrorist organisation Boko Haram.[5]

Presidential elections

At the turn of the twenty-first century, when Youssou N'Dour was the leading pop star in Senegal, if not in the whole of Africa, his home fans were wont to shout 'Youssou for president.' When asked by journalists if he had any ambition to enter politics, Youssou replied, 'I think my music is stronger than politics.'[6] But in 2011, the same momentous year that people power aimed to topple rigid regimes in North Africa, Senegal was struggling to preserve its reputation as a model for democracy in Africa and Youssou felt concerned enough to openly oppose the re-election of President Abdoulaye Wade.

In the year 2000, following forty years of government by the Socialist Party, Abdoulaye Wade of the Democratic Socialist Party (PDS) was elected on a pledge for change. Outgoing president Abdou Diouf gracefully conceded defeat and left Senegal to live in Paris, where he was appointed general secretary of La Francophonie, the Association of Francophone Countries. Soon Wade, a clever economist, began developing a free market economy, mobilising his contacts in countries like Korea, China and the Arab states to attract business and investment to Senegal. His policies, labelled Wadism, allowed the rich to get richer and the poor poorer. In 2007, as Wade prepared for re-election, money talked, and many Senegalese, including those living abroad, received money or gifts as an incentive to vote for the incumbent president. Ministers and ex-ministers in the Wade government profited from the 'sale' of lucrative contracts to shrewd contractors who offered bribes. This may go some way to explaining how a new breed of young Senegalese jet-setters could afford to drive around in expensive cars, spend 300,000 West African CFA francs (around £400) in

Dakar's Duplex nightclub on New Year's Eve or 30,000 francs (approximately £40) per person for Sunday lunch on the terraces of a chic seaside restaurant like Terrou-Bi. Dakar had become a veritable El Dorado, a destination for rich individuals from other African countries, some of them sons of African presidents, who, rather than deposit their 'dirty' money in European banks, invested it in lucrative property developments in Senegal.

Architect Pierre Goudiaby Atépa, whose award-winning design for BCEAO (the Central Bank of West African States) dominates the Dakar skyline, was appointed by Wade to oversee new millennium projects, including the modernisation of the Corniche coast road, the building of a toll trunk road out of Dakar and a new airport.

The Monument de la Renaissance, a tribute to African resistance, is an enormous bronze statue depicting an African nuclear family. Constructed by North Korean firm Mansudae Overseas Projects, it was conceived by Wade himself after he rejected a design by the internationally renowned Senegalese sculptor Ousmane Sow. Some have described it as a symbol of Wade's megalomania, since it cost a staggering 50 billion West African CFA francs (around £72 million). Standing 162 feet tall, it is a few inches higher than the Statue of Liberty in New York and, being strategically placed near the twin hills known as Les Mamelles, is clearly visible from many points around the city. On the approach to Dakar's first airport, the heroic figures of an African husband and wife cradling their child appear dramatically positioned, plumb centre above the main terminal building. However, far from being a modern or attractive structure worthy of its renaissance aspirations, it might look more at home on a mid-twentieth-century Soviet esplanade.

Wade and Goudiaby also planned a cultural park to house what they called 'The Seven Wonders of Dakar'.[7] The first two of these, a magnificent national theatre and the Museum of Black Civilisations, were financed and built by the Chinese. A concert hall, a school of architecture, a gallery of modern art, a national library and a depository for the nation's archives were also planned. Goudiaby, who believes in building dreams as well as concrete constructions, told me in 2009,

> Not all Americans are rich, but America has become the richest continent in the world because its people lived out their fantasies by building skyscrapers and Disneyland. People there know that if they work hard they can have anything they want, and it should be the same for we Africans.

Another event designed to boost the president's prestige was the third World Festival of Black Arts, FESMAN (the Festival Mondial des Arts Nègres). Wade seemed determined to emulate President Léopold Sédar Senghor, who initiated the first of these festivals in Dakar in 1966. Senghor invited 2,500 leading black artists from all over Africa and the diaspora, including his friend Aimé Césaire, whose theories of Negritude he supported, to celebrate their common heritage in Senegal. From America came choreographers Alvin Ailey and Katherine Dunham, writer Langston Hughes, jazz musician Duke Ellington and the singer Marion Williams. Representatives from thirty independent African countries and seven countries with significant African diasporic populations attended the festival.[8] The second festival, Festac '77, took place in Lagos in 1977 and featured artists including Stevie Wonder, Sun Ra, Miriam Makeba, Osibisa, Franco, Bembeya Jazz and Fela Kuti. The American jazzman Randy Weston, who was also there, commented, 'It was absolutely astonishing. And just imagine all that music. It was one of the most extraordinary experiences of my life.'[9] FESMAN, which had been postponed four times and taken six years to plan, finally took place in December 2010 with the president's daughter, Sindjely Wade, as festival director.

The scale and scope of the 2010 programme were staggering: 130 tons of stage and sound equipment were specially shipped in from France, and artists from eighty countries, including a large

9. *FESMAN poster.*

10. *Press photo from FESMAN.*

delegation from Brazil, performed in various locations – mainly in Dakar, but also in the northern city of Saint-Louis and other regional centres. Headed by Akon, the superstar son of Senegal, and former Fugee Wyclef Jean, the stellar line-up of singers, musicians and rap artists included representatives from every country in Africa and all the top names in African music: Khaled, King Sunny Ade, Hugh Masekela, Angélique Kidjo, Alpha Blondy and Youssou. There were also many leading artists from the diaspora, among them Kassav', Margareth Menezes, Chucho Valdés, and famous American jazzmen Stanley Clarke, Marcus Miller, Randy Weston and Archie Shepp. According to Aziz Dieng, who programmed the music, the festival aimed to showcase the diversity and vitality of black music and its influences throughout the world.

A sublime concert given by Cameroonian bass player and singer Richard Bona was one of a series of shows staged in a stunning open-air auditorium specially erected in Dakar at the foot of the new Monument de la Renaissance. Bona represents a younger generation of African musicians who are forging a breezy new world jazz fusion. Born in 1967 in the village of Minta in Cameroon, where his mother was the church organist, he was a precocious musician, playing first balafon and then guitar, fashioning strings from bicycle brake cables for the first one he ever played. He was discovered by a French businessman in Douala who allowed him access to his vast collection of vinyl records, mostly jazz, and the first album Richard picked out was, significantly, by American bassist Jaco Pastorius. In Paris, Manu Dibango took the fledgling jazzman under his wing. A few years later Bona moved to New York, where he owns the jazz club Bonafide and where he has collaborated with top performers including Stevie Wonder, Mike Stern, Pat Metheny and John Legend, all of whom acknowledge a new energy in his music, a keen sense of rhythm and an unmistakable spirituality in his approach. In Dakar, Bona revealed himself to be a warm, jocular and witty performer, making instant and easy contact with his audience. I remember thinking how extraordinary

11. *Richard Bona.*

it was that a young boy from a remote village in West Africa could, in a matter of years, make his way to the global stage by virtue of his incredible talent. And of course the same is true of so many of the other stars who appear in these pages, not least Youssou, who grew up in a poorer part of Dakar. Bona himself marvels at his life's journey so far:

> As a kid my dream started behind my house playing balafon all day long listening to nature and looking at the forest. I remember telling my friend Fan Thomas while looking at planes in the sky, 'I will fly in one of those one day.' He looked at me smiling and said, 'You can't even get to Yaounde! (the capital).' We were 8–9 years old.[10]

Like Bona, many of those young artists who appeared at FESMAN are based in New York. The Rwandan singer Somi came to the festival with her trio, which included the talented Senegalese guitarist Hervé Samb. Moroccan-born Malika Zarra was accompanied by her long-time collaborator, Senegalese bass player Mamadou Ba, as well as musicians from France, Surinam, Guadeloupe and Morocco. Malika's compatriot, Hassan Hakmoun, performed with a similarly eclectic band.

While FESMAN, which allegedly cost 70 billion West African CFA francs (approximately £85 million), was remarkable for the sheer number of outstanding concerts and for the quality of its art exhibitions and fashion shows staged by the sea against the sumptuous backdrop of Le Corbusier's former Meridien hotel (once patronised by Mick Jagger and his friends), it completely failed to receive the international press and media coverage it deserved.

According to rap artist Didier Awadi, the problem was Senegal's lack of coherent cultural policy or administrative infrastructure for the arts. All the same, for those who took part in FESMAN – and for those lucky enough to attend the shows – it was a magnificent event.

Added to this lack of support for the arts, Awadi feels sure that an elite has taken hold of the country's money, which is not circulating as it should. Food prices continue to rise, and life is becoming more and more difficult for most people.

12. Berber Taxi, *Malika Zarra.*

13. *Senegalese designer Mame Fagueye
Ba's fashion show at FESMAN.*

On the surface, one might assume that Senegal is a rich country, not a developing one. Strolling along the modern dual carriageway that borders Dakar's palm-fringed seafront, one is amazed by the number of four-by-fours that pass by, but it is impossible to ignore the figures in black rags sleeping face down on the pavement. My long-time Senegalese friend, Arame, put it this way: 'There are those of us who are dancing and those who are crying.'

Becoming more aware of the disparity between rich and poor, those opposed to the policies of the Wade regime began to organise themselves through the political party, Bennoo Sigil. In 2008 and 2009, several influential Senegalese citizens came together under the chairmanship of former UN Director-General Amadou Mokhtar Mbow to form the Assises Nationales, an independent group who considered alternative forms of governance and published a charter for change.

These Senegalese intellectuals, conscious that the colonial period had destroyed so much of Africa's own brand of consensus politics, felt inspired by the thirteenth-century Manden Charter, which was proclaimed in the time of Emperor Sundiata Keita at Kurukan Fuga and which obliged kings and rulers to be held to account by elders, committees and spirit mediums. It is interesting to note that around the same time, on 15 June 1215 at Runnymede near London, English barons forced King John to sign the Magna Carta, the Great Charter of the Liberties, which limited feudal payments to the Crown and protected the barons from illegal imprisonment.

In the run-up to the presidential elections in February 2012, eighty-five-year-old President Wade seemed determined to remain in power for a third term, even if it meant changing the constitution. He proposed that any candidate who gained 25 per cent of the vote could become president and, possibly with his son Karim (who already held four ministerial posts) in mind, he wished to introduce a new post of vice-president. Opposition party politicians and civil rights activists marched on the presidential palace on 23 June 2011 to vote with their feet and offer a resounding NO to Wade's planned changes. Towards the end of the year, despite lively debates about his constitutional right to stand for re-election, it looked more and more as though Wade's monarchical regime was set to continue.

When Youssou sensed the danger for his country he announced the formation of a new *mouvement citoyen*, called Fekke Maci Bolle (Since I Am Here I Am Implicated), and wrote a song with the same title to spread the movement's message: 'There's no need to quarrel; our votes are going to do the talking.' At the official party launch, he addressed the crowds gathered outside the movement's headquarters in Medina, declaring, 'There are two Senegals; one for the rich and one for the poor.' He promised to suspend his musical activities from 1 January 2012 and thereafter reveal his plans regarding the presidential election.

On 23 December 2011, as President Wade was being endorsed as official candidate at a huge Social Democratic Party rally, an even larger crowd was gathering at Dakar's Place de l'Obélisque, soon to be dubbed 'Senegal's Tahrir Square' by government critics.[11] Radical rap artists Fou Malade, Xuman and Kilifeu from the movement Y'en a Marre (Enough Is Enough) performed the single 'Faux! Pas Forcé', warning President Wade, 'You are making a mistake.'

Later that month, Youssou played his usual New Year's Eve concert at the Foire de Dakar. The programme, a medley of his greatest hits, made for a crisp, exhilarating and thrilling show, the Super Étoile proving what a brilliantly cohesive group they are.

Little did people know that this was to be the penultimate show by the core group of this legendary band. For Youssou was about to take a break from music – in order, he said, to defend democracy and a more equitable society in his beloved Senegal. Following a month of speculation, he finally threw his hat into the political arena on 2 January 2012, confirming on his own TV station his candidature for the presidential election on 26 February. His decision took most people, his musicians included, by surprise. One of them sent Youssou a text message which referred to his confirmed reputation as Senegal's king of mbalax dance music and stated 'A King is more powerful than a President.' No sooner had the news hit the airwaves than a huge media circus rolled up.

In the first week alone Youssou was the subject of around six hundred national and foreign press articles, as well as phone-ins on Radio France Internationale, a feature on the French channel TV5Monde and interviews on BBC TV and radio. While the news of his candidature aroused great interest abroad, in Senegal, the debate as to whether Youssou should have contemplated the move into politics – and whether he was indeed qualified to do so – raged on. The day after his announcement, Youssou's photograph was on the front page of almost every Senegalese newspaper. The rather tongue-in-cheek headline in *Le Grand Place* read: YOUSSOU WANTS TO BRING MBALAX TO THE PRESIDENTIAL PALACE. Some journalists suspected he had been influenced by the success in Haiti of former musician Michel Martelly, while others felt he did not have the intellectual or political clout to succeed. Others still suggested that the boy from Medina, who left school at the age of fourteen, could indeed turn things around for his country and claimed that his work ethic, his huge popularity, his entrepreneurial and managerial skills and his high-profile international contacts would surely win him votes. On the street, opinions were also divided, with remarks such as: 'He has no CV ... he only knows how to make music', 'He could get from 3 to 5 per cent of the vote and still be a kingmaker', 'How come this change of mind when Youssou once said if he were president, the people would eat stones?' and 'No, "You" Can't!'

When I met with Youssou in early January 2012, he told me about the messages of support he had received, including one that very morning from Richard Branson, and he explained his reasons for his candidacy. He said it was his patriotic duty to seek election because dictatorships and corrupt leaders bring shame on the image of Africa. In the course of his thirty-year career, despite a busy international touring schedule, he had remained in Senegal and highlighted topical issues in his songs. He had watched the people suffer and saw their despair but he also recognised the true face of Senegal, and in recent years he had come to realise that most people felt the need for change. Because he cares deeply for his country and the people who have made him what he is, he decided he must do his utmost for them. Youssou underlined his belief in free speech, saying it was for that reason he had invested in the media group Futurs Médias and then he continued,

In the past, I have been able to speak with President Abdoulaye Wade often and he has listened to my point of view. Following the events of 23 June 2011, I saw the anger on the streets, and though I was on tour in the USA, I tried to reach the president for two days but was unable to speak with him. It was then I realised it was time to act and I offered my support to the opposition. Wade is elderly. I wish him a long life, but in a year or two, even if he is re-elected, he may not be able to continue and the president of the Senate will be obliged to organise fresh elections. I am happy to let the world know the reality of what is happening in my country. Why are diplomatic passports and visas being given to families so they will vote for Wade? We have to deal with corruption. We need to reduce the number of government ministers and distribute the revenue of this country fairly. I am a successful artist. I have everything I want and need, but I am standing for election because I feel I have to. I am glad to shake the baobab.

It was clear to me that Youssou was setting about this task with the same enthusiasm, commitment and self-belief which had brought him global success as a musician, yet I was not alone in feeling apprehensive about the outcome.

It was interesting to watch the positioning of other well-known Senegalese musicians for or against President Wade's re-election. The folk duo Pape and Cheikh were among those who were most openly pro-Wade. Their song 'Goorgui Doliniou' became Wade's theme tune during the 2007 elections, and the pair were promising another winning hymn for Wade in January 2012. Idrissa Diop, Kiné Lam and Alioune Kassé also pledged their support for Wade, and the word was they were being paid handsomely for their loyalty. Didier Awadi was adamant that he would not align himself with any political party or movement, and his own agenda was clear when he told me:

It is our job to make sure that people vote and that they make an informed choice. The country will remain peaceful if we can all speak freely. No African president should be allowed to serve for more than two terms.

Awadi's clever satirical song 'Mame Boye', a YouTube hit, highlights these points.

Rap artists like Fou Malade (Malal Tall) were the real thorn in the government's side. Tall claimed he had been offered 25 million West African CFA francs (approximately £20,000) by President Wade for his support but had refused to take the money. In June 2011, he was arrested by the authorities and imprisoned for a time.

On 27 January 2012 the five so-called 'wise men' of the Constitutional Council, who were chosen by President Wade, validated Wade's candidature and that of thirteen other candidates, but did not sanction Youssou's on the grounds that he did not have the required 10,000 signatures. Youssou and his supporters were shocked and outraged. Four days later, crowds took to the streets in protest against Wade's third term and among them stood Youssou looking tired, forlorn and dismayed. In solidarity with the opposition, he was present on the street for all the demonstrations organised by the protest group M23 (whose name recalled a people's march to the palace on 23 June 2011). Tear gas was fired and a Dragon fire engine spraying boiling water appeared. Civilians and police were injured, and on one weekend alone three protestors lost their lives.

Polling day arrived on Sunday, 26 February. The elections in Dakar made the lead story on France 24, a television channel based in Paris that broadcasts in French, English and Arabic. The BBC television news did not report on the story.

It was with relief and pride that we saw queues of Senegalese calmly waiting to vote. Youssou was filmed arriving to perform his civic duty at a polling station in Medina, still limping from an injury sustained during an M23 demonstration. The turnout was said to be 60 per cent. However, it soon became clear that no candidate had gained more than 50 per cent of the vote. Wade won 34.8, Macky Sall 33.34, Moustapha Niasse 13, Ousmane Tenor Dieng 11 and Idrissa Seck 7.86 per cent. The other candidates lost their deposits, having gained less than 5 per cent of the vote. An election rerun was planned for 18 March 2012.

In the period between the first and second rounds of voting, while Youssou travelled to France to encourage Senegalese expatriates to vote again, the Fekke Maci Bolle website produced bons mots and reflections about peace and equitable societies by the likes of the Dalai Lama. In early March, at a rally in support of Macky Sall on the Place Faidherbe in Saint-Louis, Youssou told the crowds that he would not sing another note until after the departure of Wade. Nevertheless, he promised a free public concert when Wade left office. In Dakar, crowds followed Youssou to the Place de l'Indépendance, shouting, '*Sauve nous*' ('Save us').

On 25 March 2012, when votes were cast in the second round of the Senegalese elections, it soon became clear that Macky Sall was winning, and Wade quickly conceded defeat. The final share of the vote was 65.8 per cent for Sall and 34.2 per cent for Wade. Youssou gave a speech welcoming Sall as president of the entire Senegalese people while affirming that the election process and the struggle for democracy had renewed his faith in justice and freedom. He told the people he was convinced it had been necessary for him to take the initiative, to innovate, and that he had entered the fray quite naturally and with conviction. And finally, he thanked his family for their unwavering support.

On 2 April 2012, the Place de l'Obélisque was the venue not for demonstrations and anger but for celebration. Youssou performed pertinent songs from his repertoire, including 'Xale Rewmi' ('Children of our Country'). 'This is a great day for democracy,' he told the crowd. 'Now that the elections are over, we must get back to work.' And with that the Super Étoile de Dakar struck up 'Ligeey', Youssou's hymn to hard work. 'Chimes of Freedom', sung in Wolof, found the audience spontaneously waving their arms and, just in front of the stage, someone waved a very large red, yellow and green Senegalese flag.

14. *Youssou on the election trail.*

The path to prosperity

When President Macky Sall was elected on the back of the slogan 'Yonou youkkouté', meaning 'the path to prosperity', it seemed to echo the mood in Senegal as well as a prevailing optimism across the rest of the continent. There are as many Senegalese living abroad as there are at home, and they send back an astonishing 500 billion West African CFA francs every year to support their families and invest in their country. Many of these are the sons and daughters of middle-class Senegalese who have chosen to complete their studies in Europe or the USA. As jobs have become scarcer in their host countries, more of these young people are returning to Senegal after graduation, bringing with them their expertise and skills. Many are working in IT or in the rapidly developing petroleum industry, and more and more young entrepreneurs are setting up their own companies in Senegal, making use of their global contacts.

Former Arsenal and Juventus footballer Patrick Vieira, who was born in Dakar, was a driving force behind the foundation of

Senegal's first football school, the Diambars Institute, situated near the seaside resort of Saly. Along with Beninese former footballer Jean-Marc Adjovi-Boco and fellow French footballer Bernard Lama, Vieira sought sponsorship from Adidas and UNESCO for the school, which opened its doors in 2006. Pupils are taught regular school subjects as well as football and are encouraged to take part in summer exchange programmes with European children which are sponsored by Cadbury Schweppes.[12]

Part II

SENEGAL'S FIRST SUPERSTAR

15. *Youssou's parents, Elimane N'Dour and Ndèye Sokhna Mboup.*

3
A STAR IS BORN

As he emerged on the local music scene, Youssou N'Dour, Senegal's first pop idol, was often compared to American superstar Michael Jackson. Indeed, that is how he was described to me when I arrived in Dakar in October 1984. The shy, serious, talented and charismatic young man I met then was – whether he was aware of it or not – on a mission to drag his own Wolof culture out of the shadow of colonialism and to prove that, with hard work, faith, courage and ambition, it is possible to succeed and give hope to others.

Youssou was born the first child of Elimane N'Dour and his wife, Ndèye Sokhna Mboup, at Rue 31 x 22 in the Medina district of Dakar on 1 October 1959, just six months before Senegal gained independence from its French colonisers. While his father belongs to Senegal's main ethnic group, the Wolof, Youssou's Toucouleur mother is a *gawlo*, a female praise singer. *Gawlo* is a hereditary title; through his mother he can trace a musical lineage that stretches back seven generations: Yirim Diop, mother of Yaram Diop, mother of Yacine Mar, mother of Mame Ngoné, mother of Marie Sène, mother of Ndèye Sokhna Mboup, mother of Youssou N'Dour.

In general, Senegal's hereditary musicians, including those who play drums, are known as *griots*, but those who sing and play the *xalam*, the West African lute, are defined as *gawlos*. Youssou was fascinated by the atmosphere in the large *griot/gawlo* household where he grew up, the home of his maternal grandmother, Marie Sène, one of the most famous singers of her day. Here he watched with fascination all the comings and goings, the ceremonial costumes, the lavish preparations for feast days and festivals. He remembers with pride performances by his maternal grandfather,

Boubacar Mboup, and by Samba Diabaré Samb, both well-known virtuosi on the *xalam*. Youssou owes his singing prowess to his mother's family, as he told me in the early 1990s:

> In Africa, especially in the *gawlo* families, we sing with the stomach, to give out something from inside. I sing with a great deal of effort. My mother and her *gawlo* relatives learned to sing like that because it was their tradition.

One day, as he and I watched Van Morrison's blistering performance of 'Caravan' with Robbie Robertson and The Band in Martin Scorsese's documentary *The Last Waltz* (1978), Youssou remarked that, like him, Morrison sings from his stomach.

At the outset of his career, Youssou was all too aware that he came from Medina, the poorer district of Dakar, rather than the wealthy Plateau and that, as members of a casted group, his *griot* relations were considered inferior to the noble classes. Although Youssou's father is not a *griot*, the stigma attached to Youssou's mother's lineage has been challenging at times. Although as a young man he was sensitive to any implied criticism, this also spurred him on to work hard and to succeed. At the same time, he learned a great deal from his *griot* parents, whose knowledge of social mores and whose status as praise singers and guardians of history he respects. Throughout his career he has consulted them to check his Wolof lyrics or his phrasing, and in a conversation with me he acknowledged their contribution to society:

> We [the *griots*], who were once the troubadours, entertainers and chief advisers to the Mandé kings, are guardians of our culture and we have been at great pains to preserve it. We have remained quite traditional until the very last minute before opening out to the world. I am a thoroughly modern *griot*, but I know that even today music can carry a message and change people's lives.

When Senegal became independent, its first president, Léopold Sédar Senghor, poet and French academician, insisted upon high levels of education and placed special emphasis on arts subjects and music. His theory of *enracinement et ouverture* (authenticity and openness), formulated from his own experience as a writer and poet, called for a sound knowledge of Senegalese traditions together with an appreciation of Western cultural values. Youssou's percussion-based mbalax music, which is influenced by traditional songs and dances whilst integrating Western instruments and song structures, perfectly fulfils this Senghorean principle.

Youssou instinctively feels the pulse of the Senegalese people. He knows that they want to hear pop songs sung in their own language and will follow the *sabar* drums into the city nightclubs to rival the dazzle of the neon lights with their arm-flailing, high-kicking, spine-tingling dance routines. So he sings in Wolof. He sings for the people: for wealthy patrons, for market traders and the boys and girls of the Medina. He has dared create a popular music that tells old tales and modern truths, a music that makes the saddest people dance to the drums of their ancestors. The invigorating rhythms of the past are fused with the instruments and techniques of today's global music and together they provide the perfect soundtrack for a landscape of searing heat, Sahelian dust, and the hustle and bustle of one of West Africa's most sophisticated modern cities.

4

THE BEAT ON THE STREET

Youssou N'Dour gave his first public performance in 1972, aged thirteen, at the Joseph Gaye Stadium in Saint-Louis. He sang 'Mba', a homage to the eminent saxophonist Papa Samba Diop, alias Ali Mba, who had recently passed away. Many singers took part in the memorial concert, but when radio presenter Francis Cheikhna Ba introduced the young Youssou he delivered these prophetic words: 'This evening a star is born before your very eyes.'

Although most people outside Senegal can barely pronounce the word or dance to its polyrhythms, mbalax (which means 'accompaniment' in Wolof and is pronounced 'mbalagh') has become, thanks to Youssou's success, one of the most famous genres of modern African music, as representative of Senegal as soukous is of the Congo, makossa of Cameroon, or mbaqanga of South Africa. Mbalax is a syncopated music propelled by the *sabar* drums which are specific to Senegal and the Gambia and which, whether drummed by hand or struck by sticks, offer a thrilling variety of tonal colours and percussive rhythms. With its roots in popular culture, the new-style mbalax reflected the feelings and sentiments of a post-independence generation. Nonetheless, the process of integrating *sabar* drums into modern dance bands was gradual.

Latin dance music had been popular in Senegal since the 1940s, when visiting sailors first brought Cuban Grabación Victor (GV) records through the port of Dakar.[1] Salsa in particular enjoyed huge popularity and was interpreted with unique grace and sensuality on Dakar's dance floors. Nearly forty years after salsa first reached Dakar's shores, Laba Sosseh, from neighbouring Gambia, affirmed his reputation as West Africa's leading salsero when he gained a gold disc for his 1980 album *Salsa Africana*, which sold more than 100,000 copies. An intriguingly cool mix of Latin and African music later became the hallmark of the Dakar-based Orchestra Baobab, one of the most celebrated bands in West Africa.

In the late 1960s, Ibra Kassé (1927–92), owner of the Miami nightclub, where most of Senegal's popular musicians and singers started their professional careers, took the bold step of regularly drafting in *sabar* drummers for his resident groups, Diamono and the seminal Star Band. Often referred to as the father of modern Senegalese music, Kassé had lived in Paris before returning to Dakar to open a restaurant called Le Bon Coin in the Avenue Malick Sy; the restaurant then became a nightclub, the Miami, one of the hottest spots in town. Legendary musicians such as Johnny Pacheco performed there when visiting Dakar, and government ministers and foreign dignitaries came to dance the salsa, the tango, bolero, waltz and cha-cha-cha. Gradually, Zairean and Guinean music became popular in Dakar, and in the same way that Nigeria and Ghana had developed their modern highlife, Kassé set about promoting Senegal's own popular music. Gradually, salsa became salsa mbalax and Spanish lyrics were replaced by native Wolof.

In 1975 Kassé announced on the radio that he was recruiting musicians for his resident Star Band. When a gangly youth called Youssou N'Dour presented himself, Kassé told him he was too young and that he should only come back when he had his father's permission. With some difficulty Youssou persuaded his father Elimane, a local car mechanic who owned a garage in the Medina, to allow him to join the Star Band for a nightly fee of just 500 West African CFA francs (about £2), and Kassé knew immediately that he had found a golden voice. Many people have told me how Kassé, a strict disciplinarian who drank only *kinkeleba* (the local herbal tea), kept a small mixing desk by his side as he served behind the bar. If one of the musicians on stage faltered, he would simply mute their microphone. Youssou told me: 'Ibra Kassé taught me rigour.

It is like the army; it is difficult, but I learned a lot and it helped me afterwards, for it is not easy to head up a group.'

Youssou found Cuban music rhythmically acceptable but harmonically foreign, and of course he and his contemporaries wanted to sing in their own language. He was not the first to promote mbalax, nor the first to sing in Wolof (Aminata Nar Fall and Kounta Mame Cheikh had begun the trend in the early 1960s), but he knew best how to integrate the *sabar* drums, combining them with a modern drum kit, electric guitars, keyboards and horns.

Sabar drums

Elsewhere in Africa there are male and female drums, but nowhere are they deployed together as in the ensemble of Senegalese *sabars*. These drums – there can be up to eight in the traditional line-up – produce strong, distinctive rhythmic patterns and combine to produce three basic rhythms: the *mbalax* (which gave its name to Youssou's overall style), the *touli* and the *talmbat*. The goblet-shaped *mbeung mbeung bale* and its smaller counterpart, the higher-pitched *mbeung mbeung tungune*, each play a different *mbalax* rhythm. The egg-shaped *lamb*, the primary bass drum, plays the *touli* rhythm while the *gorong talmbat*, the accompanying tenor drum, plays the *talmbat* rhythm. The *thiol* can be tuned to play either the *touli* or the *talmbat*. The *nder* (a solo drum shaped like the *mbeung mbeung* but taller, sometimes as much as three feet tall) can produce a wide range of tones from a deep bass to a high-pitched stick tone, and then of course there is the little *tama*, the 'talking drum'. While Youssou's percussionist Babacar Faye plays up to four different *sabar* drums and Assane Thiam plays the *tama*, the guitar tends to replicate the part of the *mbeung mbeung* and the bass guitar the *thiol*. Counted in subdivisions of three beats, Youssou's ternary mbalax contrasts with the mostly binary rhythms of Western music. Written in simple 4/4 time, it is nonetheless played in 6/8, as if it were ternary. While Western pop music generally accentuates the first and third beats in a bar, mbalax emphasises the second and fourth beats in the same way that reggae does. The music is thus different to international standards; its inverted beat is unique, and its open forms and cyclical structures leave room for jazz-like improvisations.

The Étoile de Dakar

Back in 1977, while still a member of Kassé's Star Band, the eighteen-year-old Youssou was keen to advance his solo career and decided to form his own band. He took with him six musicians from the Star Band, including his childhood friend, percussionist Babacar Faye, Alpha Seyni Kanté (rhythm guitar), Abdou Fall (timbales), Matar Gueye (congas), Assane Thiam (*tama*) and animateur Alla Seck. He then enlisted Badou Ndiaye (guitar) as bandleader, Kabou Gueye (bass guitar), Rann Diallo (saxophone), and vocalists Eric Mbacké Ndoye and El Hadji Faye. The manager and financial backer for the group was Kabou Gueye's uncle Mohammed Ablaye Sow, known as Sow Sabor, who worked for the Dakar branch of ASECNA, the African air traffic control agency. A keen musician himself, Sow was able to provide instruments and equipment for the group.

Kabou Gueye describes the early days of the Étoile de Dakar as being fairly inauspicious. The group rehearsed at Youssou's place and made live recordings using a tape machine and microphones placed near the speakers. In this way they produced no fewer than seven cassettes in just two years. *Griot* El Hadj Faye sang with them ('Jalo' was one of his songs) and Eric Mbacké Ndoye, a friend of Badou Ndiaye, came with a collection of Cuban songs which inspired new tracks. Rann Diallo joined to play saxophone and sing backing vocals. The group were young, carefree and open to innovation. As their repertoire quickly expanded, audiences began to take notice.

Recorded at the Miami Club in 1979, 'Thiely' ('The Bird') was the first song featuring Youssou's voice to be played on the radio. Originally sung by Pape Seck and the Star Band, it was based on a melody by Puerto Rico's El Gran Combo, but Youssou's version became the song that all Dakar was talking about. 'Xalis' ('Money'), a song proposed by Badou Ndiaye and recorded at the Jandeer Club, was the first major hit for Youssou and the group Étoile de Dakar. It still retained a strong Cuban element, including the theme from 'Soy El Hombre Misterioso', but it kick-started Youssou's career and marked the transition from Cuban music to mbalax. 'Étoile', which presented the new stars in the group and became their theme song, still had Cuban overtones due to the continued presence of *toumba* and timbales, but the growing importance of *sabar* drums was unmistakable; even Kabou Gueye played his bass guitar like a traditional *sabar* drum.

Though timidly at first, dancers took to the floor with traditional Senegalese dance steps. '*C'est pour les tarés*' ('It's only for fools'), some scorned, but Youssou's mbalax was soon to become the most popular dance music in Senegal.

The song 'Thiapathioly' marked another stage in the growing popularity of mbalax. *Thiapathioly* can mean an only child, but it is also the name given to a person who is successful in their life and career, a model citizen. Here Youssou sings about Pape Thioune, owner of the Damel butcher's shop in the Rue de Thann in Dakar, a well-known victualler who supplied major outlets like the University of Dakar.

Pape Oumar Ngom replaced Alpha Seyni Kanté on rhythm guitar, and when Kabou Gueye was injured in a motorcycle accident, Jimi Mbaye was enlisted as bass guitarist and Gueye turned to directing the band, paying particular attention to the song arrangements. Remarkably, as hit followed hit, including 'Ndakarou', which celebrated the attractions of Dakar, Youssou was convincing even the intellectuals and the noble classes – who had hitherto despised the *sabar* – to follow his music. Soon they were forsaking those languorous Latin rhythms to join in the often quite suggestive mbalax dances proposed by Youssou and his band on the stage of the Balafon, the Sahel or the Jandeer Club. Étoile de Dakar's musicians were themselves inspired by the movements and impulses of the Senegalese dancers.

Hailed at first as the 'Prince of Mbalax', Youssou was subsequently promoted to the 'King of Mbalax'. His reputation as a clean-living, serious young man was to change forever the image of musicians in Senegal, previously perceived as drunkards and womanisers.

The Super Étoile de Dakar

As if to confirm those prejudices, some of the Étoile de Dakar musicians started drinking while others had let success go to their heads. In 1981, therefore, Youssou decided to set up a new group,

16. *Super Étoile de Dakar and fans in Gambia.*

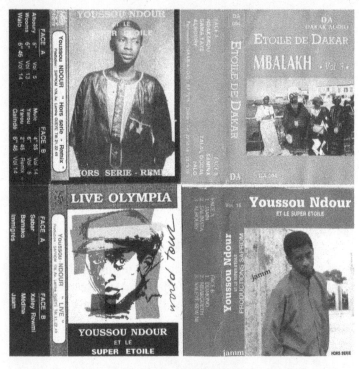

17. *Super Étoile de Dakar cassette covers.*

18. *Youssou at a Super Étoile de Dakar rehearsal in Castor, Dakar.*

the Super Étoile de Dakar, with Jimi Mbaye, Alla Seck, Pape Oumar Ngom, Babacar 'Mbaye Dièye' Faye and Kabou Gueye. The remaining musicians formed a new but short-lived group called Étoile 2000.

There had never been a music company in Senegal until Youssou created one, and Kabou Gueye played an important role in organising an administrative structure that was viable enough to support a superstar. Indeed, one of the attractions for the Super Étoile musicians was that they were now salaried and therefore had a guaranteed monthly income paid by SAPROM (the Société Africaine de Promotion), the company Youssou formed with accountant Abdoul Aziz Dièye and which was based at the new band headquarters in the Avenue Malick Sy. Feeling financially secure, the musicians were able to simply enjoy making music. Jimi, Pape Oumar and Kabou Gueye made a great guitar trio. Mbaye Dièye Faye changed over entirely from toumba to *sabar*, while Boy Gris came from Louga to play timbales.

Youssou and the Super Étoile recorded four cassettes in quick succession. They regularly performed at the Firemen's Ball on New Year's Eve, at private parties for bank officials or customs officers and began touring, playing regional towns like Kaolack, Tambacounda, Saint-Louis and Dagana. Their songs, which emanated from every courtyard and market stall in the country, felt relevant and topical.

Youssou once described the Super Étoile de Dakar as his greatest achievement – and indeed there are few, if any, African bands that have retained the same core personnel for thirty years. Performing, recording and touring together, the group's founding members came to know each other's musical abilities and strengths, and even if there were minor changes in personnel along the way they remained a well-oiled machine. The *Los Angeles Times* praised the 'joyous precision' of their Senegalese roots music.[2] Percussionist Mbaye Dièye Faye has spoken of the Super Étoile as a close-knit family with the kind of team spirit that is rare in football, let alone the music business. As a backing group they were the envy of other African stars.

19. *Touré Kunda in Paris.*

20. Best of Touré Kunda.

And yet the ultimate success of the group did not come about without some early difficulties. In 1984, after living in Paris for several years, where they had forged an international career, Senegalese band Touré Kunda decided to return to Dakar to stage a huge concert. The trio of brothers from Casamance invited as their special guests Super Diamono led by Omar Pene, and Youssou with the Super Étoile. Already one of the most popular groups on the local scene, Super Diamono received rapturous applause, but when Youssou and his band followed them on stage, they were booed. Youssou N'Dour booed! How could that be? For Youssou this was a defining moment. He realised that he needed to reinforce his line-up, and decided to do so by bringing the brothers Adama and Habib Faye into the band straight away. However, this decision was not an immediate success. Kabou Gueye recalled to me how, in the process of changing their style, the group almost lost the plot:

> I remember the first concert Youssou gave at the Sorano Theatre following the arrival of Adama Faye and Habib. They opened the show with 'Africa', a dreamily impressionistic meditation on the plight of our vast continent, once united, then carved up by colonialism, now free but splintered. Youssou's compassionate vocals, Issa Cissokho's tender saxophone solos and Adama Faye's sensitive piano accompaniment combined to produce a veritable masterpiece. Yet in the theatre people looked at each other and said, what is that?

'Africa' was indeed destined to become a timeless and classic track. It was one of the songs I heard and loved on my first visit to Dakar in 1984, and it ushered in a golden age for Youssou's music. For the next thirty years, Youssou and the Super Étoile moved forward and never looked back.

Many of Youssou's best-loved songs did not at first catch the imagination of his fans, yet each one revealed its subtle secrets over time. He himself told me once, 'I love it when an audience at

first doesn't understand the music, and listens, and is converted.'
Lamin Minte, owner of one of Gambia's busiest cassette shops,
told African music expert and journalist Dr Lucy Duran how,
when Youssou released a new cassette, people made a fuss and
criticised it:

> They will give this reason and that for why they don't like it
> but still they hang around the shop listening. They say he's
> gone too far over to a European style, or not far enough. And
> still they listen. Then all of a sudden everyone starts buying
> it. In two weeks I'm totally sold out of originals and I hide
> my last one so I can run off copies. That's Youssou's music
> every time.[3]

SUPER ÉTOILE DE DAKAR'S MUSICIANS

ADAMA FAYE (keyboards, arrangements, composition) was known
by some as the Mozart of Senegal, so exceptional was his talent.
He became a teacher at the age of nineteen, having gained his
CAP (Certificat d'Aptitude Professionelle) certificate when he was
sixteen. The Faye family's house was at 9 Rue Diourom in the area
of Dakar known as SICAP Rue 10, where many other well-known
musicians lived. Jacob Desvarieux, who lived opposite the Faye
family and later became lead guitarist of Caribbean supergroup
Kassav, learned his first notes from Adama, who enjoyed playing
versions of Jimi Hendrix or Carlos Santana songs.

Before he even owned a piano, Adama would practise on a
piece of cardboard mapped out with black and white keys. With
his special gift for transferring traditional rhythms and instruments
to the keyboard synthesiser, he recreated the sound of the balafon,
inventing a style called Marimba Mbalax that became a musical
phenomenon in Senegal. His brother Habib used the marimba
sound on Youssou's tracks, notably 'Sabar', while another brother,

Lamine Faye, promoted it with his group Lemzo Diamono. The simulation of traditional African instruments on the keyboard was further elaborated and perfected by the French musicians Loy Erlich and Jean-Philippe Rykiel, who often recorded and toured with Youssou's band.

Prior to Adama joining the Super Étoile, Youssou's style of singing and his repertoire were quite traditional, but Adama, who was influenced not only by the Rolling Stones and the Beatles but also by Herbie Hancock and Chick Corea, introduced rock, jazz and blues riffs to great effect. He also attracted a new audience for Youssou's music, especially among young people and intellectuals. Adama was an extremely generous musician, but he was also very self-effacing: when he died too young, in August 2005, the press found it difficult to find a photograph of him.

ASSANE THIAM (*tama*) is a '*Walo Walo*' from Walo, the northern region of Senegal, who has a natural sense of humour and a wide knowledge of Wolof proverbs. He comes from a long line of *tama* players who in former times performed at royal coronation ceremonies which the chief *griot* opened with seven ritual drumbeats. The *tama* players accompanied the recitation of epic stories and on the birthday of the Prophet Muhammad played a special drumming pattern called *ndond-u kere*.

BABACAR 'MBAYE DIÈYE' FAYE (percussion) grew up in Medina, near to where Youssou lived. While his father, Vieux Sing Faye, and Senegalese *sabar* master Papa Doudou Ndiaye Rose inspired him to become a percussionist, it was Alla Seck who most influenced him in terms of showmanship. Along with Youssou, Mbaye Dièye played at *kassak* circumcision ceremonies, baptisms and *mbappates* (night-time wrestling matches), and they both were members of youth theatre group Sine Dramatique, which won first prize in the Semaine de la Jeunesse (National Youth Week) competition, beating the much-fancied Cercle de la Jeunesse de Louga (the Louga

Youth Circle). Along with Youssou, he joined the group Diamono 1, before moving on to Star Band Number One, finally becoming a founder member of the Super Étoile de Dakar.

Mbaye Dièye says he gets the energy to play drums by drinking *bissap* (a sweet drink made from hibiscus leaves) and ginger. His sure-fire solution for attracting a girl is to caress the tam-tam while staring at her constantly!

21. *Babacar 'Mbaye Dièye' Faye*

HABIB FAYE (bass guitar, keyboards, arrangements and composition) collaborated with Youssou on many albums. The pair shared a house in the residential area, Cité Biagui, and together created a company called Youbib as a label for their compositions. Habib marked Youssou's repertoire with notable contributions on numerous tracks including 'Békoor', 'Sabar', 'Set' and 'Lii'. The first Senegalese musician to use a fretless bass (in 'Mbeugel', 'Mercy' and 'Ay Coona La') and the six-string bass, he replicated basslines on keyboards in 'Alboury', 'Set' and 'Wooy'. He was extremely adept at using major/minor harmonic modulations, and in 2012 he launched an ambitious solo jazz project with his album *H20*. When, on 25 April 2018, it was announced that Habib Faye, the *benjamin* (youngest) of the Super Étoile, had passed away in Paris at the age of fifty-two, his fellow musicians were devastated and the whole of Senegal was shocked by his unexpected death.

IBOU KONATÉ (trumpet) is the son of Mady Konaté, a famous saxophonist and bandleader whose group performed at nightclubs and gala evenings all around Dakar.

ISSA CISSOKHO (saxophone) was a regular musician with the Super Étoile before rejoining Orchestra Baobab in 2001, where his extrovert personality and idiosyncratic saxophone solos brought style, colour and humour to the stage. Following a performance he was often heard to say "*J'ai bombardé!*", I gave it my all. He was invited by the renowned film director Djibril Diop Mambéty to compose parts of the soundtrack for his 1994 film *Le Franc*. Issa sadly passed away on 24 March 2019.

MAMADOU 'JIMI' MBAYE (lead guitar) comes from a family of *griots*, of whom some, like Babacar Ndaak Mbaye, are storytellers. Jimi's brother, Abdoul Aziz Mbaye, also has a connection with Youssou: he was an international diplomat and president of the Youssou N'Dour Foundation before becoming Senegal's Minister of Culture. Jimi was greatly influenced by Jimi Hendrix (hence his nickname) and Carlos Santana. Around the time in 1985 that Youssou and the Super Étoile appeared with Jacques Higelin at the Bercy Arena in Paris (discussed in Chapter 9), Youssou noticed that Higelin's guitarist, Pierre Chérèze, produced a big sound thanks to an excellent technique. His remarks were a spur to Jimi, who spent ten years perfecting his own range of distinctive sounds using a Fender Stratocaster, pedal reverb, delay, chorus and effects such as picking to imitate traditional instruments like the *xalam*, *kora* and *ngoni*. Jimi eventually developed his own style, which is now as instantly recognisable as those of the guitar heroes he admires. He is most proud of his rock solo in the song 'Kocc Barma' and his intro to 'Birima'.

22. *Jimi Mbaye.*

OUMAR SOW (guitar) has a style which is a unique mix of jazz, African traditional music and modern soul, rock and blues. Born in Dakar in 1959, a few months after Youssou, he benefited from a privileged family background and a good education, and subsequently perfected his skills as a composer and arranger under jazz guitarist Pierre Cullaz at the Centre d'Instruction Musicale in Paris. When he was still a student, he formed the group Bataxal with Pape Dieng as drummer and Jean Pierre Senghor on keyboards, an exciting forum of experimentation for the young jazz apprentices. In 1985–6 Oumar played guitar on Youssou's albums *Diam* and *Nelson Mandela* and toured with the Super Étoile before opting for a freelance career. In 2006, following his participation in the albums *Alsaama Day* and *Rokku Mi Rokka*, Oumar once again became a full-time member of the Super Étoile de Dakar.

OUSSEYNOU 'OUZIN' NDIAYE (vocalist) is Youssou's uncle. His velvety voice, with its strong vibrato texture, has been an excellent foil for Youssou, and his backing vocals have been a vital element in the Super Étoile repertoire.

PAPE DIENG (drums), who is now a successful businessman and no longer performs with the group, was a natural, intuitive and hugely talented drummer and composer who brought genuine musicality and a jazz feel to Youssou's music, most notably on the album *Diam*. When Youssou supported Jacques Higelin in Paris, it was Dieng who emerged first, hoisted hydraulically with his drum kit from the basement to the centre of the arena.

PAPE OUMAR NGOM (rhythm guitar), like Youssou, comes from a *griot/ gawlo* family. His guitar links the basic rhythms and harmonies, meaning that even if the rest of the band were to stop playing on songs such as 'Thiapathioly', 'Ndakarou' and 'Immigrés' it would still be possible to recognise the song. Pape Oumar contends that each time the music follows Youssou's voice, as in 'Djino' or 'Birima', the songs seem very natural and complete, but it is less satisfying when Youssou sings over music already produced by someone else.

THIERNO KOITÉ (saxophone) comes from a long line of hereditary musicians, many of whom were expert saxophonists, including his uncle, Mamadou Mba Coro Koité. He played alongside Dexter Johnson, an accomplished Nigerian musician who lived in Dakar and influenced an entire generation of Senegalese horn players. A cousin of Issa Cissokho, Thierno began his career with the Rio Orchestra in 1969 then moved to the Star Band at the Miami Club and the Sahel at the Sahel Club before joining the group Xalam. He performed with the Super Étoile from 1985 to 2000 and guested with Cheikh Lô's band before returning to the reformed Orchestra Baobab in 2001. Blending sensitive musicality with technical virtuosity, Thierno continues to make notable contributions both in the studio and onstage.

THIO MBAYE (percussion) is a versatile and inventive performer who has worked with most of the leading groups in Dakar and toured with many of them. The title track from his solo album *Rimbax*, produced in France in 1993 by Ibrahima Sylla, was an instant hit in Senegal.

VIVIANE CHIDID N'DOUR (vocals) spent many years as Youssou's backing singer before launching her solo career. When her first cassette, *Entre nous/Between Us*, was released in 1999, it sold 100,000 copies. A role model for young Senegalese women, Viviane brings style to the stage with her designer dresses and sleek tresses (she signed a lucrative promotional contract with the Japanese manufacturer of NINA hair products). Viviane twice married and divorced Youssou's brother, Bouba N'Dour.

*

In 1987, as Youssou began touring in earnest in Europe, he created a second group, Super Étoile 2, with Kabou Gueye on bass, Ibou Cissé on guitar, Rann Diallo on saxophone and Manel Diop and Malang Cissokho on vocals. According to Gueye, it was a brilliant band, a *groupe de choc*. The idea was that Youssou could fly back to Dakar to fulfil contracts with them and avoid the expense of bringing all his Super Étoile musicians home. When Super Étoile 2 became no longer viable, the Finnish musician Khassy Wally, who often visited Dakar and was passionate about Senegalese music, arranged to take most of the musicians home with him to Finland.

5

LORDS AND LADIES OF THE DANCE

The complex polyrhythms and scintillating *sabars* underpinning Youssou N'Dour's mbalax music provide the perfect vehicle for the dancing prowess of his Senegalese fans. Typically tall and elegant, they move athletically and with ease, and even small children appear to have little difficulty in mastering quite intricate movements. At traditional *sabar* and *taneber* parties women enter the circle and they dance subtly, tracking the drum beats with their bodies, marking the rhythms with their limbs, levitating like birds of paradise, stretching towards nirvana in a flurry of ecstasy.[1] Such women were the first to promote Youssou's mbalax music.

Architect and film director Nicolas Cissé, who knows a thing or two about balance and symmetry, talked to me about how he had noted an exaltation and ultimate therapy in their dance:

> There are steps where the dancer must be in perfect harmony with her body in order to execute the dance. These complex even irrational dances seem to turn on a fake note, a subtle half beat. The dancer enters a trance-like state as she becomes aligned with the cosmos. A transcendental eroticism liberates the women physically, spiritually and sexually and the same is true of the drummers whose rhythms incite them.

The first female dancer to join Youssou onstage was Ndèye Khady Niang, who charmed audiences with her energetic and seductive routines. For Youssou, she was an obvious choice: she had been President Senghor's favourite dancer, having accompanied him on all his political campaigns, and by the early 1980s she was still the best dancer in Senegal. In 2009, a year before she died, I met her in the living room of her small bungalow in the Karak district of Dakar. Surrounded by large framed photographs of herself with President Senghor, Thione Seck, Youssou and other celebrities, she spoke animatedly about her experiences as a dancer and shared gossip from those times with me.

Youssou's first male dancer/animateur, Alla Seck, was a true original, an artist who brought instant colour to the stage whether playing maracas or dancing with his idiosyncratic shuffle. He expressed himself not only with his remarkable gravelly voice in catchy call-and-response phrases but also in the way he dressed – striped socks and patchwork robes which signified his allegiance to the holy marabout Cheikh Ibra Fall. He used profound Wolof proverbs to score witty points and mimed stories, holding out his palm as if it were a mirror while coiffing his hair, or pretending to ask a passer-by for the time while looking at his watch. Alla liked to play the role of an innocent *kow kow* (peasant from the village), newly arrived in Dakar. He was born in Gossas near Kaolack and came to the city to work with his brother as a tailor in the area known as Usine Bene Tally, but he was destined for a life in the limelight. On stage he gave one hundred per cent of himself; perhaps too much for his own good. He ate little and he smoked ganja, making the tour bus stop regularly so he could purchase his provisions. During Youssou's 1987 European tour, he fell ill in London and I drove him to the airport, unaware that I would never see him again. When he died of typhoid fever on 14 June, a month later, the stage was sad.

In Alla's memory, Youssou and his staff organised a twelve-hour, all-night benefit concert at the Demba Diop Stadium in Dakar, featuring all the major bands in Senegal. Youssou dedicated his cassette *Kocc Barma* to his cherished artist and friend, whom he described thus:

Alla Seck was from another world. He came to this earth to be an artist, and I found him at the Miami Club, where he used to

sing two songs a night or sometimes, when we were all com-
peting for our space, he might not sing at all. I saw him playing
maracas, and we persuaded Kassé to engage him in that role. Yet
whenever he came to the microphone he always had something
interesting to say, for he knew many Wolof proverbs. His dance
style was entirely his own, and when Alla died I felt obliged to
dance because the mark he made on my music was indelible.[2]

Alla has been role model and inspiration for the dancers who have
followed in his footsteps: Gallo Thielo, the original 'rubberband
man', so lithe, so witty, so inventive that his passage on to the stage
always brought thunderous applause from the floor, and Pape
Moussa Sonko, who worked with the Sorano Theatre dance troupe
before being invited to perform with Youssou at Bercy in 2006 and
who subsequently became a regular member of the touring band.

Dance has always been an essential ingredient in Youssou's
music. When he wrote 'Sabar' (sometimes called 'Wundelow',
meaning to turn round and round) it became the hit single of the
summer of 1986. In the song he warns dancers to respect the grace
and meaning of the traditional, spinning *ndawrabine*, a dance
which the Lébou people performed before the harvest to invoke
rain and ensure crops would flourish. The dancers swirl and turn,
legs high-kicking in the air, the graceful swing of their voluminous
robes complementing their movements. Despite Youssou's plea
to respect traditions, some quite suggestive, even risqué dances
have nonetheless been devised by Youssou's fans, as Moussa Joh,
a Gambian living in England, explained to Lucy Duran:

> In the early days Youssou used to sing more or less straight *kassak*
> music. This was music for what we called *sayisayi* (naughty)
> dancing which boys used to perform when they were healed
> after circumcision and were well enough to start thinking about
> girls again. They would get into the middle of the circle, hold
> their groin, and shake and wobble their legs in rascal fashion.[3]

The dance names describe their action. The pelvic and knee movements of the *moulaye chigin* exactly match the sabar breaks. Stretch your legs too far while dancing the *khoti chaya*, and you can literally split your wide Arabic-style trousers. The *reug reug bodiang* is a squatting dance, and *haj bi* is a crude imitation of a dog lifting its leg. As for *boungoun bangan*, the term conjures up a shaking posterior and the *ragajou* describes a woman rolling her eyes. In the *jelkati*, the dancer's upper arms, bent at the elbow, move in parallel motion from left to right. The highlight of an evening at Youssou's Thiossane Club was often the moment when a girl would rush on to the stage, grab a microphone stand and begin gyrating her hips suggestively. In their excitement the men would shout '*Diafondool!*' (Cling on here!) or '*Songoma!*' (Attack me!). Even the doorman felt obliged to quit his post to gawp at the spectacle and Assane Thiam, still playing his *tama*, would pursue the girl as she left the stage.

23. *Dancers in the Thiossane Club.*

6

SONGS FOR THE PEOPLE

Modern *griot* and storyteller Babacar Ndaak Mbaye told me in June 2006 that Youssou N'Dour has sung about everything:

> He has lauded with praise all the great men and women of his country. He has sung about ordinary people, about great intellectuals, the Africanist philosopher and scientist, Cheikh Anta Diop, and the incomparable Nelson Mandela. He has sung about love, about our pleasures, our sorrows, what we eat and what we drink, our folktales, our animals and the birds of the air. He has sung about politics without being political, about economics without being an economist, about humanitarian issues and life in Senegal and most of all, about peace.

Commenting as they do on issues and people, often with humour and irony, Youssou's songs have been absorbed into the collective memory so that most Senegalese fans can sing them by heart, respecting each rhythmic break and melodic inflection.

At the 1994 Dakar press launch for Youssou's album *The Guide*, writer Mamadou Traoré Diop declared,

> Today, all of Senegal waits with bated breath for a new Youssou N'Dour album. The World Bank may devalue at will the price of our raw materials, but they cannot devalue Youssou's music, which reaches places our peanuts or our phosphate or even our president's plane cannot reach.

'Nelson Mandela'

A friend of mine, university lecturer Magueye Kassé, believes that Youssou's songs are useful to the Senegalese people because they are educational as well as entertaining. A good example of this is the song 'Nelson Mandela', which Youssou wrote to explain to his Wolof-speaking mother and aunts – who were puzzled by the violent scenes being transmitted on TV from South Africa – who this great man was and what apartheid meant. It was the title track on an album produced in 1985 by Albert Koski for Magnetic Records and recorded at Studio Montmartre in Rue Lepic, down the hill from the Sacré-Cœur Basilica in Paris. This was the album that launched Youssou's international career. The songs were recorded as live, meaning that the drum kit, bass guitar, percussion and guitar were played together and then the voice and the horn tracks were added. The arrangements were by Doudou Doucouré,

24. *'Nelson Mandela'.*

a Dakar-based musician who, after studying at Berklee College of Music in Boston, moved to New York where he performed with, among others, Pharoah Sanders and James Blood Ulmer. As Doucouré told me when I met him in Dakar, there are two kinds of arranger: those who put themselves in the records, and those who follow the musician's lead. He counts himself among the latter, and believes this approach worked well for Youssou, with his traditional *griot* voice.

Following the success of the album *Nelson Mandela*, Youssou was awarded Senegal's Order of the Lion, and when Dakar's Avenue Courbet was renamed Avenue Nelson Mandela, he performed the album's title song to mark the occasion.

25. *Recording* Nelson Mandela *in Paris.*

On 11 June 1998, a major concert was held at Wembley Stadium to mark Nelson Mandela's seventieth birthday, and Youssou was invited to perform. The concert, which was televised live to 600 million viewers in sixty-seven countries, called for Mandela's release, South Africa's freedom and the end of apartheid. Among other notable African performers, Hugh Masekela sang 'Bring Back Nelson Mandela', and Youssou came on stage with Salif Keita, Sly and Robbie, and Ray Lema.

It was almost another two years before South Africa's prime minister, Willem de Klerk, gave the order that allowed Nelson Mandela – who had been incarcerated for more than 10,000 days – to walk free from prison on 11 February 1990. Later that year, when Wembley Stadium welcomed him and his wife Winnie at a joyous celebration concert, Youssou was there once again, this time singing with Peter Gabriel.

Youssou continued to show his support for the South African president, organising a show in 1996 to coincide with Mandela's planned visit to Senegal. Peter Gabriel and Bobby McFerrin were among the stars who arrived to perform at the Stade de l'Amitié (now the Stade Léopold Sédar Senghor). Film-maker Spike Lee, owner of the label 40 Acres and a Mule Musicworks, which had recently signed a record deal with Youssou, also came. Sadly the concert went ahead without the president, who was forced to postpone his visit at the last minute. When Mandela eventually arrived in Dakar, Youssou and the Super Étoile played for him on a stage specially erected in front of the presidential palace.

As well as expressing his feelings about Nelson Mandela in song, Youssou had these words to say about the president when we spoke in Dakar back in June 2006:

Black people have always withstood oppression. You only have to look at the chains on the slave island of Gorée to be reminded of how skin was torn from the arms of unwilling Africans as they resisted transportation. So Nelson Mandela was not the only martyr, there have been thousands, millions, but I chose to pay homage to that great man. Mandela is our role model, a father to us all. The first time I met him I had tears in my eyes. No one has given so much of himself in order to construct a better world. On 10 May 1994, the day he became president of South Africa, I was in Auckland, New Zealand, and when I heard the news I ran around the airport like a madman, my arms outstretched, shouting, 'Mandela is president.' When, after almost half a century spent fighting for freedom and justice, he willingly stepped down from office, it was like the cherry on the cake and I said to myself, he *is* the greatest.

When the ninth of Youssou's ten children was born on 18 July 2012, the birthday of the South African president, he named him Nelson Mandela N'Dour. Mandela died the following year, aged ninety-five.

'Set' ('Cleanliness')

In 1989, 'Set' became the theme song for a social movement called Set Setal, initiated by Joe Ouakam and the Laboratoire Agit Art to clean up Dakar and counteract careless attitudes towards filth in urban spaces. When the movement began, piles of rubbish had accumulated in the streets and in the rainy season water lay in stagnant pools. Sewers smelled so foul that people worried about their health and safety – and there was another stench, that of corruption and greed. In many ways the initiative introduced a charming spirit of neighbourhood collaboration: women began cleaning in front of their doors, while across the street, artists painted graphic murals and young people took to the streets to pick up rubbish.

The song became topical once more in the early 2000s, when fresh roadworks and rebuilding programmes introduced by

President Wade's government led to constant disorder. The urban landscape was at times apocalyptic, conjuring up scenes that would not have been out of place in an Eisenstein film. Happily, this state of affairs was only temporary.

'Békoor' ('Drought')

In the Senegalese countryside, dry riverbeds and dying trees are a reminder that too much has been taken from the land. The needs of day-to-day living – firewood for stoves or food for goats – have led to the depletion of vital resources. The continual cropping of peanuts for profit has exhausted the soil when it might easily be refreshed with local fertiliser and good husbandry.

Africa is responsible for just 2 per cent of the world's carbon emissions, yet Africans will suffer more than most from the effects of global warming due to their proximity to the equator. In the Sahel region, this will mean more drought and further desertification.

Youssou wrote 'Békoor', with its stormy percussion lines and rousing rhythms, as a wake-up call and performed it at a special concert he organised at Dakar's Iba Mar Diop stadium in support of drought victims. In the song, he outlines some measures people can take to prepare for future droughts:

> Let us plant trees and water them
> To plan is always a good thing!

In 2005, The Great Green Wall, a project developed by the African Union and supported by scientists from Kew Gardens in London, began to organise the planting of a 5,000-mile wall of thorny trees stretching across thirteen Saharan countries, from West Africa's Atlantic coast to the Red Sea at Djibouti.[1]

'Toxiques' ('Toxic Waste')

Some European companies have resorted to paying developing countries large sums of money to dispose of their toxic waste. In February 2007, an Amsterdam-based oil trader, Trafigura, reached an out-of-court settlement of $200 million (around £108 million) with the government of the Ivory Coast after thousands of Ivorians fell ill as a result of coming into contact with waste unloaded by an Ivorian waste company from one of Trafigura's cargo ships, the *Probo Koala*. Seventeen people died and the government of the Ivory Coast were forced to deal with the waste themselves.[2] Such poison is powerful for hundreds of years and can kill human beings, animals and anything living on the land or in the sea. This is what Youssou had to say about the matter in 'Toxiques':

> Rich countries
> Make toxic waste
> Why should they send it to me?
> Poor countries know toxic waste
> Why should they accept it?
> When I'm in bed
> I can't stop thinking about it
> When I'm awake
> I have to warn you
> Chorus: We say it's true
> Many of the underdeveloped countries
> Are beginning to say No!

'Immigrés'

In Senegal, as in neighbouring West African countries, the issue of emigration has taken on a new and sinister dimension in recent years. Every year thousands of Senegalese men and women who are desperate to feed their families attempt to escape to Europe by plane, by boat via the Canary Islands or overland via the North African coast. If the boats are intercepted the occupants are repatriated, although many die at sea.

Many Senegalese artists have highlighted the plight of these migrants. Back in 2002, the young Senegalese film director, Massamba Ndiaye, considered the pressing problem of illegal immigration in his award-winning short film *Banc Jaaxle* (*The Worry Bench*), inspired by the tragic story of a young Senegalese boy, Bouna Wade, who died in the landing gear of a plane along with Guinean friends.[3] The following year the Senegalese writer, Fatou Diome, highlighted the phenomenon in her powerful novel *Le Ventre de L'Atlantique* (*The Belly of the Atlantic*).[4] In 2007, Youssou made a personal appeal on Senegalese TV: 'Don't risk your life. You are the future of Africa.' In his 2016 song 'Exodus'

26. Immigrés.

he called for unity, solidarity and dignity and urged young people to stay in Africa to help construct a brighter future for all. And in 'Here' the same year, Senegalese singer Awa Ly asked the pertinent question about the possible fate of people attempting to escape by boat, 'What will you do when you find yourself in the middle of the sea?'

As far back as the 1980s, when Youssou was moved by the plight of immigrants in France – some of whom had been separated from their families in Senegal for long periods – he wrote one of his most poignant songs, 'Immigrés', to remind them of the benefits of living in their own country.

I gained some appreciation of its message when my first husband, Babacar Diouf, made his first visit home in six years. He described the impact his absence had upon him and his Senegalese family. His cousins met him at the airport and accompanied him to his house in Fass, but he asked the taxi driver to stop a little way off, as he wanted to walk in the sand, smell the atmosphere and feel the fresh sea breeze. In the courtyard, his mother jumped for joy when she saw him, then began to cry. His granny, who was in her room, pulled him to her and wept as she touched his head and his body, telling him it had been too long and that she had begun to wonder if she would ever see him again.

According to Youssou, the inspiration for 'Immigrés' came so naturally the song practically wrote itself. It began with a rhythm guitar riff from Pape Oumar Ngom and a thumping bassline from Kabou Gueye, and when the percussionists added a robust rhythm section it was on automatic pilot. The song became the title track on an album produced in France by Gilbert Castro and released by Celluloid in 1985.

When in 1988 *Immigrés* was first released in the UK on the Earthworks label, writer and broadcaster Charlie Gillett wrote the liner notes. He recognised the potential of Youssou's music on the international market:

We are not quite at the end of the decade, but this record has already staked a firm claim to be one of the landmark records of the Eighties as Van Morrison's 'Astral Weeks' and Marvin Gaye's 'What's Going On' were for the Seventies and Bob Dylan's 'Like a Rolling Stone' and Jimi Hendrix's 'Hey Joe' were for the Sixties ... For me this music follows on naturally from Dire Straits and the Police and it's just a matter of time before the rest of the world catches on.

'Sinébar' (Drugs)

At dead of night, in the murky streets of Medina, drug dealers ply their desperate trade in crack, the most addictive form of cocaine, which is widely used in Dakar. Distilled into small rocks, it is smoked in the ghettos with a makeshift pipe made from a simple matchbox. In 'Sinébar', Youssou, who decries the use of drugs and the abuse of alcohol, reminds people that there are better things to do in life. He sings: 'As for the Super Étoile, we enjoy our job better than taking drugs. We don't need it, and moreover, we are making you happy.'

'Africa Stop Ebola'

In 2014, following the outbreak of the devastating Ebola virus in Liberia, Sierra Leone and Guinea, international aid agencies were often criticised for not acting quickly enough to set up hospitals or dispatch more nurses to the area. Baaba Maal took the opportunity during a BBC radio interview to encourage Western-educated African doctors and health workers to return home in order to help tend the sick and the dying. 'Africa Stop Ebola', a reggae track produced by Carlos Chirinos for the label 3D Family and performed in French as well as local African languages by

Salif Keita, Toumani Diabaté, Oumou Sangaré, Tiken Jah Fakoly
and Didier Awadi advised Africans on how they might stop the
disease, while expressing hope for its eradication. When Youssou
collaborated with the Nigerian hip-hop star J. Martins, their video
clip 'Time is Now' opened with a fulsome expression of sympathy
for the victims of Ebola.

'Gainde' ('The Lion')

Passionate about football, Youssou wrote the song 'Gainde' to
encourage the national football team, Les Lions de la Teranga.

In 2002 the team qualified for the World Cup for the very first
time. To everyone's amazement, they beat the cup holders, France,
in the first round. Symbolically, this was a powerful moment, since
the Senegalese team had just defeated the country which had
colonised their own. According to one of the Senegalese players,
Henri Camara, Youssou would often call them on the telephone

21. *Recording 'The Lion'.*

to encourage them. They knew he was behind them whether they won or lost, and when they lost the African Cup of Nations they saw him crying, which touched them very much. Youssou also composed the official football World Cup anthem 'La Cour des Grands' ('The Court of the Great'), which he performed with the Belgian star Axelle Red on the occasion of the draw for the World Cup in Marseille in December 1997.

'Donkaasigi' ('Well-being')

In keeping with the praise-singing tradition, Youssou acknowledges well-known figures in contemporary society: Thierno Mamady Sakho ('Touré' in the song 'Wareff'); Sérigne Ndiaye Bouna in 'Alboury'; Moustapha Sy Djamil, a Tidjani marabout who lived at Fass, in 'Djamil'; the Thiam family in 'Walo'; and Bassirou Les Diagne in 'Yalla Dogal'. In 'Yarou' he sings with wry humour about Samba Gueye, known as Samba Abidjan, a Toucouleur merchant who was so rich he could afford to take over the second floor of the Concorde La Fayette hotel in Paris (now the Hyatt Regency Paris Étoile). Many of Youssou's fans found the idea of staying at the hotel so appealing they talked of staying there if they visited Paris! Thierno Diabaté (one of Youssou's most generous benefactors, whom he also lauds in song) would drive all the way from the Gambia to Dakar to attend a show, during which he would hand out large banknotes to Youssou and each of the musicians.

In the way *griots* have always done, Youssou offers advice based on common sense or age-old wisdom, making frequent use of traditional Wolof proverbs. In 'Donkaasigi' well-being is compared to a monkey's hammock, which can be hung on any tree. In other words, if your heart is in the right place and if you have the right attitude towards your neighbour and to life itself, whatever your circumstances, you can be happy wherever you are:

Everyone has a right to live comfortably
People must help each other to create a balance
So that everyone will have enough to be at ease
Unfortunately the gap between the rich and the poor is all too great
Be content and don't envy what others have.

'Sama Doom' ('My Daughter')

In 'Sama Doom', written for his daughter Thioro, Youssou sings,

Don't wish ill on others, and good only for yourself.
It is wicked to be selfish. Put others before yourself
And God before all.
Be forgiving and remember that
The love of money is the root of many evils.
In that way you will more surely follow your destiny.

28. *Thioro N'Dour.*

'Juum' ('Mistake')

The song 'Juum' is a cover version of Jimmy Cliff's 'Originator'. In it Youssou uses the Wolof line '*Nit ki dul juum amul Yalla buur bi rekka dul juum*' to express the maxim 'to err is human, to forgive divine.' In typically impish fashion, he finishes the song with the line: 'Excuse me, I think I've made a mistake...'

'Wooy' ('Woolly Hat')

'Wooy' is dedicated to children everywhere. In Dakar the song prompted the commercialisation of hats marked with an *X* to represent both Malcolm X, the American Muslim minister, human rights activist and pan-Africanist who was assassinated in February 1965 and Xippi, Youssou's music studio. Ever the astute business-man, Youssou had bought remaindered T shirts and hats from his then producer, Spike Lee, who directed the 1992 film *Malcolm X*.

There are surely few pop stars in the world who have addressed such a broad range of subjects in their songs as Youssou has done. He has written more than five hundred tracks, most of them influenced or inspired by the people he has met or current affairs in Senegal or in Africa as a whole. His voice has often been a moderating one.

7

INSPIRATIONAL FEMALE SPONSORS

Leading ladies

Senegalese women made up around three quarters of Youssou's early audiences. Following a tradition of patronage that had been established at the outset of the colonial era when rich, mixed-race businesswomen called *signares* distributed their largesse during festive occasions and set fashion trends, modern ladies of means supported Youssou with gifts of money, fine cloth and musical equipment. In return he sang their praises.

Among those who played an important role as both muse and patron was Marième Dieng Salla. Born on the banks of the Senegal River at Dagana on 23 July 1953 to a Mauritanian father and a Senegalese mother, Marième was a woman of rare beauty and charm who became the talk of Dakar. She was the guest of honour at many of Youssou and the Super Étoile's most memorable concerts, especially those which took place in her home town of Dagana, where the setting was the gardens of the former residence of Léon César Faidherbe, governor of Senegal from 1854 to 1865. On those gala evenings, held in the open air under a starlit sky, there was always an interval during which a famous *griot* or female *griotte* – such as the grand diva Adja Mbana Diop, whose ancestors had sung for the Walo kings – sang the praises of certain families who were present. From the VIP gallery, some of Marième Dieng Salla's guests would make their way to the stage to spray or dash Youssou with money, placing notes on his forehead.

Marième became the fourth wife of El Hadj 'Ndiouga' Babacar Kébé, son of a marabout from Kaolack and one of the richest men in Senegal. In 1956, Kébé began trading in diamonds which he purchased in the Congo and other African countries, and by 1973 he had established a huge import-export business in Senegal. He owned a palace in Touba, properties in the regional town of Kaolack and an apartment in the Rue de Prony in the 17th arrondissement in Paris. In Dakar he constructed the city's tallest building, the Immeuble Kébé (which is still one of the most imposing high-rise structures in central Dakar), built the Sahm shopping centre, the first of its kind, and in 1974 opened the Sahel nightclub, with its own resident band, Le Sahel. Kébé fathered twenty-two children and housed each of his wives in a separate villa in the area known as Fann-Résidence; Marième lived at Villa Kébé 7 in the Rue des Ambassades. The Senegalese people in the street watched in wonder as she drove by in the latest top-of-the-range Jaguar, a golden Mercedes 500 or a gleaming BMW.

When I arrived in Dakar in October 1984, people were gossiping that Youssou and Marième were romantically involved and that Ndiouga Kébé – who had died in a mysterious road accident on 13 March, his seventieth birthday – had been murdered by Youssou's marabouts. Then a report that Youssou had been killed in revenge by Kébé's marabouts became so pervasive that Youssou was obliged to appear on state television to prove he was still alive. Youssou, for his part, has always insisted that his relationships with Marième and all the women whom he has praised in song were based on true friendship and the highest respect.

A friend and patron of many musicians, Marième contributed financially when the Jackson Five visited Dakar in 1972 and met with James Brown and the singer Dalida when they performed at the Daniel Sorano National Theatre. She opened her home to artists, especially the musicians she admired, notably Ndiouga Dieng, Ismaël Lô, the brothers Touré Kunda – and, of course, Youssou, for whom she had special admiration and to whom she offered instruments and sound equipment.

Following her husband's death, Marième remarried but sadly died in childbirth in January 1987, aged just thirty-four. President Mobutu of Zaire and President Abdou Diouf, who were admirers, attended her funeral in Dakar and many Senegalese still describe her as 'immortal'. In May 2006, almost twenty years after her death, several society magazines compared her to Princess Diana or Marilyn Monroe. *Icône*, the jet set's glamour magazine, reproduced photographs of Marième and described her as

> part angel with a spark of genius, a person who was more than a myth and was certainly legendary ... she left behind her as many good deeds as could be counted on a string of prayer beads ... she was rich in her breeding, rich in beauty, rich because of her husband's wealth but also and especially rich because of her kindness to those less well off than herself and for the quality of her human relationships which she maintained discreetly and with tolerance.[1]

I met Alassane Mbodj, Marième Dieng's brother, at her former home in the Avenue des Ambassades. We walked the length of the avenue towards the sea, passing by the lavish, walled villas: Kébé 1, the home of Ndiouga Kébé's first wife; the home of the director general of telecoms provider Sonatel; the Dutch ambassador's residence. We talked of those earlier days when life was easy, money no object and Marième was generous to a fault. The night she died, it was Alassane who had driven Marième to the Clinique Hubert. Clearly the shock of her death had left a deep wound in his heart.

A few streets away is the home of Ndella Wade, another of Youssou's benefactors, to whom he dedicated his song 'Bes'. For him she is the incarnation of beauty, generosity, simplicity and self-effacement and retains a kind of mystery that he admires. In the traditional manner Youssou sings her genealogy:

Samba Woury, Aye Dièye, Papa Cissé, Mariama Diagne, Ndella Wade. Whoever sang it will sing it again: Birahima Jaabi, Samba Woury, Maye Dièye, Papa Cissé, Mariama Ndiaye. I hold you in the highest esteem, for no one can be kinder than you.

When Ndella Wade or Marième Dieng Salla came to Youssou's concerts at the Sorano Theatre they became his muses, inspiring him by their presence and contributing in their own way to the creative process. Senegalese journalist Massamba Mbaye told me in August 2006 how, in a spirit of gratitude and friendship, Youssou N'Dour had immortalised cherished figures from Marième Dieng Salla to Ndella Wade; people who became part of his voice down the years and who acquired their place in his repertoire through the mysterious connections we all make with each other.

By their celebrity these well-known females influenced other women who, in turn, promoted Youssou's music, helping to unite fans from populous suburbs like Pikine and those from the wealthier areas of Dakar such as Fann-Résidence.

Another well-connected lady for whom Youssou wrote a praise song was Nanette Ada, a niece of President Léopold Sédar Senghor, who was married to Ablaye Ndiack, Senghor's Minister of Information. Their daughter Colette would bring flowers to Youssou on his birthday and when he finally met Nanette, he dedicated the very next song he composed to her. It announces its subject with a boldly ascending brass fanfare followed by tripping *tama* and staccato *sabar* phrases topped by Youssou's wailing vocals and washed over by Adama Faye's rippling keyboards. 'Nanette Ada' takes pride of place on Youssou's magnificent cassette *Africa Deebub*.

One of Youssou's earliest patrons, Absa Gueye Yaye Dior, was the subject of the song 'Absa Gueye', which he composed with the Étoile de Dakar in 1979. A well-known beauty who was always dressed to the nines, she would arrive at his shows with a huge star denoting her support for the band emblazoned on her boubou dress, turning every head in the hall. She helped Youssou purchase instruments and introduced him and his music to an affluent new audience from the central Plateau area, where she lived on the Rue Carnot.

Absa Gueye was the daughter of Ibrahima Gueye Kato Diagne, a wealthy businessman who made furniture for the marabouts of the Sy family at Tivaouane and owned a fleet of cars, limousines and convertibles which he rented out to French governors and *colons* in the years before independence. An elegant dandy who wore three watches, one on each wrist and one around his neck, Ibrahima had four beautiful wives – including Aminata Niang,

29. *Absa Gueye.*

the mother of Absa Gueye – each of whom played a traditional instrument in the family orchestra. Absa Gueye inherited her father's business acumen, travelling all over West Africa to buy textiles, mainly in the Ivory Coast, Togo, Mali and Ghana. When I met her at home in the Mermoz district of Dakar, she told me, 'Youssou is very wise and well-behaved, and his success is due to the fact that he loves and respects his mother.'

Youssou's mother, Ndèye Sokhna Mboup, believed in him and always supported him, especially in the early years of his career and despite his father's objections to his becoming an artist. Ever mindful of this, Youssou wrote 'Jimaamu' especially for his mother. *Jimaamu* means modesty, one of the cardinal rules in the Wolof code of honour.

It was Youssou's maternal grandmother, Marie Sène, however, who was his primary musical inspiration. For her he composed 'Yaakar' ('Hope'), a melodious tribute which features the *asiko* percussion of the late Ismael Thiam, otherwise known as Billy Kongoma, founder of the Ballet D'Afrique Noir in the 1950s. Journalist Massamba Mbaye eloquently summed up the significance of Youssou's maternal lineage and *griot* heritage when he told me:

> The legacy of his mother in the wake of his grandmother is more than simple syntax; it traces a direct link and a bridge to an antique Africa of grand deeds; a world where there were no satellite dishes but caravans and caravels.

Awa Gueye, another of Youssou's supporters, told me with pride that the first time she heard the song that bears her name was during a gala performance by Youssou and his band at the Sorano Theatre. On that occasion she had felt quite overcome with emotion. A joyously limpid, bluesy, blowsy shuffle, the song grooves with a slow rock 'n' roll rhythm and is eminently danceable by Senegalese and non-Senegalese alike. Awa Gueye's mother, Aissatou

Sow, a Toucouleur lady from the Fouta area around Saint-Louis, was the first Senegalese woman to buy embroidered cotton from Europe and Awa followed her example, travelling to Paris, Italy and Switzerland to buy textiles for sale in her shop in the HLM5 district and her stall in the Castor market. Knowing that Youssou liked to be stylish onstage, she offered him literally kilometres of magnificent cloth for costumes. She passed away in 2011, but her song illuminated its time and is one of my own favourite pieces.

Such discerning female trendsetters were the forerunners of Senegal's modern fashion designers like Linn Senghor, Collé Ardo Sow, Dasha Nicoué or Claire Kane, whose subtle yet distinctive creations in *pagne tissée* (traditional woven cloth) have been worn onstage by Youssou.

One designer who regularly works with Youssou is Diouma Dieng Diakhaté, who gave up her secretarial job at air traffic control company ASECNA to pursue her passion for making clothes, initially setting up shop in her garage with just one sewing machine. Today, Shalimar Couture, the company she founded, is one of the most successful in Senegal. Diakhaté, herself a model of poise, charm and beauty, has dressed African heads of state and their wives and designed outfits for Barbara Bush, Hillary Clinton and Oracene Price, mother of tennis stars Venus and Serena Williams. I first met her when Youssou and I visited her workshop to select stage costumes, and when I later asked Madame Diakhaté to give me her impressions of Youssou's career, she received me in her office in the Boulevard de la République. She invited me to sit on one side of her desk while on the other side she drew up her usual chair, a Swiss ball. As she sat down, she pointed to her flat stomach, exclaiming, 'How else do you think I keep this trim?' At her fashion shows, whether in Abidjan, Paris or Tokyo, Madame Diakhaté – who is patron of *L'Observateur*, the newspaper run by Youssou's company Futurs Médias – used Youssou's songs for her soundtrack. A recipient of Senegalese TV station RTS's Woman of the Year award, she has invested money in social initiatives, including maternity hospitals and a morgue. When she announced her divorce from her long-time Senegalese husband, the gossip columns linked her romantically with the Congolese singer, Kofi Olomide, who had dedicated a song to her. She was a candidate in the 2012 presidential elections (an ill-advised move, perhaps, since she lost her deposit after gaining just 0.12 per cent of the total vote). A consolation was her appointment the same year as roving ambassador for Senegal by the newly elected president, Macky Sall.

The women whom Youssou describes in 'Jigééni Rééw Mi' ('Women of my Country') are well aware that they are no less worthy than their menfolk. Some serve as government ministers, some work in the fields, some in the marketplace, some stand over the cooking pot, some pound grain and some are in the sea at Bargny, pulling nets alongside their men. Certainly many Senegalese women are beautiful, but other qualities, including serenity, sensitivity and inner strength, also make them attractive. 'Women are the salt of the earth, the backbone of the nation,' sings Youssou. As architect and film-maker Nicholas Cissé told me in June 2006, a Senegalese woman learns how to keep a secret in her heart. She can find something very displeasing about her husband, yet keep it to herself forever.

Signare courtesans

Strong independent women have long been a force to be reckoned with in Senegalese society. Since colonial life was solitary for early European traders and administrators who travelled to Africa, they entered into arrangements with local chiefs and elders to marry African women for the duration of their service in Senegal. Those wives, who were chosen for their beauty and poise, lived with their husbands in Saint-Louis, the former capital of Senegal, or on Gorée Island, where they became wealthy courtesans and enjoyed the benefits of a luxurious lifestyle. The children of such intermarriages produced successive generations of increasingly more beautiful and charming *signares*, a name once given to noble ladies of the Portuguese court of Joseph the First. As befitted their station, the *signares* lived in large colonial houses and defined good manners and high fashion. Adorned with elegant headdresses and elaborate jewellery and wearing their most alluring costumes, fashioned from the finest silks and cashmere, they could be seen promenading along the bank of the Senegal River at five o'clock for their afternoon *takussanu*. Many of them expressed their independence and emancipation by smoking a pipe. One of them boasted that she had had as many lovers as the pearls on the beads which covered her hips. She even doubted whether she had enough sets of beads to count them all.

Looking beyond the stock images of *signares* as graceful and beautiful concubines, historian Jean-Luc Angrand has presented a revisionist view of their lives. Highlighting their business acumen, he describes these women as the *Mama Benz* of their day. They were highly organised traders in gum arabic, gold and indigo. Some of them owned their own boats, and at the end of the seventeenth century they exported up to 150,000 hides a year to Holland. They rented out workshops to craftsmen whose woven products were transported in *signare* ships to ports on the African coast. Thus the *signares* were rich, often more so than their European husbands.[2]

At traditional Christmas and New Year's Eve parades called *Fanals*, the *signares* presided from their balconies while specially constructed floats, decorated wooden models of landmark buildings lit up by lanterns, filed past below. *Griots* and *asiko* percussionists animated the parade, singing praise songs to their *signare* patrons in the hope and expectation that they would be showered with gifts of money.

Although the practice of *Fanal* parades finally lapsed, Marie Madeleine Diallo, one of the most famous actresses in Senegal, who appeared in *Dékal Ndar*, Senegal's most popular television soap opera, was instrumental in reviving the *Fanal* parade as part of the millennium celebrations in her native city. Youssou dedicated his song 'Marie Madeleine' to the actress.

Signare culture also inspired Fabienne Diouf, the daughter of Senegal's former president Abdou Diouf, a friend and early supporter of Youssou who introduced him to Stevie Wonder and other well-known musicians when they came to Senegal. Fabienne is an astute businesswoman of exceptional energy and drive. She renovated a typical Saint-Louis *signare* town house to create La Maison Rose, a luxury hotel. With considerable flair and exquisite taste, she developed a line of high-quality modern tableware, shawls and jewellery inspired by traditional Senegalese designs and made by craftspeople in Saint-Louis, where her company – aptly named Signare – was based.

30. *Marie Madeleine Diallo.*

Heroines in history

The heroines of yesteryear have gained renewed relevance through Youssou's songs. 'Miss', for example, co-written with Pape Dieng, is a piece that conveys the pathos of Greek tragedy in both its lyrics and the manner in which Youssou sings it. It tells the story of two remarkable and legendary women, the first of whom resisted the French colonisation of Senegal.

Aline Sitoe Diatta was born a Diola princess in 1920 in the Kabrousse area of Mosor in the province of Casamance. She led a fierce resistance movement against Portuguese colonial domination, later protesting against the French colonisers who were demanding that Senegalese farmers produce large quantities of rice and meat for the World War II effort in Europe. Carrying an emblematic baton, she moved from village to village opposing the payment of taxes and boycotting the planting of peanut crops. She opposed the drafting of Senegalese foot soldiers (known as *Tirailleurs Sénégalais*), 93,000 of whom served in Europe during both world wars. Aline Sitoe Diatta was arrested by the French and deported to a prison in Timbuktu, Mali. She died in captivity in May 1944 but remains a symbol of resistance, especially for the people of Casamance in Senegal's southern province. Even after her death, she represented the spirit of revolution for communists who formed the political party Ande Dieuf, which was popular with Senegalese students in the 1980s. The main female campus at Cheikh Anta Diop University in Dakar is named after her, and the stadium in Ziguinchor also bears her name.

The second subject of 'Miss' is Yacine Boubou, the queen who sacrificed herself so that her son might inherit the throne and become *damel* (king). She was the consort of King Madior, who had several wives, all young and beautiful. When the king dreamt that one of them must be sacrificed in order to perpetuate his reign, the first, second and third wives all refused, but Yacine Boubou did not hesitate to pay the ultimate price, giving up her own life so that her son might succeed his father.

Another example of Youssou giving prominence to heroines of the past is in his song 'Nelson Mandela', where he compares the plight of apartheid victims in South Africa to a group of brave Senegalese women from Walo who, upon receiving news that their husbands had been captured by an invading Trarza king, gathered in a hut and set fire to it rather than be raped and taken hostage. It is said that not one of these women screamed or uttered a word while suffering immense pain.

8

EMPERORS AND KINGS

Griot praise singers, keepers of history and entertainers

Listening in 2006 to the modern *griot*, storyteller and historian Babacar Ndaak Mbaye explain to me how West Africa was ruled in the days of the great empires, I began to understand that Youssou's interest in democracy and justice is as much a part of his heritage as singing. Mbaye stressed the importance of the word in the *Penc*, the place where people came to listen to the king through his spokesman the *griot* and to cast their vote in the *Wariyu*, the assembly composed of all social classes which ensured that the people had their say in all decisions – ancient African democracy at work. In the evening, wrestling matches took place in the same *Penc*, and singers and musicians came to demonstrate their talents. There was a *Penc* in each village and up to twelve in the region of Dakar alone. Mbaye believes that colonisation destroyed those traditions and along with them social structures that were different from – and, in his opinion, perhaps just as effective as – modern Western democracy.

Nowadays there are no kings, but there are still *griots* in the Republic of Senegal. Practising *griots* from hereditary families (including the Kouyatés, the Diabatés, the Mbayes, the Secks and the Sambs) are still called upon to perform at baptisms, weddings, *kassak* circumcision ceremonies or wrestling matches which resemble ancient Greek or Roman tournaments, and they help families with genealogy when marriage is on the cards. With their innate gift for oratory, many *griots* have found a modern role in broadcasting, and more recently in politics.

Even though Youssou's modern repertoire has been inspired by Wolof history and legend, his songs are topical, often praising the virtues of well-known public figures with whom he is personally acquainted. In 'Ndiadiane Ndiaye', his tribute to the first Wolof king, he also praises Lamine Nar Diop, a friend who helped him in the early stages of his career by bringing influential members of the government to see him perform.

Ahmadou Ndiaye, who became known as Ndiadiane Ndiaye, was born in the thirteenth century to a Berber saint. Ahmadou was a virtuous man, and legend has it that soon after his father died he manifested mystical signs and spiritual powers. (When the King of Sine heard about these mysteries he was apparently astonished and exclaimed '*Ah Ndiadiano*', meaning 'Isn't that amazing!') Ndiaye founded the first Wolof kingdom, where Wolof and Serer noblemen served him before separating into independent kingdoms. He gave a structure to the Wolof empire by federating these kingdoms and creating a capital at Tcheng, with Wolof the lingua franca.

Ndiadiane Ndiaye's descendants reigned until Alboury Ndiaye became the last Wolof king in 1875. Alboury, who had twelve wives, was said to have had lemon-yellow eyes that turned red when he went into battle. A man with the heart of a lion, who concluded it was better to die than to live in ignominy, Alboury was killed by a poisoned arrow at the age of thirty. Youssou sang about Alboury at the outset of his career in the Miami nightclub, and a revised version of 'Alboury' recorded in 1989 praises the king's grandson, millionaire businessman and entrepreneur Sérigne Ndiaye Bouna (who is also the cousin of Abdou Diouf, Senegal's former president). At first Bouna made his money selling second-hand clothes in street markets like the present one at Colobane. Then he set up the company SPCA Thubet, which imported cars and represented Honda and Brezza in Senegal. Today he owns the duty-free shop at Dakar airport and imports petrol from Saudi Arabia and other Arab countries. When Libyan president Muammar Gaddafi visited Dakar to take part in the 2006 Independence Day celebrations he was a guest at Bouna's mansion in the Dakar suburb of Almadies. The epic nature of Youssou's piece is emphasised by a grand intro similar to the fanfare that welcomes Spanish toreadors to the arena before a bullfight.

In his song 'Birima', one of the most impressive in his entire repertoire, Youssou recalls another famous king and brings the song right up to date by evoking his friend Aziz Mbaye, brother of the Super Étoile guitarist Jimi Mbaye; as mentioned in Chapter 4, Aziz Mbaye was once the president of the Youssou N'Dour Foundation before becoming Minister of Culture in the government of President Macky Sall. Furthermore, Aziz Mbaye's wife is called Birima. The name, itself a form of Ibrahima, is given to both females and males in Senegal, just as Evelyn, Hilary or Valentine are unisex names in the UK or Ireland.

The story of 'Birima' dates back to the early thirteenth century, when a select group of families produced kings. Although the kingship was not hereditary, the throne passed to the one who was judged the most worthy, and this occasionally led to rivalry. In Cayor, where the kings were chosen from the Fall family, Birima Ngoné Latyr was the charismatic son of the *lingère* (queen), Ngoné Latyr Fall. He was the nephew of Amary Ngoné, King of Bardial, and grandson of Birima Maissai Tend Dior, who reigned over the kingdom of Cayor from 1855 to 1859. When Birima fell out with his cousin Thieyacine his uncle intervened, but Birima felt he was not impartial and decided to leave Cayor instead. He went to Sine, from where – with the help of the *bour* (king) – he organised raids on the lands of Cayor and Baol, burning the crops. He fought his uncle in the Battle of Ndiop and thus gained the throne of Cayor. As king, Birima spoke to his people once a year on the occasion of a grand feast day celebrated with wine, meat and sweetmeats. On this day, he would emerge from his house to make his speech and then return indoors immediately, and for this he became known as *Birima Mathia Bene Batba* (Birima Who Had One Message). An efficient administrator, he was known for his dignity, his courage and his discretion. A Ceddo aristocrat, he represented the values and honour of the Ceddo soldiers who resisted Islam.[1] He refused to collaborate with the French colonisers and died in 1860 – poisoned, it was said, on the orders of Faidherbe, governor of Senegal.

During the recording of the song 'Birima', a vocal tour de force, Youssou entered the recording booth and delivered a full demonstration of all his musical capabilities, stretching his voice to new high notes at the top of his four-octave range. After all his years of singing, confident in every aspect of his instrument, he closed his eyes and imagined he was in a village long ago, a traditional singer in the court of the *Penc*. Like the villagers who once gathered around the baobab tree, the sound crew and the musicians assembled in the control room were visibly moved by his performance.

Performing 'Birima' in April 1997 in the Stade Léopold Sédar Senghor, Dakar's largest stadium, in front of 100,000 ecstatic young fans and in the presence of President Abdou Diouf, Youssou seemed more popular than the head of state, and his showcase song had virtually become a national anthem.[2]

The popular song 'Kocc Barma' was written about Kobthie Barma Fall, a well-known Senegalese philosopher and master of proverbs who was born Ibrahima Fall in 1585 in the village of Ndiongué Fall. He was so talented that he earned the nicknames 'Kocc', meaning clever, and 'Barma', another form of Birima. He liked to play draughts with the king, a serious rival. One day, Kocc appeared with his head shaven save for four curious tufts, each tuft representing a proverb:

> *Jigeen soppal te bul woolu*: You can love a young wife, but do not tell her everything.
> *Burr du mbokk*: A ruler can betray anyone, even his own family.
> *Doomi jittle du doom*: An adopted son is not a real son.
> *Mag matnaa ba cim reew*: The elders are the wisest in the community.

31. *Kocc Barma.*

The king was apparently intrigued, but Kocc played for a time before revealing the secret of his hairstyle. Impatient, the king bribed Kocc's young wife with a gold casket to reveal the secrets. Vexed when his wife betrayed his confidence, Kocc realised that the first proverb had been fulfilled. Kocc was, in fact, a half-brother of the king, so he recognised the second proverb when the king arrested him and sentenced him to death. As Kocc was being led to the gallows, his young stepson was brought before the king in the hope that that would soften his heart, but no. Then the child, thinking of his own gain, asked the king to give him Kocc's clothes, making the third proverb a reality. When an old man arrived to plead for Kocc's release and the plea was granted, the final proverb came true. Kocc Barma died in 1665 at the age of eighty but today one can visit his mausoleum in the village of Ndiongué.

32. *Youssou in his Kocc Barma costume.*

Performing 'Kocc Barma' on stage, Youssou wore a patchwork jacket and peaked cap, and during one of his more convincing dance routines would twirl and doff his hat in homage to the great sage.

Another early king who features in many of Youssou's songs is Lat Dior, King of Cayor. In October 1886 at Derklé, the king, who had opposed the building of the railway line from Dakar to Saint-Louis, went into battle with the French colonisers knowing that he would surely die. 'I prefer that people talk about my death,' he declared. 'I prefer that fate than to live in a Cayor dominated by foreigners ...: on the plains of Derklé I will leave something that will always be remembered, that is my name, and the name of my birthplace, "Niani".' Having uttered these words, he removed his protective gris-gris talismans and entered the fray.[3] Through his death he became a hero of the resistance, and to this day, the youth hymn of Senegal is 'Niani Bagne na' ('Niani Refused').

*

Wolof kings and princes reigned in pomp and style, heading up a complex and fascinating hierarchical society with a strong moral code dictated by rank. Each social group was sensitive to the judgement of the others; they all adhered to strict rules of conduct based on dignity, composure and stoicism, attributes which even today the Senegalese call *mougne*. Their code of honour prescribed respect for ancestors, love of parents, honesty, modesty, discretion, hospitality, generosity, courtesy and sociability. It included formal salutations and abstinence from certain foods, especially the totem animal of the clan.

Garmi aristocrats, who had soldiers, slaves, women and other so-called inferiors in their power, were the courtiers. Nobles (*geer*), who included *laman* chiefs (the word means 'master of the land' in the Serer language), oversaw lands and extracted mineral wealth. The middle-class bourgeoisie were called *jaambur* and the peasants *badolo*. Casted artisans, known collectively as *nenyo*, who lived in a separate part of the village, included *teug* silversmiths and ironworkers, *wuude* shoemakers, *lawbe* carpenters, *sen* coopers and *rabb* weavers. *Griots*, the storytellers and keepers of social history who played a central role in court society and were considered part of the elite, were also casted – and even within their own ranks there was a recognised hierarchy. Some *griots* accompanied their sovereign on expeditions and kept oral records of battles in which they also participated. They exhorted the indecisive to act bravely and the brave to act like heroes, and when they returned from battle they recounted epic stories, balancing tragedy with comedy.

Every Friday *griots* took part in a royal salute for the king and his courtiers, singing the praises of the royals and reciting their genealogy. If a *griot* recited fewer than seven generations he was not rewarded. At meals in the royal household, when wedding guests were served according to the rules of etiquette and rank with specified pieces of meat, *griots* divided the meat and in return received offal or innards, money or a boubou, the Senegalese equivalent of a kaftan.

The chief of the royal *griots*, Fara Dundun (the *dundun* was the drum of war), lived in the capital, where he guarded the royal drums. These drums were used every day by two chief *griots*, who drummed the reveille for the king in the morning and sang his praises. *Griots* were also called upon whenever the king had gallant company and they sang and played for the queen, the *lingère*, when she held dance parties with other noblewomen. The queen had her own drums (*ganben*) and her own special rhythms (*n'diagabare*). The *griots* were close to the *lingère* in the same way that female *griottes* were confidantes to the king. Princes were nursed by *griottes*, whose milk was said to give them power and influence. This reinforced the association between *griots* and kings, and a king without a powerful *griot* was not held in high esteem. The status of *griots* at court was such that they could manipulate public opinion and use their knowledge of political secrets to stir up rumour and rivalry among the vassals or feudal tenants. *Griot* families married among themselves in order to guard the secrets of their profession.

In the *griot* tradition love songs were rare and, though they are few and far between in Youssou's repertoire, his song 'Djino' describes the power of love, personified by the character Capitaine Borom, who pledges: 'If I had an aeroplane, I would give it to you and then I would pilot it for you. Wherever you wish to go, there we will go.' The bassline throbs passionately while Jimi's guitar solo pulls at the heartstrings and the keyboards flutter fancifully. The horns in the coda strike a note of resignation before the final frenzied crescendo of sabars underpins Youssou's enthralled repetition of the words, 'What else can I do to please her?'

Youssou, who has always insisted on keeping his personal life as private as possible, has surely known the joys and vicissitudes of love. Particularly touching was his attachment to the young lady who, by all accounts, is the inspiration for the girl he calls Ami in his song 'Hey You!' The problem was that her parents, being nobles, were unwilling to sanction a marriage to a person whom they regarded as casted. Still a schoolgirl, Ami was walking home from class with a friend when they passed by the Sahel nightclub, and there, standing in the doorway, was Youssou. Their eyes met and as she moved on she chanced to look back and saw that he was following her with his gaze. So began their ill-fated courtship. Youssou's song 'Salimata', where a woman says no to her lover, is perhaps based on a similar story of unrequited love.

9

ALL THE WORLD'S A STAGE

In the summer of 1985, while Youssou was on tour in the UK, Peter Gabriel invited him to record vocal lines for a track on his album *So*, produced by Daniel Lanois.

On the appointed day, I travelled with Youssou to Gabriel's studio in Wiltshire, where the recording of his vocal lines for 'In Your Eyes' was completed in a matter of hours – just in time for tea and croquet on the lawn.

In the evening, back in London, Peter and Daniel joined us at a lavish party in the sumptuous surroundings of a private house in Chelsea's Glebe Place, where Youssou and the band entertained the guests of art dealer Martin Summers and his wife Nona. Youssou's appearance at the party was organised by James Fox, author of *White Mischief*, a story of murder in the British colonial community in Kenya.[1]

33. So, *Peter Gabriel*.

34. *Recording 'In Your Eyes'.*

The following year, when Youssou and the Super Étoile de Dakar were the support act for Peter Gabriel's North American tour, I accompanied them on the first leg of the tour in my capacity as translator. It was winter, and the first thing Youssou's manager, Verna Gillis, did when the musicians arrived in New York was to buy thermal underwear for each of them. In a series of one-night stands, the tour took us to Boston, Philadelphia and Cleveland, Ohio, where, driving through avenues of snow-covered white clapboard houses, we arrived at the Coliseum.

Youssou and the musicians were constantly teasing each other, swapping stories and jokes. On the tour bus, amid the general spirit of bonhomie and good-humoured banter, they would play cards and listen to music, especially 'The Way It Is' by Bruce Hornsby and The Range, a new-found favourite. After each show, as the bus travelled on to another town, the guys would sit up into the early hours replaying a cassette of their earlier performance, listening intently, looking for flaws and discussing improvements before retiring to their bunks for a few hours' sleep. Even when the bus broke down and the temperatures fell well below zero, morale was invariably high.

35. *Youssou enjoying a game of croquet.*

36. *The concert at Glebe Place.*

37. *Youssou and musicians on tour in the USA.*

Peter Gabriel's show was polished and powerful, a carefully choreographed piece of musical theatre. Each night he astonished the auditorium by making a backward flip from the stage into the audience, allowing himself to be passed around the crowd like a parcel. 'In Your Eyes' really came alive on stage as the first encore in his set. *Melody Maker* magazine described how Gabriel's rousing duet with Youssou was an exhilarating demonstration of how easily two cultures can come together in a common inspirational sound, adding,

'Nelson Mandela', Youssou N'Dour's tribute to the South African anti-apartheid hero, had a striking jazz-pop melody line floating seductively over hurricane percussion. And while N'Dour sang the whole set in Wolof, there was a universal glow to his clear, urgent vocal that suggested Michael Jackson wailing away under a bright African sun. N'Dour had also cast his vision of African music westward.[2]

Backstage, during the Madison Square Garden show in New York, I snapped a symbolic picture of Youssou in the company of the exalted kings of rock and pop, Elvis Presley and Michael Jackson.

On a sunny summer day in 1987, Youssou and I drove up to Highgate in north London for lunch at the elegant town house of Sting and his wife, Trudie Styler. We ate in the family kitchen then chatted with Sting in an oak-panelled sitting room where the grand piano took pride of place. Acknowledging his enthusiasm for African music, Sting nevertheless refused to categorise it as

38. *Youssou at Madison Square Garden.*

ethnic music. It was clear he would like to see the removal of all musical barriers, favouring a kind of music without borders, a mingling of global styles, traditions and rhythms. He reminisced about his childhood in Newcastle in the north of England, where he had found his voice as a delivery boy, with one street cry for the morning milk round and another for the evening newspaper. He was later to write music for *The Last Ship*, an album and stage show featuring his home town, but at the time of our visit he was preparing the album *Nothing Like the Sun*. Nine years later Sting invited Youssou to appear with him on the French TV show *Taratata*, where they performed Lennon and McCartney's 'Ob-la-di Ob-la-da', later released by Sony as a single.

In March 1987, the London Palladium was the venue for the Secret Policeman's Third Ball, an event organised by Amnesty International to raise awareness of human rights abuses. The star-studded line-up of comedians and musicians was filmed for television and recorded for an album released by Virgin Records. Jackson Browne and Paul Brady (one of my favourite Irish musicians) performed Browne's 'El Salvador', while Mark Knopfler and Chet Atkins offered a sensitive, sympathetic version of John Lennon's 'Imagine'. Lou Reed sang 'Voices of Freedom', with Peter Gabriel on piano and Youssou contributing backing vocals.

The evening ended with Gabriel's 'Biko', a powerful protest song about Stephen Biko's death in police custody in apartheid South Africa. Peter was joined on stage by Youssou, Pape Oumar Ngom on rhythm guitar and Habib Faye on bass, but Youssou was annoyed when his microphone failed to respond during the final climactic chorus. What the audience did not see was the chaos backstage: a lack of dressing rooms meant that artists were obliged to wait in the wings; some found chairs to sit on, though Bob Geldof and his wife, Paula Yates, settled for the corridor floor. Peter Gabriel was looking for somewhere private to change into his stage costume as Ruby Wax, who was presenting the TV show, rushed by with a film crew in tow.

Youssou continued to support Amnesty International; on 2 September 1988, he joined Bruce Springsteen, Sting, Peter Gabriel and Tracy Chapman at London's Wembley Stadium for a photocall and press conference to announce the charity's *Human Rights Now!* world tour. It is not every day you get to sit opposite 'The Boss', as I did on the short bus journey from the hotel to the press conference!

Following the opening concert in London, the 200-strong caravan of musicians and crew travelled to France, Italy, Spain, Bulgaria, the USA, Hungary, Zimbabwe, the Ivory Coast, Japan and India, ending up in Buenos Aires in mid-October. At each concert, Amnesty distributed booklets outlining the thirty articles in the Universal Declaration of Human Rights drawn up by the United Nations and signed off in Paris in 1948. For Youssou and the Super Étoile, the only non-Western group on the bill, the tour provided a unique opportunity to understand Amnesty's message and to witness their humanitarian work in the various countries they visited. It also served to broaden their musical horizons and allowed them to share their music with new audiences. As for Bruce Springsteen, the stadium concert in Abidjan in the Ivory Coast was the first time that he and his musicians, the E Street Band, had played to an all-black audience. He described it as 'the greatest celebration of mutual discovery that I have ever experienced.'[3]

Youssou defined the importance of musical collaborations to me thus:

> When I meet a musician or a musical style, it leads me somewhere else, and helps to regenerate my career. Some periods have produced a host of ideas born of extraordinary meetings in Senegal or elsewhere, defining moments on tour or even the clash of cultures, and when I have something to express

I don't hold back. I think that collaboration is very important
for musicians in general, for African musicians in particular,
for myself and even for humanity.

In 1983 Youssou took a break from the Super Étoile and from Dakar
to record an album, *Diongoma*, in the government-sponsored
Studio de la Nouvelle Marche in Lomé, Togo. The producer was
Gerard Theus, an African American who had collaborated with
Tamla Motown and who had established a label called Mandingo
to record albums with some of Africa's major artists, namely Mory
Kanté, Aicha Koné and Mamadou Doumbia. His partner in this
venture was Ablaye Soumaré, a Senegalese sound engineer who had
worked with Stevie Wonder. The producers employed Senegalese
musician and arranger Doudou Doucouré as artistic director for
the project, and a group of top African musicians from Ghana,
Cameroon and Togo were chosen to back all of the singers. This
same team produced the first version of 'Yé Ké Yé Ké' by Mory
Kanté, a piece that was subsequently rerecorded in France, where
it topped the charts as a dance single.

As for Youssou, a scheduled week of rehearsals had to be
cancelled because of hitches in his travel arrangements, and his
album *Diongoma* was recorded in just one day and mixed the next.
In the circumstances, and given the complete change in singing
style demanded of Youssou, the results were astonishing. There is
a pan-African feel to this album, a planned structure and a certain
universality that presages Youssou's later work with Peter Gabriel,
Ryuichi Sakamoto, Deep Forest and other international stars. Key
tracks are 'Massamba', 'Saf Safati' and 'Mba', the song that had
launched Youssou's singing career.

This was also the year that Youssou first visited Paris to perform at the Phil One Club in La Défense at the invitation of the
Association of Senegalese Taxi Drivers, whose members had saved
their money in order to bring the group to France. When the French
lost their colonies, they encouraged their ex-servants to come to the

metropolis as street cleaners, domestic staff or to work in factories. Many immigrants lived in foyers in Montreuil and Belleville or the neighbouring suburbs of Mantes-la-Jolie and Les Mureaux, where they were employed in the Citroën and Renault factories. Others worked as street traders, taking advantage of their natural Senegalese talent for commerce. The more he travelled, the more Youssou realised that many Africans had left their country for Europe or America thinking they would find the promised land, but in reality they were often immensely lonely and their lifestyle could be extremely difficult.

In October 1984, when BBC film director Peter Bate and I went along to Dakar's Sahel Club to watch Youssou and the Super Étoile perform their Sunday night show, he arrived just after midnight looking dapper in a cream striped blazer offset by a white flower in the buttonhole. He crossed the floor to greet us with a hearty handshake. Halfway through the concert the band struck up 'Immigrés' and Peter, recognising its merit immediately, said to me, 'That's the track!' Not only did that music catch on, it has endured. Thirty years after its release, a live version of 'Immigrés', which was filmed in Athens in 1987 when Youssou and the band supported Peter Gabriel on his *So* tour, was released by Real World as part of a DVD/CD package entitled *Fatteliku Live*.

The year 1984 was a pivotal one in Youssou's career. In May, he was invited by Mamadou Konté, founder and director of the promotion company Africa Fête, to support the popular Ghanaian group Osibisa at the Pavillon Baltard in the Parisian suburb of Nogent-sur-Marne. Youssou agreed on condition that he close the show, a decision he came to regret when he heard Osibisa play, such was their professionalism and the brilliance of their music. In the audience was Peter Gabriel, an Osibisa fan, who was so bowled over by the 'liquid velvet' of Youssou's voice that he vowed to meet him. Later that year Gabriel made a special journey to Dakar in the company of Senegalese producer George Acogny to seal what was to become a close friendship (each is godfather to the other's son) and to lay the foundations for future collaborations.

Meanwhile, Youssou and the Super Étoile musicians continued their mini European tour with concerts in Switzerland, Norway and Sweden, where he met the young Neneh Cherry, daughter of Sierra Leone musician Amadu Jah Sierra Leone and Swedish artist Monika Klassen (who later married the American jazzman Don Cherry). Then just twelve years old, Neneh marvelled at Youssou's voice and told him, presciently, that she would like to sing with him one day. In London Youssou appeared at The Venue, near Victoria station, as part of a series of *African Nights* concerts which also featured the inimitable Pierre Akendengue from Gabon. Youssou then performed at France's biggest festival, the Fête de l'Humanité.

On 31 December 1984 another providential meeting took place in Dakar. Jacques Higelin, one of France's most famous rock stars, who was on tour in Africa, showed up on New Year's Eve at Youssou's Bal des Sapeurs Pompiers, the Firemen's Ball. Higelin spoke of being impressed not only by the magnificence of Youssou's music but by the style and grace of the Senegalese revellers. The following year, when Youssou and the Super Étoile appeared with Higelin in a series of shows at the Bercy Palais Omnisport stadium, he remarked on Youssou's human qualities of warmth, energy and humour and was astonished by his ability to know exactly what he does and doesn't want.

Youssou and his contemporaries Salif Keita, Angélique Kidjo, Khaled, Papa Wemba and Thomas Mapfumo, whom one might term 'the independence generation', modernised the traditional music of their countries and were the most prominent African artists on the international stage for more than thirty years. They were lucky enough to be picked up by Western record companies who invested in their careers, offered them tour support and introduced them to new audiences around the world.

Throughout his career Youssou has engaged a series of managers, including Verna Gillis and Thomas Rome in America, Michelle Lahana in France and Dudu Sarr in the UK. In 1997, he asked me to meet up with Rob Hallett of the London music agency, Marshall Arts, whom he had met briefly when Rob accompanied Herbie Hancock to the Saint-Louis du Senegal jazz festival and who had expressed a wish to become Youssou's touring agent. We lunched at a north London restaurant near his office and it soon became clear that Rob and his agency, who have represented stars like Paul McCartney and Lionel Ritchie, could indeed offer new platforms and audiences to Youssou and raise his profile among pop and jazz enthusiasts. Following this meeting, Youssou began working with a highly professional touring team and playing ever larger venues in Europe. When Hallett joined the entertainment company AEG Live, Youssou's schedule included shows at the O$_2$ in London.

As they became better known internationally, Youssou and the Super Étoile de Dakar appeared in Australia at WOMADelaide, organised by Peter Gabriel's pioneering WOMAD (World of Music and Dance) festival. They also became popular in Japan and performed at Tokyo's Kani Hoken Hall, where they met up with Youssou's friend Miyoko Akiyama – who has photographed him so often she boasts a collection of over two thousand images! Meals were provided after each show in a different restaurant in the neon nightscape of Shinjuku, and the group lodged at the Prince Hotel in the Roppongi district close to small coffee shops with miniature gardens backing onto artists' studios selling ceramics and pottery. After their final performance in Tokyo, as the musicians took their bows, the girls in the audience came forward to shower Youssou with flowers and exquisitely wrapped gifts, chanting, 'I love Youssou.'

In the USA, the New York-based agency Concerted Efforts booked shows for Youssou. In 1994, Don Snowden of the *Los*

Angeles Times attended Youssou's concert at the famous corrugated iron-clad House of Blues, where a surprise guest caused quite a stir. 'Youssou N'Dour's two-hour performance', Snowden wrote,

> was a total package which simply lacked flaws on any level, visually, musically or theatrically. The ten-piece Super Étoile de Dakar was a well-oiled machine with a loose, jamming feel. Stevie Wonder traded wailing Islamic vocal lines with N'Dour on a traditional Senegalese piece with the band members seated on the stage in white robes. But N'Dour had already transfixed the full house with canny audience participation routines that had everyone eagerly joining in.[4]

Afterwards, in the green room, which was predominantly pink and plushly upholstered with sumptuous mirrored Indian fabrics, Wonder sipped champagne and pineapple juice, his favourite tipple, and posed for photographs with Youssou and his musicians, and with me! The tour bus left early next morning, but I spent Independence Day, Sunday 4 July, with Stevie and his then girlfriend, Ghanaian-born Akosua Busia. Akosua and I attended Sunday service at the Pentecostal West Angeles Church of God in Christ, where A-list Hollywood stars like Denzel Washington and Samuel L. Jackson worship. When Stevie asked me what I thought of the gospel choir and the music, I replied, 'Now I know where rock 'n' roll came from.' He is such an iconic performer that his supreme talent effaces his disability, but in his presence one cannot ignore his blindness or the constraints imposed on him by his fame. Akosua described the enormous pleasure he experienced walking barefoot along the shoreline when she organised his first ever trip to the beach. Most striking of all is his irrepressible and infectious good humour. Driving with them through the streets of LA, I was allowed a sneak preview of 'Rain Down Your Love' from the soon-to-be released album *Conversation Peace*, which includes tracks inspired by Stevie's visits to Ghana.

'Seven Seconds'

In 1994, true to her word and ten years on from their first meeting in Sweden, Neneh Cherry invited Youssou to sing on the track 'Seven Seconds'. His vocal lines were recorded in the north London home of Cherry and her producer husband, Cameron McVey. Released as a single, it topped the charts in several countries, including Italy and France, where it remained at number one for a record-breaking sixteen consecutive weeks. It notched up more than 2 million sales worldwide, gained seven gold discs, and was named Europe's Song of the Year at the 1995 World Music Awards in Monaco. The track, which had introduced Youssou to an entirely new pop audience, was released on Youssou's album *The Guide* and on Neneh Cherry's 1996 album *Man*. What distinguishes Youssou's success with 'Seven Seconds' is that in contrast to his predecessors, like Miriam Makeba and Hugh Masekela, Manu Dibango or Mory Kanté, who achieved success when living in the US or Paris, his chart-topping tune arrived while he was based – as he has always been – on his home soil of Senegal.

Youssou's father Elimane N'Dour told me his proudest moment was the day Youssou arrived at Dakar airport with his first gold disc. Thousands of fans and a battery of photographers and cameramen turned out to line the route from the airport. Elimane and his wife, Ndèye Sokhna, drove Youssou around the streets of Medina in the yellow Mercedes car which he had bought for them, until they arrived at the house of Youssou's grandmother, Marie Sène. 'That was just the best day,' enthused Elimane to me later, 'but the celebrations continued for weeks afterwards.' Youssou said the success of 'Seven Seconds' made him proud to be Senegalese and to have honoured his country. In December 2007, at Ellis Park in Capetown, Youssou and Annie Lennox performed a spirited version of 'Seven Seconds' during a televised concert in aid of Nelson Mandela's Aids charity 46664 (Mandela's prisoner number on Robben Island).

The international hits continued. In 1997 Youssou joined Massimo di Cataldo, the Italian singing star, for another chart-topping duet, 'Anime'. He also recorded 'Diabaram' with Ryuichi Sakamoto, 'Undecided' with Deep Forest and Neneh Cherry, 'A United Earth 1' with Alan Stivell and 'How Come' with Canibus and Wyclef Jean. He sang with Alicia Keys in New York at a concert for the charity Keep a Child Alive. Such appearances undoubtedly enhanced his reputation as an international star.

The *Jololi Revue*

In the summer of 1996 David Jones from the London agency Serious proposed a label tour along the lines of the Motown Revues, and so I organised the first *Jololi Revue* tour in Europe featuring Youssou, Cheikh Lô and Yandé Codou Sène.

39. Jololi Revue *poster.*

Born in 1932 into a Serer family of traditional singers, Yandé Codou Sène joined her mother's choir to sing in the polyphonic style that is typical of Serer music. They performed praise songs on ceremonial occasions, recited family genealogies and recalled historical events. The first Senegalese president, Léopold Sédar Senghor, was, like Yandé Codou, a Serer and a Christian, and in May 2006 she described to me her first meeting with him:

> After we were introduced, Senghor signalled to me to pour him a drink. From that day forth, whenever he organised a political meeting, he called upon me to be present and before he made his speech, he would ask me to sing the praises of his Serer ancestors. Then I would entertain the crowd, singing with my choir and drummers. During his presidency Monsieur Senghor granted me an audience each year.

Yandé Codou's inimitable voice and forceful personality greatly impressed Youssou, whose ultimate tribute was to record an album with her. *Gainde* was released by the German record company World Network in 1995. In October 1996, Youssou and Yandé Codou were the stars of a concert to celebrate former president Léopold Senghor's ninetieth birthday, which was staged in his hometown of Joal. Yandé Codou Sène passed away in 2010.

During the *Jololi Revue* tour, Youssou, as was his wont, used days off to compose new songs with his musicians. The acoustic guitars of Pape Oumar Ngom, Jimi Mbaye and Habib Faye, and Jean Philippe Rykiel's significant contribution on keyboards, created the semi-acoustic concept that defined Youssou's album *Lii!*

When, on 8 November 1996, the *Jololi Revue* reached London's Festival Hall, the concert was reviewed by Nigel Williamson, who wrote in *The Times*:

> Most of the audience had come to hear Youssou's pop oriented hits, such as *Seven Seconds* but he thrust the spotlight on

40. *Dimi Mint Abba.*

41. *Doura Barry.*

the slender, dreadlocked figure of Cheikh Lô. Nobody was
disappointed for what we witnessed was the British debut
of a rare talent destined to become one of world music's
biggest stars.[5]

The second edition of the *Jololi Revue*, featuring Cheikh Lô, Dimi
Mint Abba from Mauritania and Doura Barry from Guinea,
was scheduled for 1997. I made a special trip to the capital
cities of Nouakchott and Conakry to persuade the singers to
join the tour.

Nouakchott, Mauritania's capital, has the air of a new town, its
low, flat-roofed buildings constructed systematically in squares and
blocks. The proximity of the desert makes it dusty; the overriding
colour is grey, with the sun faintly visible through a constant white
haze. Dimi, whose father had composed the Mauritanian national
anthem, lived in some comfort with her extended family in a new
house on the outskirts of the city. Ali Farka Touré's favourite singer,
she enjoyed the patronage of Mohammed V, the king of Morocco,
who frequently invited her to perform at his court in Casablanca.
She also appeared in Las Palmas, where she loved to play bingo.
Sadly, she died in 2011.

In Conakry, the capital of Guinea, I met with Doura Barry,
who drove me around the city in the Chevrolet he had bought
from the Canadian ambassador. Apart from the Novotel, with its
harbour views and the splendid pavilions built to house heads
of state during the 1984 Organisation of African Unity summit,
Conakry struck me as dreary and down at heel.

Kirikou and the Sorceress

In 1998 Youssou composed and recorded music for *Kirikou and
the Sorceress*, Michel Ocelot's acclaimed animated children's film
set in the magical world of Africa's plains and forests. The real

discovery was the pleasing voice of the young Boubacar Mendy, who was supported by Oumar Sow on guitar. The sound technician was Philippe Brun, who has worked with Youssou on very many of his recordings.

42. *Philippe Brun and Oumar Sow.*

'Amazing Grace'

The well-known hymn 'Amazing Grace' is sung to music adapted by Edwin Excell from a Scottish-influenced American folk song with words penned by John Newton, a former slave trader. The transatlantic slave trade involved some 36,000 voyages from Africa to the New World, during which an estimated 12.5 million slaves were taken on board; 10.7 million arrived at their destination and the rest died at sea in appalling conditions. In 1748, Newton, who traded slaves from Sierra Leone, was sailing back to England on board his slave ship the *Greyhound* when it was caught in a severe storm off the coast of north-west Ireland, began taking on water and almost sank. At the cathedral in Londonderry, Newton prayed to God for salvation and in thanksgiving later wrote 'Amazing Grace'. The hymn has been famously interpreted as a gospel spiritual by Mahalia Jackson and Aretha Franklin, and in 2017 President Barack Obama sang it during the eulogy for Reverend Clementa Pinckney, who was killed in a shooting at the Emanuel African Methodist Episcopal Church in Charleston, South Carolina.

On 25 March 2007, the UK marked the 200th anniversary of the Anti Slavery Act passed by Parliament after William Wilberforce, Thomas Clarkson and others had campaigned tirelessly for more than twenty-five years to abolish the slave trade. The feature film *Amazing Grace* (2006), directed by Michael Apted, tells the story of Wilberforce and the anti-slavery lobby. It stars Ioan Gruffudd as Wilberforce, as well as Michael Gambon, Benedict Cumberbatch, Romola Garai and Rufus Sewell. Albert Finney plays John Newton, and Youssou made his acting debut in the part of Olaudah Equiano, an African slave who bought his freedom and settled in London, where he wrote a bestselling account of his life before joining Wilberforce's campaign to end slavery.

Le Grand Bal

Since 1999, events organised for largely Senegalese audiences in the diaspora by Youssou and his Dakar production team have grown ever more ambitious in scale. These include the Grand Bal at Bercy Arena (now the AccorHotels Arena) in Paris and the annual African Ball at the Hammerstein Ballroom in Manhattan, massive all-night parties that begin at 10 p.m. and finish at dawn. One of the most memorable was the Grand Bal of 2008. Suspended on a flying harness and singing 'Pitche Mi' ('The Bird'), Youssou descended to the stage like an Olympian god. With his Super Étoile musicians solidly behind him, he was jovial, exuberant and warm in his welcome for his special guests, who included Thione Seck and Carlou D. He showed himself to be at the peak of his powers, holding the stadium audience in the palm of his hand. The entire night was a joyous celebration of Senegalese song and dance, of friendship and national pride.[6]

43. *Youssou performing at Le Grand Bal.*

10

THERE'S NO PLEASING
ALL OF THE PEOPLE ALL OF THE TIME

Buried in Youssou N'Dour's worldwide success is a musical conundrum. Can mbalax music be successfully exported? Do its complex polyrhythms make it too difficult for anyone to dance to other than the Senegalese? Youssou himself would argue that mbalax contains reggae and jazz and every kind of music, or perhaps they all contain mbalax! Habib Faye claimed in one of our conversations that the Senegalese style is compatible with any music, be it Japanese or Latin American, and confirmed that, in any case, the Super Étoile musicians can make any musical style sound mbalax!

Over the years Youssou has signed contracts with major record labels – including Virgin and Sony Columbia in the UK and 40 Acres and a Mule Musicworks and Nonesuch in America – but Senegalese fans have often complained that he oversimplifies his music for the international market. They have been irritated when a song which was a huge hit at home seems to have been watered down on its international release, 'Gainde', 'Set', 'Birima' and 'Ligeey' being oft-cited examples.

Lawyer Bara Diokhane contends that when African artists are 'lucky' enough to be offered a record deal by a multinational company who then delegate producers who understand nothing about African music but are supposed to know what will sell in the West, there is a problem, for in general they distort the music. For Diokhane, the song 'Set' was a case in point. The original cassette, which was launched in Dakar at the Club Aldo in 1989 on the back of a social movement called Set Setal, was one of Youssou's greatest successes in Dakar. According to Diokhane, that first version of 'Set', an absolutely fabulous piece, had delighted everyone. It created a link between Youssou's traditional audience and his new fans, including young people, intellectuals, men and women. Yet Diokhane told me in June 2006 how he feels that the version produced by Michael Brook for the international album *Set* (released on Virgin Records) destroyed the song. Despite sales of more than 60,000 copies and some rave reviews – Rick Glanvill, for whom Brook was an inspired choice as producer, described *Set* as an 'unpolished gem of an album that approaches genius'[1] – Virgin lost confidence in the project and released Youssou from his contract.

In a perceptive article in the *New York Times*, Jon Pareles observed how an intricate, eclectic music can be dumbed down on albums by nervous producers, and he offered his solution to the problem – hear the music live.[2]

It is true that Youssou's Western record companies have tried at times to tame the mbalax rhythms and tailor his songs for a pop market. For example, there is not a Senegalese *sabar* drum within earshot on 'Seven Seconds', his duet with Neneh Cherry, and Doudou Doucouré observed that the song has nothing to do with African music, yet it sold over two million copies.

On the other hand, Youssou's album *Alsaama Day*, a thoroughly home-grown product, presented Senegalese fans with a selection of fast and furious dance tracks which they found wholly satisfying. However, the prevalence of searing *sabars*, unusual harmonies and the seemingly trite English lyrics on 'Del Sol Dal' could be rather off-putting to Western ears.

Joko: From Village to Town, possibly Youssou's most Westernised album, received generally mediocre reviews, one of which slammed its 'bland grooves, MOR ballads and plodding cameos by Sting, Peter Gabriel and Wyclef Jean'.[3] It was a commercial flop and led to Sony dropping Youssou. And yet the album contains what I consider to be a near-perfect crossover track, 'She Doesn't Need to Fall', produced by Pierre Bianchi, arranged by Jérôme Lemonnier and co-written by Youssou, Prince Charles Alexander and Boubacar

44. *Poster advertising* Alsaama Day.

N'Dour. Youssou's cascading vocals weave in and out of tripping, groovy rhythms magically propelled by drummer Manu Katché and Lemonnier's keyboards.

Youssou expressed his own reservations about his dealings with multinational record companies when he told Mark Hudson:

Western record companies haven't always dealt with African musicians in the best way. Giving them a lot of money and telling them they're going to be bigger than Phil Collins is the wrong way to do it! ... Even if they don't tell you which songs to play, you're aware that it's their money, and you feel pressure to produce a certain kind of sound. I wouldn't say I was disappointed by *Joko*, but I wanted to find a new way of working.[4]

He was soon to sign a deal with Nonesuch in New York, an agreement that gave him greater artistic freedom and allowed him to record in his own studio in Dakar.

Egypt

The renowned Senegalese scientist and philosopher, Cheikh Anta Diop (1923–86), believed that the Wolof are a Nilotic people who travelled across North Africa and south to Senegal and whose dialect was close to ancient Kopt. The region which lies along the borders of the Senegal River, taking in the modern towns of Saint-Louis, Podor and Dagana, is deemed to be the birthplace of Wolof civilisation, rich in tradition and influenced in bygone times by Egypt and the royal courts of the pharaohs.

Knowing that Wolof culture has links with the Nile valley – and inspired by Oum Kalsoum, the Egyptian diva his father was a fan of and who he had listened to as a child – Youssou set out to create a fusion of the two countries' music in his album *Egypt*. He used Wolof lyrics to highlight the peaceful way Islam is practised in his country, and in this respect he was assisted by Kabou Gueye who, through his family connections, has links with both of the main brotherhoods in Senegal. Gueye's mother, Fat Thioune Khoudjia Yade, was a well-known *griotte* who animated *Fanal* ceremonies in Saint-Louis, while his father, Saliou Gueye, was an imam. Kabou is a Mouride but on his mother's side he is Tidjiane: his maternal grandfather was close to the founder of the Tidjani movement in Senegal.

After several years of planning, Youssou finally got together with Fathy Salama and his orchestra to record *Egypt*, bringing with them an unlikely assortment of instruments – seven violins, two cellos, a double bass and oud, together with *sabar* drums, a balafon and a kora. The album was completed in 2001, the year the Twin Towers in New York were destroyed by Islamic extremists, so Youssou felt it would be inappropriate to release it immediately. In line with Cheikh Ahmadou Bamba's pacifist views, Youssou said in an interview in *Songlines* magazine that it should not be necessary to kill even one person in the cause of Islam, and he has also expressed his concern about the way Islam is perceived: 'My religion needs to be better known for its positive side. There's a lot happening in the world that has been bad for the image of Islam, and the key question is how to change that.' Speaking specifically about his album *Egypt*, he said, 'Maybe this music can move us forward towards a greater understanding of the peaceful message of Islam.'[5]

While the album received a lukewarm reception from Youssou's Senegalese fans at home and even some criticism from the Muslim brotherhoods, who objected to what they considered to be the commercialisation of Ahmadou Bamba, it finally appeared on the Nonesuch label in 2004 and won Youssou his first Grammy award the following year. Yet while the New York record company was happy to release *Egypt*, they declined to distribute *Dakar–Kingston* (presumably because they did not rate it), and it was finally released by Universal France.

Back in 1990, *Rolling Stone* magazine had predicted that if any third-world performer had a real shot at the sort of universal popularity last enjoyed by Bob Marley, it was Youssou N'Dour, a singer with a voice so extraordinary that the history of Africa seemed locked inside it.[6] Youssou would be the first to admit that Bob Marley was a unique and consummate artist. His reggae was indeed universal, and he was well supported and promoted by Chris Blackwell and Island Records. However, Youssou's own reggae project, *Dakar–Kingston*, somehow missed the mark. The original premise was to show that, at its source, mbalax uses the bass drum to emphasise the strong beat in the same way that reggae does. But since Youssou's album was recorded mostly in Jamaica with some former members of the Wailers, there is nothing intrinsically Senegalese about this reggae. Youssou failed to create African reggae in the way that Alpha Blondy or Tiken Jah Fakoly of the Ivory Coast, or the South African Lucky Dube, or indeed the pioneering Senegalese group, Touré Kunda, inspired by the *Djamba Dong* (leaf dance) rhythms of Casamance, managed to do. In the case of Blondy, the universality of his reggae music was confirmed by the journalists Sylvie Clerfeuille and Nago Seck:

> Blondy sings in Diola, a language understood all over West Africa from Tchad to Senegal, but he also sings in English and French. Like all reggae men he carries a rasta message, but it is adapted to his African public, especially through his use of proverbs. Nevertheless his reggae, with its new sounds, reaches a universal audience.[7]

On the other hand, Harry Belafonte, who was born in Trinidad and made a brilliant career singing calypso, considered making a reggae album but realised that no one can emulate Bob Marley: 'I saw no way to bring a stamp of my own to what he did. You either did reggae the way Marley did or you didn't do it at all.'[8]

With the release of the album *Africa Rekk* (*Africa Now*) in November 2016, Youssou surprised his fans. He seemed to have freed himself from all restrictions and contradictions and to have found the right recipe for combining his Senegalese mbalax with other styles from around the African continent and the diaspora. Here he is completely at home singing calypso, rumba, blues, reggae, salsa and soul music. During the album's recording, Youssou immersed himself fully in all aspects of its production, as composer, producer, lead vocalist and backing vocalist. His experience and musicality shine through every track, from the haunting harmonica blues of the first song to the Afro-Cuban calypso of the last.

In 'Exodus' Youssou calls for unity, solidarity and dignity and urges young people to remain in Africa to help construct a brighter future for everyone. He reminds them that money is not the be-all and end-all. In a clever remake of his 1979 hit 'Xalis', a piece which boasted the attractions of money, 'Money Money' decries those whose sole aim is to increase their wealth. Family life counts for more, especially when one remembers the cruel separation of men and women in the House of Slaves on the island of Gorée during the Atlantic slave trade. He offers some fatherly advice to young women in 'Be Careful', while 'Serin Fallu' underlines Senegal's reputation for religious tolerance. The spiritual guide in question, the second son of Cheikh Ahmadou Bamba, founder of the Mouride Muslim brotherhood, was a good friend of President Léopold Sédar Senghor, a Christian. On a personal note, in 'Jeegel Nu' Youssou seeks God's pardon for his sins and asks forgiveness of his peers and all those whom he has wronged.

45. *Tiken Jah Fakoly.*

11

THERE IS BUT ONE GOD

'I never had a master plan,' Youssou once told me. 'I cannot even explain how most things happened. I met the right people or I was in the right place at the right time. I believe in God and I followed my destiny.'

Proud to be a member of the Mouride Muslim brotherhood, Youssou is a *talibé*, a devotee of the religious guide Cheikh Ahmadou Bamba, the so-called Gandhi of Senegal, whose saintly virtues have undoubtedly contributed to Senegal's reputation as one of the more open, democratic and tolerant societies in Africa. Referring to the Senegalese brotherhoods of the Tijaniyyah, Muridiyyah, Qadiriyyah and Layenne, Youssou told me, 'God blessed us greatly by giving us religious guides who have worked for peace and solidarity in our country.'

On a personal level, Youssou has found the example of Ahmadou Bamba to be a powerful motivator in his own life. Bamba defended Islam against his French colonial masters, built the holy city at Touba and spent his humble life promoting peace. Youssou's faith in God, his work ethic, his sense of community and even his belief in his own abilities are very much inspired by Mouridism. Furthermore, Ahmadou Bamba himself, his philosophy and his legacy, are the subjects of many of the songs in Youssou's repertoire.

Ahmadou Bamba Khadimou Kassoul (1853–1927) was born Ahmad ibn Muhammad ibn Habīb Allāh in the village of Mbacké, the son of Habibullah Bouso, a marabout from the Qadirriyah, the oldest tariqa (Sufi order) in Senegal, and Maryam Bousso, both devout Muslims. In 1883, he broke away from the Qadiriyyah, a Sufi branch of Islam founded in Iraq in the twelfth century and spread by its missionary shaykhs into Asia and Africa, to form the Sufi brotherhood, the Muridiyyah. Mouride is a French spelling of the Arabic term *murid* (disciple or novice), one who is reaching towards paradise. In 1886 Bamba married the daughter of Lat Dior, *damel* (king) of Cayor, with whom he had five sons and a daughter. Small in stature, noted for his determined gait and rapid footsteps, he was always simply dressed and led the humble life of an ascetic, spending his time in prayer, meditating, walking alone and writing. He conducted his religious classes in the open air, illustrating his lessons with signs drawn in the sand. He ate frugally but enjoyed drinking tea, and especially coffee sweetened with *telsi* sugar. The man whose name in Wolof means 'the one who protects' rekindled the Muslim religion just as French colonisers attempted to quash it. By his unshakeable faith and the miracles he allegedly performed, he gave Islam the fervent soul of Africa and validated the beliefs of black Africans who were often despised by their Arabising, fairer-skinned neighbours to the north of the continent.

Rallying his followers to make a peaceful protest against the French, Bamba maintained that man did not create life and therefore should not take it, not even the life of a worm. He believed that in war there are never any winners and he proved, by his resistance to efforts by the French to stamp out Islam, that he could obtain what he wanted without shedding any blood. Adversity only served to deepen his respect and admiration for the Prophet Muhammad and to draw him closer to God. Through his devotions, his faith and his vision, Cheikh Ahmadou Bamba was regarded as a saint in his own lifetime. He himself claimed that all the saints knew he was one of God's miracles and a very close neighbour of the Creator of the Universe.

Arrested in 1895 by the French authorities, who feared his power over the Senegalese people, Bamba was taken to the governor's office in Saint-Louis du Senegal and then exiled to a French army camp at Mayumbe in Gabon. Because he was not allowed to pray on the boat which took him there, legend has it that he performed a miracle; he laid his prayer mat on the sea and prayed, and when he returned to the boat the governor's wife, who was present, marvelled at the sand on his forehead. This scene and others from Bamba's life are often depicted on Senegalese *suwer* glass paintings.

In Gabon, Bamba concentrated on his devotions in order to withstand his loneliness, to purify himself and to draw ever closer to God. Called to face a firing squad on the beach in Mayumbe, he remained unharmed: the story is that the soldiers desisted, claiming they had seen a vision of angels mounted on horses and were filled with dread. In 1902, after seven years in exile, Bamba was allowed to return to Senegal. As he had so far defeated all their efforts to quash his reputation, the French decided to deport him to Mauritania, where they hoped the Maures would despise him and kill him themselves. That exile lasted from 1903 to 1907, and when Sérigne Bamba finally returned to his village he remained under house arrest, but he was determined to found a holy city called Touba (*tuba* means 'bliss' in Arabic) at a place in the wilderness where he maintained he had seen an apparition of the Prophet Muhammad.

Bamba asked his followers to commemorate his first exile with a *Grand Magal* (an annual pilgrimage) to Touba, so they could pray, read the Koran and recite the *Khassayid* verses which he wrote. Pilgrims should offer food and gifts to the Prophet Muhammad and hospitality to fellow brotherhood members. Since 1928, when the first *Magal* took place, pilgrims have habitually filed past their saint's tomb, touching the rails, throwing coins and banknotes and making their vows; many believe that anything they ask for at Touba will be granted.

Cheikh Ahmadou Bamba's son, the marabout Moustapha Bassirou Mbacké, a tall, distinguished figure who exuded power and privilege as well as a certain charm and an unmistakable mystique, was in charge of arranging the 1984 pilgrimage. I met with him to seek permission for our BBC crew to film the ceremony.

48. *Alexis Ngom's* suwer *painting of Cheikh Ahmadou Bamba.*

47. *Touba.*

While I was waiting to see him I saw his followers, or *talibés*, queuing up to be blessed; mothers carried sick babies, hoping they would be healed by saliva from the marabout's spit.

On the actual day of the *Grand Magal*, a special train left Dakar so packed with pilgrims that young men stood or crouched on the roof. When some of them saw us filming the train as it passed through a railway junction at Thies, they began to throw stones in our direction. In an instant a voice spoke these salutary words in my ear:

> There are two things you white people should understand. Many of our African ancestors were forcibly taken into slavery and our foot soldiers known as *tirailleurs*, who were drafted by the European Allies to serve in both world wars, were used as cannon fodder.

Before I could see his face, the man had disappeared and stones continued to rain down from the roof of the train. The incident said much about the perceptions of a people who had felt exploited by slave traders and colonial rule.

Youssou kept a life-size portrait in his office of Sérigne Mourtalla Mbacké, the youngest son of Cheikh Amadou Bamba. The Sérigne, who died in 2005, was for Youssou a true guide who prayed for him, and with whom he could discuss any problem. 'Islam or its influence has always been in my music,' confirmed Youssou to me:

> In Senegal we are lucky to have an enlightened Islam. Although the Senegalese population is ninety-five per cent Muslim, our first president, Léopold Sédar Senghor was a Christian, so we have proven that Islam can be open and tolerant and that is what makes our Islam different. If I wore a turban one might suspect that I was a fundamentalist but I have shown openly who I am; I am not a fundamentalist but a Muslim son of a Muslim.

I stand for tolerance, understanding of others and peace because that is how I am. Ours is a secular country where religious groups practise freely, and that is what I try to describe in my songs. We can sing in clubs about the founder of our Mouride Brotherhood, Ahmadou Bamba, and watch girls dance, and the following day we can go to the mosque. That is what Bamba did for us, and it is positive for it gives us an outlet for our feelings and prevents fanaticism.

'Jamm' ('Peace'), one of the most memorable songs in Youssou's entire repertoire, is about peace as it is summed up in the Islamic greeting *salaam alaikum* (peace be with you). It is the title track on an album in which every track seeks gloriously and majestically to convey that peace. Most notable is 'Ale Samba', on which Youssou duets with his uncle Ouzin Ndiaye, their voices supported by Thierno Koité's sympathetic saxophone riffs. Then there is the hymn-like, harmonious song 'Yonent' ('The Prophet'), remarkable for the interplay of Oumar Sow's subtle guitar lines and Pape Dieng's persistent and pervasive drum patterns.

Recorded live at the Thiossane nightclub by El Hadj Ndiaye's mobile recording unit, 'Yonent' begins, 'Millions and millions of people believe in him, Mohammed Rassoul Allah, Muhammad the messenger of God.' Mongoné Touré, a perceptive and gifted writer, helped Youssou clarify the texts.

When Irish academic Donal Cruise O'Brien wrote a doctoral thesis about the Mouride brotherhood in Senegal, he compared their work ethic to that of European Protestants, particularly those in Northern Ireland. As a committed Mouride, Youssou has never shied away from hard work. On the contrary, work – combined with his considerable talent – has been an essential component in his success, as he explains in his song 'Ligeey' (Work):

Hard work is the only way to success
No matter how routine that work may be

> I cherish it more than anything else
> Let us work for the benefit of our families
> As we work, we strengthen our faith
> Work is the duty of every person
> The world we live in requires us to work

In the Arab world, the feast day which occurs approximately seventy days after the end of the holy month of Ramadan is generally known as Eid ul-Adha, but in Senegal it is called Tabaski. The celebration has its origins in the Old Testament story of Abraham and his son Isaac, whom the Muslims call Ishmael. In the story, God tests Abraham by asking him to sacrifice Isaac, and since Abraham's faith in God is perfect he makes all the necessary preparations and is about to slay his son at a place called Moriah when the Angel of the Lord calls out to him to stay his hand. Noticing a ram nearby, Abraham sacrifices it instead. On the morning of Tabaski, custom dictates that a sheep or a goat be ritually slaughtered by every Senegalese family. Given that the population in Senegal is overwhelmingly Muslim that adds up to innumerable animals, but it is said that every sheep longs to be killed on that day, for it will go straight to heaven. Once blessed, the meat is shared and offered as a sign of peace and forgiveness. The greeting *Deweneti* (Happy New Year) is used by all who hope that the incoming year will be at least as happy, prosperous and successful as the outgoing one. All the same, when times are hard, such celebrations can seem more of a burden than a blessing for the poorest, who struggle to keep up appearances. In his song 'Tabaski', Youssou defines the essential spirit of the feast day:

> On the day of Tabaski
> We kill the sheep
> We wish each other well
> On that day, if someone hurts us
> We must forgive him

For devout Muslims, Islam offers a perfect path to happiness and peace through submission to God. Those who are in a state of gratitude are content and able to live in the present; having done their best, they are pure and free from yesterday and have no fears, desires or expectations for tomorrow. Based on 'Akhirou Zamane', a poem by Cheikh Amadou Bamba, the message of Youssou's song 'Deuge' ('The Truth') is 'Live in the moment and live it to the full, for it could be your last.' He also describes how the Prophet was concerned about that period in human history between his death and the end of the world, when men might lose their faith. But as the song says, the cycle of religious teaching – from the Old Testament of the Jews to the New Testament of the Christians, to the Koran of the Muslim world – was complete following the Prophet Muhammad's death. Since then, he believes, men and women have had all the knowledge they need to find their way to God. They should simply read the Holy Scriptures, listen to the enlightened, and become religious in the true sense of the word, bound to God.

'Deuge' points the way to a search for the truth and reality behind every living thing and behind the elements themselves, the sea, the sky and the land. In his lyrics Youssou implies that through this kind of awareness, people can feel acutely the guiding spirit during every second of their daily lives:

> God is always recreating his world, from the simplest
> blade of grass to the greatest elements in nature.
> Look at the sky, and the clouds. Look up at the moon,
> Look down to the sea, look right into the depths,
> Look round at the forest. God is truth.
> Find truth in everything.

Like the Mouride brotherhood, the other main Sufi orders in Senegal – including the Layennes (followers of Seydina Mouhammadou Limamou Laye, 1843–1909) and the Tidjanes (the Tijaniyyah was founded in Morocco by Cheikh Ahmed Tijani, who lived from 1735 to 1815) – are led by a hierarchy of religious leaders or marabouts. Even though Youssou is Mouride, he does not hesitate to recognise and sing about the other brotherhoods. 'Djamil' is Youssou's praise song about Senegal's religious guide, Moustapha Sy Djamil, known as Seydi Djamil, a Tidjani marabout who lived at Fass in Dakar. In the song Youssou also pays homage to Djamil's father, Sérigne Babacar Sy, to his grandfather, El Hadj Malick Sy, and their immediate family for their religiosity.

In September 1997, the Senegalese people mourned the death of Sérigne Abdoul Aziz Sy Dabakh, the youngest son of El Hadj Malick Sy. Nature seemed to mourn him too; I was on the beach at Ngor that day and experienced the signs for myself: the dusty fog that covered the entire country and the watery pale white sun which resembled the moon that had eclipsed the sun the previous week. The owner of the press group Walfadjiri wrote in his newspaper that these signs had been foretold in the sacred book *Al-Asrar* and in the prophecies of Abderrahmane Ashami Al Maghrebi:

> When one of the four poles or one of the four keys to the divine treasure disappears, the angels descend from the sky en masse to attend the funeral and present their condolences, and as they pass, the sun becomes as pale as the moon.[1]

Youssou's repertoire is inspired by subjects which concern everyone: death and the afterlife, peace and non-violence, women and marriage. In relation to this last topic, Youssou has never openly discussed the widespread practice of polygamy in Senegalese society. In 2006, the superstar, who has always been a role model for his fans, surprised many of them when he took a second wife, Aida Coulibaly. Sadly, he could not save his marriage to his first wife, Manocoro 'Mami' Camara, which ended in divorce.

Polygamy has been a sensitive issue for other Senegalese musicians, such as Thione Seck and Carlou D, the former rapper with

48. *The mosque at Ouakam.*

49. *Babacar Lo's painting of a marabout.*

Positive Black Soul, now a successful solo artist, who expressed his views in his song 'Namenala' ('I Miss You'), a haunting and tender lament for his mother, who died when he was twenty years old. In the sleeve notes of his album *Muzikr* he writes:

The thing I loved most about her was how she was completely and madly in love with my father, whom she married when she was fourteen years old. One day my father decided to take a second wife, and though we all lived happily together for a while, none of it was real; it was the *sen regal* spirit. Then all of a sudden my father and his second wife left us and we never heard from them again. My mother became ill from the stress and,

50. *Carlou D.*

shortly after, she died. I miss her every single day; she believed in me and my music when no one else did.[2]

Thione Seck remembers the discord in his father's compound at Gueule Tapée, where four wives and twenty children shared the same space. Having grown up in that charged atmosphere, Thione decided he would never take more than one wife. He remained true to his word and is married to Kiné, with whom he has six children, the eldest of whom, Wally, is now a pop star in his own right.

One artist who seemed to achieve harmony in his ménage, despite having three wives, was Ndiaga Mbaye, a singer who was highly respected for his views on life and was much admired by

51. *Ndiaga Mbaye.*

Youssou, who also became his producer. A devout man, and a true believer, he educated the audiences of the weekly radio show he presented in all of life's virtues. His maxims were: patience leads to tolerance; politeness pays; take care to cultivate kindness, openness, modesty, simplicity and understanding; be discreet and never speak ill of another; open your heart; practise forgiveness; be happy with what you have; you can do anything you wish if you really want to ('*vouloir c'est pouvoir*'); and never hide your love, for hidden love is a great burden. Ndiaga's recipe for a happy marriage included good communication, one of his favourite phrases being '*Il faut toujours causer*' ('It's good to talk').

12

ROLE MODEL AND ICON

British photographer Iain McKell's eloquent black and white portrait of Youssou N'Dour wearing Ray-Ban sunglasses and headphones along with a traditional Senegalese straw sun hat and embroidered boubou perfectly captures Youssou's ancient musical heritage as well as his own style of modern pop music. The celebrated photographer of celebrities like Brad Pitt, will.i.am, Gilbert & George, Grayson Perry and Vivienne Westwood took the publicity shot in the mid-1980s during a photo shoot in a warehouse studio in Shoreditch in east London. Following several changes of costume and many different poses, McKell made this one and knew immediately he had the image he was seeking.

52. *Iain McKell's portrait of Youssou.*

One day in the late 1980s Youssou introduced me to a man he described as his biggest fan. Issa Samb, alias Joe Ouakam, artist, philosopher and art critic, whose Lébou family once owned large swathes of land around the village of Ouakam, was walking his dog along the seafront near Youssou's house when he stopped to speak with us. I subsequently met Issa on many occasions, often in his Laboratoire Agit Art on the Rue Jules Ferry in central Dakar. On one of these occasions, he defined Youssou's place in modern Senegalese life and art thus:

> Youssou speaks for at least three generations. He comes from Medina, a place apart with its own history and habits, a place stamped with the mark of independence where boys turn up their coat collars and walk defiantly and with attitude. Youssou is an innovator who has always surprised us and will continue to surprise us. He is capable of working with any musician on the planet. That deep emotion, that sensitivity, that humanity, that pragmatism which is never arrogant can only come from an exceptional being, a person with what we call genius. He seems continuously to renew his inspiration, making gigantic efforts

53. *Joe Ouakam.*

to advance his music beyond the borders of Wolof culture and out onto the international stage.

Senegalese architect and film-maker Nicholas Cissé thinks there is a strange inevitability about Youssou's success, and that this relates to his *griot/gawlo* heritage. He told me in Dakar in 2006:

> There is no such thing as a minor *griot*. All *griots* have inherited the same gifts of singing, playing instruments or talking. Their feats of memory are remarkable; the power of their words awesome, their proverbs ring true like Shakespearean couplets. Each generation sings and speaks and plays and the words accumulate until the day when a plethora of words falls on one *griot* who receives the ultimate gift and becomes a megastar called Youssou N'Dour.

Retired linguist and translator Souleymane Diakhaté told me that he believes Youssou is one of God's chosen ones, chosen to show other Senegalese musicians that it is possible to succeed and even to become a superstar. Good looks, charisma and a natural reserve have all contributed to the mystique surrounding Youssou, especially at the outset of his career. Growing notoriety forced him to retreat from the usual routines of everyday life in order to escape being mobbed by crowds. Ironically, he was freer to live a 'normal life' during his visits to London, New York or Paris than in his home city.

In 1992, an assassination attempt targeting Youssou recalled a similar attack on Bob Marley in Jamaica in December 1976 or the cruel killing of John Lennon in New York in December 1980. Since Youssou was on tour in Germany he escaped, but the world's press carried the report that a man intending to stab the Senegalese pop star rushed into the singer's Dakar office and seriously wounded one of his friends, a young man nicknamed 'You 2' because of his physical resemblance to Youssou. Then the perpetrator turned himself in to the police, saying he had just killed Youssou N'Dour. The victim was a young man named Abdou Ndiaye, who subsequently died of his injuries.

Thanks to his work ethic, patience, pragmatism and an eye for an opportunity, Youssou understood what it took to advance his career and secure his place on the international music scene. Promotional tours involved journeys on planes and trains and nights in hotel rooms followed by hour upon hour of interviews and photo shoots. Gradually, Youssou became a role model for a new generation of Senegalese artists. His serious, clean-living image broke the mould and rendered the music profession, once frowned upon as the preserve of drunkards and womanisers, respectable.

Like many performers, when Youssou is onstage, the one place he feels really free, he transcends his natural timidity and the instant response of his audience gives him an extraordinary power. Clearly he has that indefinable attribute we call 'star quality', and this epithet, 'star', has followed him from the outset of his career: Star Band, Étoile de Dakar and finally Super Étoile de Dakar. The core group of musicians who made up his backing group and recorded his albums remained together for more than thirty years.

The enigma that is Youssou N'Dour

Youssou is notoriously inscrutable. 'I must have met him at least 10 times,' British writer Mark Hudson noted in 2004,

> and while he is always friendly, even jovial in a blokeish high-fiving way … he tends to be infuriatingly circumspect and diplomatic. At times I've felt that I've pushed ever deeper into what makes him tick; at others I've wondered whether I've recorded one sentence that reveals who he really is.[1]

Hudson also suggested that Youssou must have known from the beginning he was not an ordinary person. As mentioned in the Preface, it is true that in the early years his Senegalese fans would shout that he was more than a human being and that everyone wanted to touch the hem of his coat.

Senegalese journalist Massamba Mbaye offered me this perceptive comment about Youssou:

> Despite a meticulous perusal of this peerless artist's work, there is still something profoundly unfathomable in it. Look at his eyes. Youssou does not look at the present, he looks into the future. But the mirror which reflects his regard has been polished down the centuries. He belongs with the inventors, those who know how to turn the pages of time ever so carefully, for each page is precious.

Mbaye's press colleague Khalil Gueye told me, simply: 'No one is perfect, especially an artist who creates perfect art.' And renowned sculptor Ousmane Sow commented that

> Youssou endures because he is clever. He deftly manages every project, never taking on too much and always keeping his feet on the ground. He has never allowed his fame to go to his head, for he is exactly the same person he always was, and that is a mark of his intelligence.

Interviewed for the Senegalese newspaper *Le Quotidien*, Youssou admitted that the one person who knows him best is his mother. 'My mother and I are very close,' he told the newspaper.

> She knows everything about me, and like all mothers she lives only for me. She knows what I am capable of and what I will never do. She is also a partner who makes things go smoothly for me. As for my father, he is a very rigorous and straight man and I am afraid of him even today.[2]

When asked in the same interview, 'Who is Youssou N'Dour?' Youssou had this to say:

> I really find it difficult to answer that, but each person has a mission. My mission is to show that it is possible to succeed. I believe sincerely that whether one is born in New York, in Singapore or Dakar, one can be successful and give hope to others. I take care, as we all must, to show our young people that they should have principles. They too can aim high, and they too can be fulfilled. I find it difficult to talk about myself because I forget easily, and that is maybe a good thing. My father used to say that to make progress in life one should not focus on the past. So I go forward. I am lucky to make my living through music, which is my passion.[3]

I have immense admiration for Youssou as a singer and musician. As a person he is extraordinarily even-tempered – I have only once seen him angry, and that was when a tour manager made an unfortunate mistake. He is an extremely private person who shows little emotion, though he demonstrates great tenderness towards his children. In the way of the *griots* he reads other people very well; a shrewd negotiator, he conducts his business affairs on the basis of give and take, his motto being only to give when you can get something in return. His attachment to his country, his hopes for the future of his people and for Africa in general are genuine and are reflected in his own achievements.

Self-made millionaire

It quickly became clear that Youssou had the rare ability to combine artistry with a head for business. Latyr Diouf, his former manager in Dakar, says he was always impressed by Youssou's belief in himself and with his capacity for hard work. In his view, every year from

1981 onwards – when Youssou launched his solo career with the Super Étoile de Dakar – was an epic one for multiple reasons, and each year was more glorious than its predecessor.

In March 2016, the website Buzz Senegal published a list of the five wealthiest men in Senegal. Youssou's name was fifth on the list, with a supposed fortune of 95 billion West African CFA francs (around £96 million).[4] In May 2014, the website Constative stated that Youssou was the richest African artist, with a net worth of $135 million.[5] This is unsurprising when you consider what he has achieved over the years. A man of ideas and an innovator, he built a recording studio in Dakar before establishing the record label Jololi and a music promotion company, Xippi Inc. Through his various enterprises – the Thiossane Club, the newspapers *L'Observateur* and *La Sentinelle*, Radio TFM, the Youssou N'Dour Foundation and the television company Futurs Médias – he employs more than 800 people.

When he initiated the Joko ('link/connection' in Wolof) programme to provide internet access in villages across Senegal, Youssou was optimistic about the internet's potential to help African economies leapfrog industrialisation and aspire to more equitable partnerships in the world economy. In February 2008, with support from the Italian company Benetton, Youssou launched a microcredit scheme, Birima, to support small business enterprises in Senegal, declaring, 'Africa doesn't want charity, it wants repayable subsidised loans.'[6]

In the autumn of 2009, just before Youssou's fiftieth birthday, I met him backstage at the O$_2$ Arena in London and asked him what his ideal birthday present would be. After a brief reminiscence about Phil Collins's fiftieth birthday party where, after the guests had assembled, a curtain was opened to reveal Peter Gabriel and the other members of Genesis seated at their instruments ready for Phil to join them, Youssou said without hesitation that his best birthday present would be the unveiling of his new TV station in Dakar.

On the basis of a government promise to grant him a licence for an independent TV station, Youssou bought the necessary equipment, but suddenly the licence was refused and no explanation given. So he set about gaining 10,000 signatures – mostly from his fan base – in order to back his bid, and a licence was finally granted to Télé Futurs Médias. The station, TFM, went on air in May 2010.

Some people have described Youssou as being ruthless in his business affairs, but my friend Souleymane Diakhaté's view is that Youssou has needed to be rigorous and forceful in order to succeed in an unstructured and informal economy.

He has also been accused in some quarters of nepotism. However, given that Senegalese tradition expects the *taaw* (eldest son) to set a good example so that the rest of the family will

54. *Some of Youssou N'Dour's siblings as children.*

succeed, it is hardly surprising that as the eldest son Youssou has made use of his family's talents to support his business interests. Far from seeing it as nepotism, he is proud that his brothers and sisters – and now his son Birane – are working for his media and music companies. Youssou's sister, Ngoné N'Dour, studied sound engineering in London and became chief executive of Xippi Inc., with her brother Bouba N'Dour as artistic director and her sister Marie N'Dour as the company's international representative in France. With her brothers Prince Ndiaga N'Dour and Ibrahima N'Dour, she formed Prince Arts, a production company for the promotion of local artists through events, films and recordings. In 2016, Ngoné was elected PCA of the Senegalese copyright and related rights society (SODAV). Prince Ndiaga is chief technician at Télé Futurs Medias, where Youssou's son Birane is associate chief executive. Ibrahima also played keyboards on Youssou's album *Rokku mi Rokka* and really came into his own as arranger on the 2016 album *Africa Rekk*. He told me,

> I listen to all kinds of music. For example, I discovered a style which resembles mbalax but which is simpler and instantly appealing. It is the *bachata* from Puerto Rico, and I introduced this rhythm along with others in *Africa Rekk*. I also like to keep abreast of new talent.

Youssou's sister Aby N'Dour, a singer and designer, has set up her own fashion house in Dakar, and in August 2018 she released a new single titled 'Ni Lay Sante' ('This Is To Say Thank You').

Despite his meteoric rise to superstardom, Youssou has also been pleased to endorse the careers of emerging singers and musicians, especially in Senegal, where Cheikh Lô, Viviane, Pape and Cheikh, Carlou D and Daara J were among his protégés.

When I left the BBC in 1996, Youssou promptly invited me to work with him, an invitation I was delighted to accept. And so I headed to Dakar for a prolonged stay. Planes flying south to the city hug the Senegalese coastline, providing passengers with a bird's-eye view of fishing villages and the Lac Rose, its pink-tinged mineral waters clearly visible from the air. On its final approach, the aircraft circled over Gorée Island then glided down over the rooftops of Mermoz and Ouakam to land at Léopold Sédar Senghor airport.

My job title was International Liaison Manager for Youssou, his record label, Jololi, and his commercial recording studio. I lived in a room at the top of Youssou's three-storey house in Almadies, which was designed by architect Nicholas Cissé to resemble a West African kora, and I had my office on the second floor. Youssou and his family lived in the same building and he himself was closely involved in running the music business. When, in high summer, there were frequent power cuts, we would sit outside in the court-yard to get some air and Youssou's wife, Manacoro 'Mami' Camara, who has a keen sense of humour, would entertain us all with witty stories from her days as a bank official while some of Youssou's close friends regaled us with tales of their youth. On these occasions, the congenial atmosphere reminded me so much of an Irish ceili (house party) that I felt very much at home.

Nowadays Youssou no longer lives in the house at Almadies; the entire complex has become the busy headquarters of Télé Futurs Médias, a site bustling with eager young journalists, technicians and television presenters.

Youssou N'Dour, Minister of Culture, Tourism and Leisure

When upon his election in 2012 President Macky Sall announced the appointment of twenty-five new ministers, half the number that had served in the previous government, Youssou was named Minister of Culture and Tourism. Sceptics wondered if he could succeed in a post for which he had no formal training. I remem-bered what Pape Dieng, former drummer with the Super Étoile had once said, 'Youssou always has an idea and he has always relished a challenge,' but questions remained: would his quick intelligence, pragmatism, contacts and experience of the world allow him to initiate and carry ideas through? Even though he is no bureaucrat, would his entrepreneurial skills and his flair help him to open up the ministry, encourage collaboration with the private sector and mobilise other people's talents?

In one of his first speeches, Youssou defined the importance of his mission, stating that Senegal may not yet have mineral resources or petrol, but that it has cultural and intellectual riches instead.

Then early in 2013, Youssou was replaced as Minister of Culture by Abdoul Aziz Mbaye but retained the portfolio for Tourism and Leisure. He claimed that his worldwide reputation would be useful in his new role, but an editorial in the newspaper *Le Pays au Quotidien* was moved to comment somewhat caustically:

> Is it enough to have sat at Bono's table for the perception of Senegal as a tourist destination to change? Is it sufficient to have attended the G8 as a spokesperson for Africa to imagine that everything he touches will turn to gold? Tourism will not flourish through the aura of the man charged with reviving it, for it is an eminently economic sector ... Tour operators may adore You the artist but You the Minister must find the means to convince them that Senegal as a destination is not only attractive but competitive in price too.[7]

The same journalist questioned whether Youssou himself felt comfortable in his ministerial role and averred that as a political figure, Youssou would be a target for more criticism than he ever faced as a musician or media mogul:

> If the Senegalese people discover that the present government's policy of 'Yonou Yokkouté' [The Path to Prosperity] changes

their lives for the better, Youssou's political odyssey could be described as glorious. On the other hand, he could be written off as an inglorious politician involved in a misadventure which interrupted his legendary career. He may then take comfort in listening again to his back catalogue! Legends do not die, but they can lose their way.[8]

Return to the stage

In February 2013 it was announced that Youssou had been given permission by the president and the prime minister to resume his musical activities while retaining a ministerial post, this time as special adviser to the president. Youssou explained how that worked:

> I carry out missions, I take part in strategy meetings, I suggest ideas, I alert the president and advise him on all issues. This work demands less time which allows me to return to my music. However, my political life remains important.[9]

Back on tour in Europe he revealed some disillusionment with the processes of government when he told Mark Hudson, 'When you're outside politics, it's very easy to say, "Why didn't they think of that?" or "Why are they so slow?" But when you get inside, you realise how complicated the processes are.'[10]

In the interim, the rift which had developed between Youssou and his long-time musicians Habib Faye and Jimi Mbaye, who were dismayed at the manner in which he had left his superstar band in the lurch while pursuing his political aims, had now left an obvious gap. Into the breach stepped the young guitarist Moustapha Gaye, while Cameroonian bass player Christian Obam Edjo'o replaced Habib Faye.

On 12 October 2012, the morning of the eleventh Grand Bal at Bercy, Youssou was the guest of Catherine Ceylac on her France 2

TV show *Thé ou Café*. The elegantly directed studio programme reviewed the high points of his career before showing footage of recent rehearsals at the Palais des Beaux Arts in Brussels, an established classical music venue that is now as familiar to Youssou as the Royal Albert Hall in London or the Opéra Garnier in Paris. Despite the continued absence of Jimi and Habib, Youssou assured his interviewer that he had all the human resources he needed. Yet, in what seemed a veiled reference to his former stalwart colleagues, he alluded to his discomfort when musicians take up too much space. Given the long term cohesion of his group and the considerable contribution the Super Étoile musicians made to Youssou's recordings and stage shows down the years, the implied breach of confidence was clearly painful, as painful as any separation between people who have been close for a long time. However, the story had a happy ending: in November 2017, all the Super Étoile musicians, including Habib Faye and Jimi Mbaye, performed on stage with Youssou at that year's Grand Bal.

55. *Youssou with Barack Obama.*

Always keen to project a positive image of Africa, Youssou invited Ms Ceylac to visit Senegal to experience the welcome of its legendary *teranga*, its vivid colours, creativity and exuberance. Joined by Senegalese singer Julia Sarr, he finished the live show by singing 'Africa Dream Again': 'Wake up, stand up, Africa … dream again … smile again.'

In July 2014, during a speech at the US–Africa Summit in Washington, President Barack Obama toasted the New Africa, inspired, he said, by a song of that name that he had first heard in Senegal.

Cultural ambassador

Youssou has been an ambassador for UNICEF and the World Food Organization and has pioneered music projects for the Red Cross and the UN. Through his friendship with Bono and other high-profile performers he joined the ranks of musicians working for the good of humanity. When Bob Geldof organised Live Aid in July 1985, Youssou was onstage at Wembley Stadium with Salif Keita and Sly and Robbie.

Youssou later joined Geldof and Bono in lobbying world leaders for the cancellation of debts accrued by developing countries. According to Geldof, the Make Poverty History resolutions passed at the Gleneagles G8 Summit in 2005 – including the cancellation of debt and doubling of aid to Africa – mean that seven of the ten fastest-growing economies in the world are now African.[11] On stage the same year at the Live 8 concert in London's Hyde Park, Youssou made this plea: 'The debt cancellation is OK. The aid is OK, but please open your markets.'

So Why?, an album co-written and produced by Wally Badarou for the International Committee of the Red Cross, was released in 1997 and carried messages of protest against ethnic cleansing and war in Africa. It includes contributions from Youssou who,

58. So Why?

to the tune of Bob Dylan's 'Chimes of Freedom', sang about unrest in the beautiful but troubled province of Casamance in southern Senegal. Papa Wemba (Congo), Lourdes Van-Dúnem (Angola), Lagbaja (Nigeria), and Jabu Khanyile and Lucky Dube (South Africa) made equally significant contributions.

In 2000, refugee artists from a variety of countries gave a concert in Geneva to mark the fiftieth anniversary of the United Nations High Commissioner for Refugees (UNHCR). The following year, in his role as artistic director for the event, Youssou invited eleven refugee musicians – including the Liberian Peter Cole, who had settled in Senegal, and the Zimbabwean Chartwell Dutiro who had fled to Britain – to record the album *Building Bridges* in his Dakar studio. When the album was released, Youssou said that he would like this music to reach out to all people, helping them to realise that exile could also happen to them, so that maybe then people would do more to help refugees.

In the same year, Youssou organised and headlined a concert in Dakar in support of efforts to combat malaria, a disease which is most prevalent in West and Central Africa and which at that time was killing around 1 million Africans each year. The Rollback Malaria concert, which also featured Angélique Kidjo, Salif Keita, Baaba Maal, Corneille, Orchestra Baobab, Oumou Sangare and Tiken Jah Fakoly, was filmed for television by British director Mick Csáky. The Senegalese designer Oumou Sy dressed 'Mosquito Men' on stilts who strode through the crowd, dancing with the audience.

Youssou continued his fight against malaria, appearing at a Malaria No More benefit concert at the IAC building in New York City in November 2010 in the company of other performers, including Goldie Hawn. Through his involvement with the campaign, he found himself drinking coffee in the Oval Office at the White House in Washington with George Bush, the man whose politics he despised (in 2003 Youssou cancelled a thirty-eight-week tour of the USA in protest at America's invasion of Iraq, as he believed America had upset the entire world by waging that war without the support of the UN). Yet Bush proved sensitive to the cause, and as a result America doubled its support for the fight against a disease which has killed more humans than all wars, famines, plagues or natural causes put together.[12]

Youssou welcomed the election of Barack Obama not because he was black, but because he felt Obama was the best candidate. 'Obama', he remarked to me in Dakar in December 2010,

> has set about rectifying ruptured relations between the United States and the rest of the world and that has a calming effect, like tropical rain after a period of intense heat. He understands that the future of Africa is in the hands of Africans. We will be asking Obama to help us trade freely so that we can receive a fair return for our products.

Along with Malian artist Rokia Traoré, Youssou has been a leading figure in the Association of Professional African Musicians. In Paris in February 2007, they both attended the Afrique Avenir forum to defend the interests of professional musicians and to promote investment in good causes.

When Yoko Ono donated the rights and music publishing royalties to some of John Lennon's songs so that Amnesty International might encourage a new generation to stand up for human rights, Youssou chose to interpret the track 'Jealous Guy'. It was one of twenty-eight tracks on a double album entitled *Instant Karma: Save Darfur*, which included contributions by U2, REM, Snow Patrol, Corinne Bailey Rae, Jackson Browne and Christina Aguilera.

International recognition

According to Senegalese academic Oumar Sankhare, author of *Youssou N'Dour: Le Poète*,

> Youssou N'Dour's art is harmonious, melodious, euphonious and eurythmic, a unique example in Senegalese music. The name of this singer will henceforth be written in the universal pantheon of great artists who have succeeded in imposing their particular aesthetic view on humanity. His international recognition is eloquent testimony to his universality.[13]

International journalists have lauded Youssou, praising his powerful voice, his talent and his ability to fuse world and pop music. Jon Pareles described him in the *New York Times* as 'a musician who acts globally and hears locally'.[14] In his 2008 biography *Youssou N'Dour: le griot planétaire*, Gérald Arnaud lauds Youssou's 1992 album *Eyes Open* as 'a treasure of soul music comparable with the most beautiful discs of Marvin Gaye, Al Green or Curtis Mayfield.'[15]

Thirty years on from his first ever trip out of Senegal, in May 2011 Youssou received an honorary doctorate from Yale University, which came with this citation:

As a singer, songwriter, and composer, your music melds African rhythms with traditions ranging from Cuban samba to hip-hop, jazz, and soul. You have created Africa's leading ensemble, performed with great artists around the world, sung about tolerance, and acted with conviction, all the while remaining true to your own faith and culture. Understanding the power of music to liberate, heal and united [sic], you have organized and performed in concerts that call attention to injustice, poverty, and disease. With your extraordinary sound, you give voice to hope and our common humanity. We salute you now as Doctor of Music.[16]

The prestigious Polar Music Prize, which is worth 145,000 Swedish kronor (nearly £12,000) to each recipient, was founded in 1991 by the late Stig 'Stikkan' Anderson, the musical entrepreneur and former manager of ABBA. Previous recipients include Ray Charles, Bob Dylan, Peter Gabriel, Gilberto Gil, Quincy Jones, Paul McCartney and Miriam Makeba. In 2013 it was awarded jointly to Finnish composer Kaija Saariaho and Youssou and was presented by King Carl XVI Gustaf of Sweden at a gala ceremony at the Stockholm Concert Hall. Youssou's citation was read by Swedish footballer Henrik Larsson:

A West African *griot* is not just a singer but a story teller, poet, singer of praise, entertainer and verbal historian. Youssou N'Dour is maintaining the *griot* tradition and has shown that it can also be changed into a narrative about the entire world. With his exceptionally exuberant band Super Étoile de Dakar (Dakar Star) and his musically ground breaking and political solo albums, Youssou N'Dour has worked to reduce animosities between his own religion, Islam, and other religions. His voice encompasses an entire continent's history and future, blood and love, dreams and power.[17]

Youssou did not perform at the televised ceremony; instead, he enjoyed the luxury of watching Neneh Cherry, Carlou D and other artists interpret his music.

A further feather in his cap came in September 2017 when Youssou was presented with Japan's Praemium Imperiale international arts prize, worth $136,000, for outstanding contributions to the development, promotion and progress of the arts. Following a ceremony in New York, where he received a gold medal and testimonial letter from His Imperial Highness Prince Hitachi of Japan, Youssou dedicated the award to the whole of Africa, with a message to African youth to believe in themselves and the continent. He also pledged to share a portion of the prize money, 75 million West African CFA francs (around £100,000), with his fellow Senegalese musicians. As UK journalist Rick Glanvill wrote of the star, 'Senegal shaped a unique man.'[18]

Part III

YOUSSOU N'DOUR'S MUSICAL HINTERLAND

13

THE SOURCE

Always conscious of the deep well of inspiration available to him through the musical gifts of his *griot* ancestors, musicians who served as entertainers, advisers, and keepers of history and lineage in the great courts of West Africa's kings and emperors, Youssou N'Dour has often defined himself as a modern *griot*. Indeed, the notable success of his music and that of other musicians from Senegal, Mali, Guinea and Mauritania during the world music era can be attributed directly to that rich seam of music which has its source in the thirteenth-century royal courts of West Africa.

Salif Keita

The greatest patron the *griots* of West Africa ever had was Sundiata Keita (*c.*1217–55), who founded the Mali Empire, a federation of the Mandé people that endured for more than 200 years from its foundation around 1240. Its territories eventually extended right across the region from the shores of the Atlantic to the ramparts of Timbuktu and included modern-day Mali, Senegal and the Gambia, as well as parts of Mauritania, Guinea, Guinea-Bissau and the Ivory Coast. Sundiata's court brought kingship to its highest level, as he was regarded as all-powerful; it is said that if he sneezed, his subjects beat their breasts in sympathy. The penalty for wearing sandals in the emperor's presence was death, and all were required to cover their heads with dust as a mark of humility. The emperor alone wore a headdress and his regal clothing befitted his wealth and status, yet he never raised his voice. During Sundiata's reign, the courtly traditions which allowed the *griots* to play a pivotal role as historians and entertainers were devised and developed.

Salif Keita's noble family trace their lineage back to Sundiata Keita. Like his illustrious ancestor, who did not walk until he was seven years old, Salif emerged from an unpromising childhood to become one of the great soul voices of West Africa. Born in 1949 in the village of Djoliba, some fifty miles from the capital Bamako, he was an albino child who faced all the superstition and prejudice associated with such a condition in Africa; on the continent, albinos have even sometimes been sacrificed in order to bring good luck. The birth of an albino son so shocked and shamed Salif's father – it was said such a child would bring bad luck for seven generations – that he initially banned his wife and baby from his compound, before relenting and taking them back. When, at Salif's baptism ceremony, the hair on his head was shaven, the village women fought over it so they could sow it in the fields to fertilise the crops. As a result of his own condition (he describes himself as a black man with white skin), Salif Keita hopes for a world of mutual understanding and multiculturalism, and set up the Salif Keita Global Foundation to work for the fair treatment and social integration of people with albinism.[1] Imagine his great pride when his niece Nantenin Keita, also an albino and whose photograph appears on his 1995 album *Folon* (*The Past*), represented France at the 2016 Paralympic Games in Rio de Janeiro and won the gold medal for the 400 metres.

Musically, Keita has achieved a remarkable fusion of Western and African traditions in his music. In Mali he listened to Pink Floyd and Rod Stewart, but his mighty album *Mandjou*, composed with Les Ambassadeurs in 1978, was an immediate hit in Africa. His next album, *Soro*, which was produced in France, was hailed as a classic crossover album which, together with Youssou's album *Immigrés*, heralded the dawn of the world music era.

57. Folon.

In the spring of 1988, I travelled to Paris with TV journalist Robin Denselow and director James Marsh (who went on to make *Man on Wire* (2008), *The Theory of Everything* (2014) and *The Mercy* (2018)) to shoot a short film, *Paris, Africa*, about the rising popularity of African music in the French capital.[2] Africa's reggae-man, Alpha Blondy, provided the soundtrack with his song 'I Love Paris', and we interviewed the award-winning Senegalese band Touré Kunda. They were among the first West African musicians to bring their music to the capital, where they recorded seven LPs and a double album and gained three gold discs. Filmed at night against a backdrop of an illuminated Eiffel Tower, the trio looked as though they owned the place. North African music was represented by the Algerians Khaled and Fadela, and then we spoke with Salif, who was living in the suburb of Montreuil (popularly known as Little Bamako) and had just recorded *Soro*. A remarkable fusion of Western and African styles arranged by François Bréant and Jean-Philippe Rykiel, it was produced by Paris-based Senegalese producer Ibrahima Sylla. Robin Denselow described *Soro* in the programme as 'a mix of synthesizers, subtle rhythms, brass and chanting African choruses, all topped up with one of the greatest soul voices to be heard anywhere in the world.'

In *Paris, Africa* Salif defined the global importance of African music using the image of a tree: 'The roots are African music; the tree trunk is jazz and the branches and the leaves are funk, reggae, hip-hop and other modern styles.'

In 1989 I met Salif again, this time in Mali when I joined another BBC television crew led by director Chris Austin and cameraman Chris Seager to film *Destiny of a Noble Outcast*, a documentary for the arts series *Arena*.[3] We were introduced to Salif's mother and father in the village of Djoliba, where the apparent simplicity and harmony of their life gave no clue to the emotional turmoil they had experienced when their eldest son was young. Throughout Salif's childhood, *griots* came to the Keita household to sing the praises of that noble family. It seems Salif was a brilliant pupil at school but his poor eyesight prevented him from following his chosen career as a schoolteacher, so he overturned all the rules of the caste system to become a singer like the *griots* who praised him.

58. Soro.

(He would later boast that singing is the most noble of professions, but in those early days it was tough going for him.) He slept in the market in Bamako; he listened to Pink Floyd and Rod Stewart; he sang in bars, strumming his own accompaniment on an acoustic guitar, someone slipping a coin beneath the guitar strings every now and again. Whenever it all seemed hopeless, Salif would sit alone on a hill above the city and reflect on his fate. At last he joined the Rail Band at the Buffet de la Gare and began to find his way. In the railway station's courtyard, the Rail Band, who were paid as civil servants, performed for local punters, who were joined at two or three in the morning by passengers arriving at the station on their way to or from Senegal and Niger. So popular was the group that some people would leave Dakar on a Friday night and take the train to Bamako in order to dance to their music. During a brief absence, Salif's place was taken by a certain musician and singer called Mory Kanté, who would later gain international acclaim for his kora playing and the hit song 'Yé Ké Yé Ké'. So Salif turned on his heel and went down the road to the Motel to join Les Ambassadeurs, his only stipulation being that they should buy him a Mobylette moped. The group's musicians came from Guinea, Senegal, the Ivory Coast, Burkina Faso, Cameroon and Ghana as well as from Mali, hence their name. Under the coloured lights of the open-air stage, they serenaded visiting diplomats and tourists with their interpretations of the latest Charles Aznavour, Otis Redding or James Brown hits; in short, every kind of music except African. Salif wanted to change all that and modernise the traditional music of Mali, with all its riches. In 1978, following an attempted coup in Mali, he left the country in the company of Kanté Manfila, Ousmane Dia, Sambou Diakité, Ousmane Kouyaté and Alpha Traoré. They headed for Abidjan in the Ivory Coast, at that time the centre of all the musical action, and it was not long before they had created their first and most famous song, 'Mandjou', a praise song dedicated to Sékou Touré, the Guinean president. It became the title track on an album that was an immediate hit in Africa. Listening to it for the first time in my flat in Chiswick, the magic of 'Mandjou' kept me housebound and spellbound for an entire weekend:

> Touré don't cry. Touré don't be sad, for God has given
> you all the gifts he has to give, including that of making music.

We filmed Salif walking in the fields around Djoliba, projecting his powerful voice in the way he had as a young man to strengthen his vocal chords. We filmed him in the marketplace in Bamako, at the Buffet de la Gare, and at the abandoned Motel.

Back in London, when the film returned from the processing labs, two key sequences were missing. The first featured a ritual dance by village hunters including Salif's father, Sina Keita, and Salif himself, all dressed in full ceremonial costume and bearing guns. The second sequence contained footage of Salif at the cliffs of Bandiagara in remote Dogon country, an area well known for its deep spiritual traditions. Dogon legends describe the visit of extraterrestrial *nommos*, a race of mermen and mermaids who came from the Sirius star system.[4] Could it have been that the solitary figure who appeared on a cliff just as Salif performed a song to his own guitar accompaniment had been angered by our intrusion upon this sacred site? Whatever the reason, it seemed clear we had contravened some local law, and so the director and the cameraman returned to Mali to reshoot both sequences, this time with the necessary permissions.

Although most Malians embrace the Muslim faith, many also believe in what they call 'African realities'. When we met Salif Keita's mother-in-law, Tenin Traoré, a well-known healer and clairvoyant and the subject of his song 'Tenin', she offered to read her cowrie shells for us. She explained that she had inherited her spiritual powers from her grandfather, Adama, and claimed she had met Mamiwata, West Africa's legendary water spirit. Tenin prescribed for me the sacrifice of a goat and a ritual herb bath. She then poured

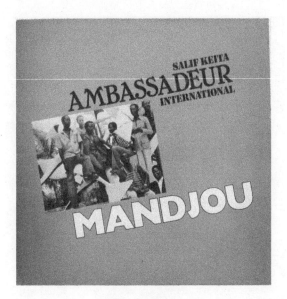

59. Mandjou.

60. *Salif Keita with the author.*

61. *Tenin Traoré*.

a murky potion over my body and I accompanied her by the light of the moon to the local cemetery to bury the goat's eyes.

Miriam Makeba, whose mother was an *isangoma* (traditional healer/diviner), defined those realities thus: 'The spirits of our ancestors are ever-present. We make sacrifices to them and ask for their advice and guidance. They answer us in dreams or through a medium like the medicine men and women we call *isangoma*.'[5] Zimbabwe's top musician, Thomas Mapfumo, who was brought up a Christian, thinks that those who have passed on are closer to God. When I interviewed him, he explained the spiritual nature of his *chimurenga* music and described his respect for his ancestors: 'They can speak with Him; maybe they are living with Him. So, through mediums, we have to consult our ancestors and tell them what messages we wish to convey to God.'[6]

In her book *Obama Music*, Chicago-born writer Bonnie Greer notes how that same African spirituality was carried by the slaves and their music to the Americas. She writes,

> The blues has this quality of the 'other world', of that great African Triad of the living, the dead, and the unborn.
>
> This Trinity exists together and at once in the African consciousness and it was brought over with the Passage.
>
> The blues are full of the knowledge of this.
>
> Growing up, we respected the dead because, well, they weren't gone.[7]

Perhaps it is these deep atavistic connections with the land and the spirit world that are beguiling to Westerners like myself, who, once we visit Africa, feel drawn again and again to the continent. Traveller and writer Ryszard Kapuściński puts it this way:

> For centuries people have been attracted by a certain aura of mystery surrounding this continent – a sense that there must be something unique in Africa, something hidden, some glistening oxidizing point in the darkness which it is difficult or well nigh impossible to reach.[8]

My lasting memory of my first trip to Mali was the feeling of humility and awe that came from standing alone beneath a starry sky looking out over the savannah plains of that immense land mass. Doris Lessing, who grew up in Southern Rhodesia (now Zimbabwe), summed up this sense of vastness when she said, 'Africa gives you the knowledge that man is a small creature, among other creatures, in a large landscape.'[9]

On his first visit to Mali in 1983, Youssou was moved by the enthusiastic and generous welcome he received. In fact, the attraction was mutual: Malian star Ali Farka Touré joked that the divorce rate increased sharply after Youssou's concert, so numerous were the Malian women who defied their husbands to attend! The trip held special significance for Youssou because it was the first time he had played outside of Senegal. To receive such a warm reception in a country with extremely high musical standards gave him enormous confidence and an assurance that his music could travel. He was also thrilled to meet Fanta Damba, a singular and unsurpassed singer whom he regarded as the first lady of Malian music, and whose song, 'Haye Hane', he later reprised in his own majestic composition, 'Wareff'.

I remember driving through Dakar with Youssou at the wheel and Fanta Damba's cassette playing in the tape deck and Youssou humming and gently moving his shoulders in time to that sublime music. It is clear from Youssou's song 'Bamako' just how much Mali held him in its spell. The image of a lady wrapped in her shawl is enveloping and alluring; she appears to be Youssou's muse and

62. *Fanta Damba.*

inspiration. Could it be that he is in fact referring to Fanta Damba? Feelings of mystery and nostalgia pervade the song as Youssou's voice soars to its topmost notes above the sweet voices of the Martyr of Luganda church choir. He repeats his longing in the phrase '*Duma fatte, fatte, fatte Bamako*' ('I shall never forget Bamako').

Ali Farka Touré

The late Ali Farka Touré greatly admired Youssou's enterprising spirit and his voice. Youssou pays homage to Ali Farka in the style and tone of his 2007 album *Rokku Mi Rokka* (*Give and Take*), which features the gifted Malian *xalam* player Bassekou Kouyaté on many of its blues-tinged tracks.

Before he became a full-time musician, the great Malian blues-man was a farmer, a radio engineer, a driver, a desert guide and an ambulance boatman. He might equally have been a healer, a marabout, or even a king, as he came from a noble line of Songhai and Amarak warriors and generals. Ali was the youngest of ten children but the only one to live to manhood. When he was two his father died from injuries sustained fighting on the French side in the trenches of World War II. A pacifist, a teacher, a nature lover and an artist, Ali refused conscription when his time came. When he played the *N'jarka* fiddle, he conjured up the desert landscapes, the haunting solitary places where he loved to hunt. He told me that it was by a lake near his village that he first encountered the *Ghimbala*, the powerful water spirits that took hold of his little *djerkele* guitar, sending him into a trance as he played it.

His grandmother, Kounandi Samba, priestess of the *Ghimbala*, passed on to Ali the secrets and rituals of her traditional religion, but when he was eighteen he was, in his own words, 'cured' by a religious marabout and renounced these practices, pledging his allegiance to Islam at the great mosque at Timbuktu, the fabled city founded in *c.*1080 by the Tuaregs. From then on Ali prayed five times a day; if he missed a certain prayer, he would make up for it with extra prayers in the early morning. He might pray all night if he had a special trip to make. These rituals were as important to him as tuning his guitar or checking sound levels. I recall how he gave me a mantra, presumably one he used himself, which I still recite for safekeeping while taking off and landing in an aeroplane. Indeed, Ali never travelled without his protection kit – a bundle of herbs and resins to cure all aches and pains and a collection of talismans, each with a special significance, carefully tied to his body or pinned to his dress before every concert. An acute awareness of evil eyes may have accounted for a certain irascibility, and he was known to berate his audience if he thought they were not listening or appreciating as they should! His pride would not let him forget any behaviour which was less than generous towards him or his music.

The *N'jarka* and the *djerkele* were to remain his primary source of inspiration, providing a seemingly endless spring of melody. He transferred the same technique he used to play these simple instruments to the acoustic or electric guitar, tuning them in his own mysterious fashion, much to the bewilderment of those schooled in orthodox tuning methods. Although austere in his religion, he smoked cigarettes and savoured the odd tot of whisky, especially when he was in Scotland. His prodigious memory made up for the fact that he could not read or write – he could give you a day and date for every event in his own life, or for important events in his country. He danced the rumba or the bebop with enormous ease and elegance, just as he did any of Mali's many traditional dances.

Among Ali Farka Touré's favourite artists were Ray Charles, Stevie Wonder, Otis Redding, Jimmy Cliff and James Brown. When he first heard John Lee and Albert King he swore they must be Malian, so closely did their music relate to his own. Nevertheless, he learned a great deal from them in terms of technique. 'If one day I am lucky enough to meet John Lee Hooker, I shall die happy,' he said.[10] Yet he would never deny the root source of his own inspiration – the natural blues of his desert songs; the dance rhythms of the nomads, the mysterious men in blue; the lore of eight different dialects including Tamashek, Songhai, Bambara and the Arab inflections which are echoed in his guitar lines.

Ali was a many-faceted man who, over the years, brought home tales of his trips to Russia, Bulgaria and many European countries, and since he was a keen photographer, he had albums full of snaps to prove it. Also in his luggage would be a new tailored suit or a remarkable hat, for he prided himself greatly on his appearance. In London he had his eye on a tuxedo complete with patent black shoes and bow tie; since cotton materials came cheaper in the shops in Willesden Green or London's New Street market, his Malian tailor would soon be busy with yards of heavy cotton *bazin* in brilliant royal blue, deep russet, or pure white, fashioning long, flowing boubou robes.

63. *Ali Farka Touré with the author.*

When Ali's first wife died in childbirth he was grief-stricken and swore he would never marry again; he did in time, of course, and his son Vieux Farka Touré is now a well-known musician. He also married Henriette Kuypers, a young Dutch woman, with whom he had three children, and it was touching to see her dancing onstage during Vieux Farka Touré's concert in Amsterdam in 2011.

Always extremely courteous towards women, Ali would gallantly say, '*ce que femme veut, Dieu le veut*' ('whatever woman wishes, God wills'). A good friend and a gentleman in the true sense of the word, he used to tell me I was a Peul from among the herding nomadic people of West Africa and he would tease me by calling me 'Jenny Diallo', a name common among that ethnic group. And then, of course, I married a Senegalese man named Sow – who is in fact Peul!

Ali was also generous; old and young came to his house each morning to receive the few coins that would support them through the day. He always spoke fondly of his farm on the shores of the Niger River at Niafunké near Gao in Northern Mali, where his entire family were engaged in farming, tending flocks and growing crops. In 2012 and 2013, the area around the cities of Gao and Timbuktu was occupied first by MNLA (National Movement for the Liberation of Azawad) rebels who aimed to establish an independent northern state for the Tuareg and later by Islamist groups including Ansar Dine, who imposed strict sharia law. Ali's wife and many of his family moved to Bamako for a time, though most of them later returned. When, in late 2015, Vieux Farka Touré was asked how his father would have felt about the violence, the political instability and the financial ruin in his cherished homeland, he replied, 'I can't say, it would have hurt, but he wouldn't have left Niafunké, that's for sure. He would have done everything to stop the destruction because, believe you me, it's been devastated.'[11]

Ali won his first Grammy award for *Talking Timbuktu*, the album he recorded with Ry Cooder, and a second for *In the Heart of the Moon*, his collaboration with ace kora player Toumani Diabaté, who traces his *griot* ancestry (*griots* are known as *jalis* in Mali)

64. *Vieux Farka Touré.*

back in an unbroken line through seventy-one generations to the first kora player, Tiaramagau.

When he was diagnosed with cancer Ali faced his illness with stoicism and exemplary bravery. He insisted on leaving all his affairs, including his Niafunké farm, in good order. I attended his final concert at the Barbican in London in June 1995 and spoke again with him in Paris not long before he died on 6 March 1996, aged sixty-seven.

Baaba Maal: *yela* and reggae

Rising in the Fouta Djallon mountains in Guinea, the Senegal River passes through Mali, embraces Senegal in a large curve, forming the border with Mauritania, before flowing into the Atlantic Ocean at Saint-Louis. The river played a crucial role in the Atlantic slave trade, becoming a highway for the transportation of slaves from territories in the interior to the seaport. It has been a constant source of inspiration for Baaba Maal, who was born in 1953 in Podor, a town that sits on the banks of the Senegal River. His father was a fisherman and a muezzin, who with his sonorous voice called the faithful to prayer, while his schoolteacher mother taught him the customs of his own Toucouleur people, their dances and their songs. Baaba spent many years with a group of traditional musicians, the Lasli Fouta, travelling up and down the river and gaining first-hand knowledge of daily life in the region; of the men and women who work in the Walo flood fields where millet is grown from November to June and in the Dyeri lands higher up. He noted how the village girls made themselves pretty for the arrival of a relative or friend on the riverboat, the *Bou El Mogdad*, which made the round trip from Saint-Louis to Kayes in Mali. During their regattas, the northern fishermen would call up the spirits of the sea with their *pekane* music. The warrior caste sang about their heroes in a style called *gumbala*. The butchers had their own *sawali* music and the weavers plaited their threads to the *dilere*. The Toucouleur people dance the *ripo*, the *tiayo*, the *ndadali* or the *odi boyel*, while the dance of the virgins, the *wango*, is so strenuous that only the unmarried are supposed to be able to perform the high-kicking steps.

Listening to the praise songs the *griottes* sang at weddings or those of women pounding grain in family compounds, Baaba discovered the *yela* which was to become his trademark, a swinging beat regarded by Jimmy Cliff as the original reggae.[12] Indeed 'reggae' in the African Soninke dialect means 'to dance'. Explaining the evolution of his own musical style, he had this to say:

> If you listen to the women of the Bundu in Southern Senegal as they sing and dance their *yela*, you will notice that the way they clap their hands resembles the beat of the rhythm guitar when we play it and the alternating drumbeat represents their

accompaniment played on a simple kitchen calabash. When Africans are modernising their music, they bring out what is in their own traditions, and there are definite similarities between that music and the music of black people in Jamaica or America.[13]

As with so many African rhythms, it is likely that *yela* went to the Americas with the slaves and eventually became a universal beat, achieving ultimate worldwide popularity through the music of Bob Marley.

A clever student, Baaba read law at the University of Dakar, then music at the city's arts school and later at the École des Beaux Arts in Paris. In 1985, he formed the group Dande Lenol, meaning 'The Voice of our People', to reflect the particular lifestyle of the Pular-speaking ethnic groups of his own region. The Peul and the Toucouleur were pastoralists, although the Peul guarded their nomadic status longer than the Toucouleur, who intermarried with sedentary Serer groups to settle in the region called Fouta Tooro. When Baaba Maal and his group celebrated their first anniversary with a concert at the Sorano Theatre in Dakar in 1986 they quickly acquired a nationwide following, and when Baaba later signed a recording contract with London label Palm Pictures, a subsidiary of Island Records, Youssou now had a serious rival both at home and abroad. In Mansour Seck, a blind *griot* musician, Baaba found a musical companion with whom he wrote songs for a moving and memorable acoustic album, *Djam Leeli*. It was this music that first seduced international audiences, especially in the UK. When they showcased the album at London's Hackney Empire, the concert was filmed for the BBC's television series *Rhythms of the World*.[14]

In the same week, Peter Gabriel invited Baaba Maal to record vocal lines for the soundtrack which he was composing for Martin Scorsese's film *The Last Temptation of Christ* (1988). My friend Lucy Duran and I drove him to the Real World studios. Lucy was at the wheel, Mbassou Niang, Baaba's manager, was in the front seat, and I sat in the back between Baaba and his keyboard

65. *Baaba Maal at the Real World studios.*

player, Hilaire Chaby. We chatted along the way and then Baaba, who rarely spoke about his personal life, began telling me about his mother, whom he clearly adored, who had supported him in his chosen career, and who died when he was a student in Paris. Describing her warmth, generosity and kindness, he said fondly, 'I think about her every day. What hurt me most was the fact that I was unable to return home from Paris to see her before she was buried.' As he spoke, tears welled up in his eyes, and my heart went out to him. Afterwards we sat silently side by side, yet he seemed to take comfort from the sharing of such a profound loss. As if to diffuse the sadness Lucy stopped the car at a lay-by, and we stepped out to admire the breathtaking view down the By Brook valley towards the village of Box.

66. *Baaba Maal with the author.*

On Peter Gabriel's album *Passion*, Youssou's voice is heard on the title track alongside that of the great Pakistani qawwali singer Nusrat Fateh Ali Khan and English boy soprano Julian Wilkins.

Baaba's recording for 'A Call to Prayer' reflects his own spiritual nature and appears on the companion album *Passion – Sources*. His contract with Palm Pictures afforded him the freedom to collaborate with producers and artists from the world of pop and electronic music on albums such as *Firin' in Fouta*, *Missing You (Mi Yeewni)*, *Nomad Soul*, *Television* and, in 2016, *The Traveller*, produced by Johan Hugo Karlberg. Baaba Maal's soaring vocals echoed over the Wakanda hilltops of the much-publicised 2018 blockbuster movie *Black Panther*; Swedish composer Ludwig Göransson spent a month in Senegal familiarising himself with African music and making recordings which included Baaba's significant contributions to the film score. The soundtrack won the Oscar for Best Original Music Score at the 2019 Academy Awards ceremony in Los Angeles.

Alpha Blondy

Youssou and I travelled to the Ivorian capital, Abidjan, to attend a meeting. While we were there we lunched with his friend Alpha Blondy, the country's leading reggaeman, voice of the dispossessed and idol of the gangs in Abidjan's Treichville district. We drove in Blondy's pale blue Volkswagen Beetle to Cocody, the seaside suburb which gave its name to his album *Cocody Rock!!!* As we sat at a beachside restaurant under the shade of coconut trees, I reflected that Blondy had come a long way since his troubled childhood when he had been moved from pillar to post, from Dimbokro to Odienné and Boundiali to Korhogo, where he was eventually expelled from his secondary school.

Born Seydou Traoré on 1 January 1953 to a single mother, he was brought up by his grandmother Nagnêlê until his mother married a man named Koné whom he disliked but who gave him a new surname. Then he formed a band called The Atomic Vibrations and took on an entirely different identity, that of Elvis Blondy. He was just twenty when he moved to Monrovia, where he learned English and taught karate to the sons of the future president, Samuel Doe. From Liberia he travelled to New York, where he faced altogether new challenges and where his frustrations resulted in a spell in a psychiatric hospital. The French journalist Hélène Lee, who knows Alpha well, said, 'He is not mad, he belongs to another world, that of the extraterrestrials or simply that of Africa's tomorrow.'[15] All the same, it was at Central Park in 1975, during a Burning Spear concert, that he discovered his true vocation.

By a quirk of fate, he was spotted in a Greenwich Village club singing 'War' by Bob Marley's producer, Clive Hunt, who was briefly interested in working with him but failed to follow through on the idea of creating the first ever African reggaeman. Disillusioned, Blondy returned to the Ivory Coast, turned another page in his career and adopted a new name, the one that stuck: Alpha, meaning the beginning. In Abidjan, he worked at the TV station and engineered an appearance on a show called *Première Chance*, where a TV producer, George Benson, arranged a recording session for him which culminated in the album *Jah Glory*, sung in English, French and his mother tongue, Diola. One magic track, 'Brigadier Sabatier', about police brutality, sent shock waves around the country and the whole of West Africa. Ten years later, his song 'Apartheid is Nazism' set a precedent for many of his overtly political songs.

In 1986 he travelled to Kingston, where he recorded the album *Jerusalem* accompanied by the legendary Wailers, Bob Marley's group, and produced by Tuff Gong. Then with his own band, The Solar System, he recorded *Revolution* (1987), *The Prophets* (1989) and *SOS Guerre Tribale* (1991), all of which contained lyrics that denounced dictatorships, division, repression and tribalism. Asked why his songs are so political, Blondy replied that he is an ordinary Ivorian who reads newspapers, watches TV and listens to the radio. As for religion, this son of a Muslim father and Christian mother claimed that he respects all religions that respect God. 'God is against war and the people that want to fight holy war are mistaken. They are going to hell because God said, don't kill.'[16]

67. Apartheid is Nazism.

Released in 1998, an album named after and dedicated to the assassinated President of Israel, Yitzhak Rabin, confirmed Blondy's fascination with a country where Jews, Christians and Muslims try to coexist. It featured vocals by Rita Marley and Marcia Griffith and was produced by none other than Clive Hunt, whom Blondy had met again by chance in a hotel lobby in Paris. One of the tracks, 'Guerre Civile', offered a prophetic warning of the dangers of civil war between ethnic groups in Africa, and as it turned out, in the Ivory Coast.

14

THE GREAT WEST AFRICAN ORCHESTRAS

Orchestra Baobab

Early in the year 2000, a miracle happened. Nick Gold, managing director of World Circuit Records in London, who had already licensed tracks by Orchestra Baobab for the album *Pirates Choice*, had for some time been mulling over the idea of reuniting the group, which had disbanded in 1987. When I was asked to propose Senegalese bands for a Dakar Night at the Urban Vibes festival at London's Barbican Hall, I immediately suggested a comeback concert by Orchestra Baobab. By then I was working in Dakar as international liaison manager for Youssou's music operations and

68. *Orchestra Baobab with well-known Senegalese photographer Behan Touré.*

he was fully supportive of the idea of a reunion: the Orchestra, along with other legendary West African bands including the Senegalese group Xalam, Guinea's Bembeya Jazz and Gambia's Super Eagles, had been a seminal influence on his early life and career.

I telephoned Barthélémy Attisso in Togo and persuaded him to return to Dakar for rehearsals. Balla Sidibé, Rudy Gomis and I met him off the plane at Dakar airport, and a meeting over lunch at Terrou-Bi in Dakar, where we were joined by Issa Cissokho, Latfi Bengeloune and Thierno Koité, sealed the idea of a comeback. Thus the legendary Orchestra Baobab came back to life, intact save for the voice of the late lamented Laye Mboup who, at Youssou's suggestion, was replaced by a remarkable young singer called Assane Mboup (no relation). The London concert was deemed a success. Writing in the *Guardian*, Robin Denselow described it as a 'subtle, charming, triumphant reunion', although he thought the group's green floral-patterned shirts made them look like an old-fashioned hotel band.[1]

Orchestra Baobab were originally formed in Dakar in 1970 when a group of Senegalese personalities, including Ousmane Diagne, Dame Dramé and government minister Adrien Senghor, decided to create an intimate club where they could meet with their friends. They took over the basement of number 144 Rue Jules Ferry, a stone's throw from Independence Square and the presidential palace. The ceiling and walls, moulded to resemble the knotty trunk and branches of a baobab tree, were decorated with monkey skins and wicker lampshades. The Baobab Club was quite simply the trendiest and chicest venue in the city.

Baro Ndiaye (saxophone), the first bandleader, and Sidathe Ly (bass guitar) chose the other band members. Moussa Kane played congas and *toumba*; Bitèye was the kit drummer while Barthélémy Attisso from Togo, who was studying law at the University of Dakar, became lead guitarist. The singers Balla Sidibé (who also played drums, guitar and congas) and Rudy Gomis were enticed away from the Star Band at Ibra Kassé's Miami Club. Laye Mboup, the charismatic star of the National Troupe at the Daniel Sorano Theatre, came with his stunning good looks, his local *griot* singing talents, perfect pitch and a wealth of Wolof songs.

By the late 1950s, Senegal and neighbouring countries, including Guinea and present-day Mali (then called French Sudan), were seeking independence from colonial rule, and their growing political links with Cuba served to popularise Cuban music. Cuban *son*, which emerged around 1905, spawned other Cuban, Latin American and Caribbean styles including cha-cha-cha, mambo, rumba, pachanga and merengue in the Dominican Republic, calypso in Trinidad and Tobago and eventually, in the 1960s, salsa. This dance style first emerged in Venezuela and was popularised in New York by Johnny Pacheco, Ray Barretto and Rubén Blades. When it reached Senegal, salsa was played by the local groups Star Band and Miami, and became all the rage. What came to define Orchestra Baobab's repertoire was their intriguingly cool mix of pachanga, salsa, cha-cha-cha and African music. Initially the group animated the Baobab Club at weekends, but they quickly gained so many fans that they were playing every night and the dance floor was full by ten o'clock. Since the musicians were drawn from many ethnic groups, they had an extensive repertoire of popular songs which included something for everyone. Balla Sidibé and Rudy Gomis and later Charlie Ndiaye (bass guitar), who were all born in the southern Senegalese province of Casamance, contributed Mandinka, Mandiago and Diola folk songs. Médoune Diallo represented Toucouleur music from the north of Senegal. Issa Cissokho (tenor saxophone) and his cousins, Mountaga Koité (drums) and Seydou Norou 'Thierno' Koité (saxophone) drew inspiration from their Malinké relatives in Mali. Latfi Bengeloune (rhythm guitar) was born in Saint-Louis of Moroccan parents, while Peter Udo (clarinet) was Nigerian. Barthélémy Attisso added touches of Togolese, Congolese and other Central and West African musical styles to his arrangements. Laye Mboup and Ndiouga Dieng, Wolof singers from the major ethnic group in Senegal, came with the praise-singing traditions that put the final Senegalese stamp on the music.

During the 1970s Orchestra Baobab were hailed as the best band in Senegal if not in Africa, enjoying a status similar to Bembeya Jazz in Sékou Touré's Guinea. The founding members stayed firmly with the group, but they welcomed regular guest musicians and singers. Despite his natural talent, Laye Mboup was unreliable, finding it difficult to cover his commitments with both the Sorano Theatre and Orchestra Baobab, so the group looked around for a stand-in singer. At his audition, the young and very promising Thione Seck sang 'Demb', a tribute to his mentor Laye Mboup, and was accepted without hesitation, as was his younger brother, Mapenda Seck. In 1975, when the twenty-seven-year-old Laye Mboup was killed in a tragic car accident, rumours of a spell cast by a jealous husband surrounded his death.

Apart from the Baobab Club, the group were invited to play on state occasions, such as a soirée to celebrate the nomination of Abdou Diouf as prime minister. They were the star attraction at glamorous army and navy dress dances at the *Mess des Officiers* and they also appeared at the Lions Club, the Zonta Club and the Soroptimist Club. They livened up the New Year's Eve Ball in the southern town of Ziguinchor, which was held to raise funds for municipal improvements there. In 1978 they played at the wedding reception of Pierre Cardin's daughter in an expensive venue frequented by the glitterati near the Arc de Triomphe in Paris. Four years later they performed on the *Casamance Express* passenger boat during its inaugural trip, travelling from Dakar to Ziguinchor and on to Conakry in Guinea, where they appeared at the Palais du Peuple. The Guineans, who were seduced by Barthélémy Attisso's rapturous guitar solos, loved 'On Verra Ca' ('We'll See About That'), as did President Sékou Touré, who made a habit of using that phrase in his daily discourse.

In 1979 the Baobab Club closed down and Orchestra Baobab moved to the Ngalam nightclub at Point E, next door to the fashionable Lebanese-owned patisserie Les Ambassades. A small but delightful venue, its mirrored walls reflected the revellers on the intimate dance floor. It was here in 1981 that Moussa Diallo from Thies recorded a live session with his four-track Nagra and the musicians signed a recording contract with Mbaye Gueye. Wahab Diawo, the owner of the Jandeer nightclub (later called the Kilimanjaro), invited Orchestra Baobab to play at his place. Madame Michelle, who ran the Balafon, booked the orchestra for her club at the Immeuble Macodou Ndiaye. At the height of their popularity, Orchestra Baobab commanded a very respectable fee of 1,800,000 West African CFA francs per night (about £3,000 in today's money).

In 1982, the twenty-three-year-old Youssou N'Dour, who had formed his first band and introduced a new wave of popular mbalax dance music based on the rhythms of traditional *sabar* drums, emerged as a surprise rival to Orchestra Baobab with their more leisurely and languid dance grooves. By 1985, in what proved to be a vain attempt to update their style, the group introduced *sabars* and female singers, but in 1987, after a difficult tour in France, Orchestra Baobab began to disintegrate. One by one the musicians left to join other bands, and Issa Cissokho and Thierno Koité joined Youssou and the Super Étoile de Dakar. Barthélémy Attisso resumed his work as a lawyer in Togo. Balla Sidibé joined Pape Fall and his group African Salsa, while Rudy Gomis took a day job as a teacher. So ended the first chapter of the Orchestra Baobab story.

In 2001, when a new album, *Specialist in All Styles* (the very title indicated a renewed confidence in their music), was recorded by the revived Orchestra Baobab at the World Circuit studios in London, Youssou co-produced it and sang on the track 'Hommage à Tonton Ferrer' along with Ibrahim Ferrer of the celebrated Cuban group Buena Vista Social Club.

The album topped the world music charts and earned Orchestra Baobab the prize for best African group at the BBC Radio 3 Awards for World Music. It also assured the musicians of regular

69. *Nick Gold and Barthélémy Attisso.*

70. *Youssou with Ibrahim Ferrer.*

international tour dates. In March 2003 they performed at the charity event Le Bal de la Rose, organised annually in Monaco by Princess Caroline in aid of the Princess Grace Foundation. For this event, staged at the Monte-Carlo Sporting Club on the Avenue Princesse Grace, the band wore costumes designed by my sister-in-law, the late Fama Sow Cama, each one distinctive, each one imaginatively created with a fabric chosen to suit the individual musician. The costumes would have been scrutinised by Karl Lagerfeld, who was a guest at the ball. Dutch photographer Christien Jaspars took moody black-and-white photographs of the group and Matar N'Dour snapped them posing around a painted *car rapide* bus. It was no sinecure, however, to manage twelve macho men who had once told me, 'If you had been a Senegalese woman, we would never have allowed you to do this job!'

At the end of March 2017, Orchestra Baobab released a brand-new album dedicated to Ndiouga Dieng, one of their original vocalists, who had passed away in November 2016. In the sleeve notes, Nigel Williamson wrote, 'As enduring as the mighty African Baobab tree from which the group derives its name, the veteran

11. Tribute to Ndiouga Dieng.

core of the band remains as strong and sturdy as ever.' Caressed by their languorous, well-tempered dance grooves, soothed by the warm welcoming voices of Balla Sidibé, Cheikh Lô ('Magnokouto') and Thione Seck ('Sey'), charmed by lyrical guitar lines and glissando kora riffs, thrilled by Issa Cissokho's exuberant tenor sax and Thierno Koité's blowsy, bluesy sax solos, I realised once more why African music had seduced me all those years ago.

Xalam

The Senegalese group Xalam II, who inspired Youssou to open his own music to new ideas, were at the height of their fame in the 1980s, rivalling Osibisa, Fela Kuti and Hugh Masekela. The Afro jazz fusion for which they became famous may have been influenced by Cream, Led Zeppelin, James Brown and Ray Charles, but it began as a truly innovative experiment in modernising traditional African tunes and songs. Who of their ardent fans can forget 'Ade', 'Sidy Yella' or 'Djisalbero'?

In late 2008, the musicians, many of whom were now living in France, came together again in Senegal for rehearsals at the Quai des Arts in Saint-Louis, followed by reunion concerts in that charming city and in Dakar. At the invitation of Henri Guillabert, I was delighted to spend Christmas and New Year in their company. Abdoulaye (Ablo) Zon, an exceptional young drummer from Burkina Faso with a similar feeling and technique to that of the late Prosper Niang, had come on board. Jean-Philippe Rykiel had travelled from Paris. Vocalist Ibrahima Coundoul was there as, of course, was the inimitable Souleymane Faye, an original artist with a singular voice. At their eagerly awaited, sold-out show at the Just 4 U Club in Dakar, Souleymane Faye brought piquant humour, sartorial surprises and a suitcase to the stage. His costume had been fashioned to his own specifications by a local tailor from ten metres of luminous green taffeta. He later removed an outer boubou with matching scarf to reveal flared trousers and a bodice with an askari-style pleated skirt. In the audience was Pierre Hamet Ba, for whom Faye is the soul of the group. In a Dakar interview in January 2009 he told me,

Faye's pictures of daily life derive from a very simple view of the phenomenon of human existence. He is very profound; he is very intellectual though his university has been the school of life and he is a complete artist. Others work at their art, but Faye is a natural genius.

72. *Souleymane Faye with Xalam and suitcase.*

In 2011, Youssou showed his respect and affection for Souleymane Faye by offering him a 4 x 4 vehicle to replace his ancient Citroën 2CV.

The Xalam story began on a tide of optimism and political fervour. The years following Senegal's independence on 4 April 1960 were infused with a spirit of black pride, respect for indigenous customs and openness to whatever influences the outside world might bring. In the capital's nightclubs Aminata Fall was singing her moody blues. Laba Sosseh, from neighbouring Gambia, was affirming his reputation as West Africa's leading salsero by gaining a gold disc for his single 'Seyni'. Dexter Johnson was in residence at Ibra Kassé's Miami Club. Music stores like Radio Africaine and Disco Star were selling vinyl LPs imported from Europe, Cuba and the USA. An emerging bourgeoisie, who had settled in suburban villas at SICAP Amitié, attended Friday night music clubs, sharing their love of American soul, R & B and jazz. The groundbreaking group, named after the traditional African lute, was created by Professor Sakhir Thiam, an aspiring guitarist who subsequently became a minister in the Senegalese government. He was of a generation who listened to the *Voice of America Jazz Hour* presented by Willis Conover, broadcasting music by Count Basie, Benny Goodman, Louis Armstrong or Duke Ellington. By 1970, the original Xalam formation featured Cheikh Tidiane Tall on guitar and Ayib Gaye on bass, Bassirou Lo (flute) and Diego Kouyaté (alto sax). The frontmen were Magaye Niang, Tidiane Thiam and Mbaye Fall. Their repertoire included salsa, paso doble and cha-cha-cha dance tunes as well as cover versions of James Brown, Otis Redding, Cream, Led Zeppelin and Jimi Hendrix, and they also flirted with jazz. Flamboyantly dressed in Sixties-style floral shirts, Abraham Lincoln jackets and flared trousers, the band set out on a year-long tour of neighbouring African countries, performing in Mali, Guinea, Sierra Leone, Liberia and the Ivory Coast. Senegalese impresario Tanor Dieng, who organised the tour, remembered, 'I was their doctor, psychologist, social worker and manager.'

73. *Xalam.*

Back in Dakar, while Orchestra Baobab were pulling crowds at the Baobab Club and the Star Band were still the main attraction at the Miami, leading musicians from Europe and the US regularly staged concerts in the city. Johnny Hallyday, Max Roach and Stanley Cole were among those who came to see Xalam at the Gamma Club, a popular venue situated on the corner of Rue Carnot and Rue Wagane Diouf.

Eventually the original Xalam musicians were eclipsed by their own protégés. Known as Xalam II, the new group was managed by Dani Gandour, son of a Lebanese peanut farmer from Casamance. Prosper Niang played drums, with Henri Guillabert on congas and guitar, and Ibrahima Coundoul joined Khalifa Cissé on percussion and vocals. The arrival of three talented graduates from the art school – Yoro Gueye on trombone, Ansoumana Diatta on saxophone and percussionist Moustapha Cissé – prompted a radical change of musical direction. Samba Yigo's guitar was naturally funky and rock, while Ansoumana's phrasing was uniquely his own and contributed significantly to the overall sound. Baye Babou, the bass player, who was inspired by James Brown and Ray Charles, set about deconstructing the harmonic patterns of jazz classics in order to understand them better. Percussionist Moustapha Cissé grew up in Dakar's Fass district, where he began drumming during Lébou Ndeup and Mandinka Djina Fola rituals. Then, through his work with the National Theatre's African Ballet and Mudra Afrique (Maurice Béjart's modern dance school, directed in Dakar by Germaine Acogny), he amassed a repertoire of regional rhythms, especially those from Casamance. What also set him apart from other Senegalese percussionists was his knowledge of jazz, as his father owned an extensive collection of jazz LPs.

Xalam II found a house in the suburb of Liberté 6 which was quiet and spacious and where they could live and work together under one roof. Here they invited Fanta Sakho, Lamine Konté and other traditional singers to help them understand Sose, Serer, Wolof, Toucouleur, Mandinka and Pular traditions and language. Young, handsome and talented, they became the resident band at the New Experience Jazz Club and soon gained a growing fan base. 'They were our Beatles,' says my friend Clarice Mbodj. 'We were all in love with them.'

In 1979, when Hugh Masekela invited Xalam to perform at a festival in the Liberian capital Monrovia, which was organised by the African National Congress (ANC) to raise funds for South African exiles, they arrived with a new song, 'Apartheid'. Fela Kuti was there and Miriam Makeba together with her husband, Stokely Carmichael, the American civil rights and black power activist, who drove the Xalam boys home in his limousine after the show.

In the same year, Volker Krieger, a German musicologist and jazz-rock guitarist who was touring West Africa, asked Xalam to perform during the first part of his stage show in Dakar. Dressed in shrill red satin shirts, the group made a dramatic entrance from among the stadium crowd, raising a percussive storm of African rhythms as they approached the stage. They joined Krieger and his musicians for a big-band version of their own composition

'Ade'. Krieger then invited them to take part in a festival in Berlin alongside the Brazilian star Gilberto Gil, and while they were there they used their concert fees to record their first album, *Ade: festival horizonte berlin '79*, a calling card that would launch their international career.

During a Jazz Festival at the Club Med resort in Dakar, they found themselves eating at the grill bar with Dexter Gordon, Dizzy Gillespie, Jimmy Owens, Kenny Clarke and Stan Getz, who jammed with them onstage. Dizzy loved their track 'Kanu' for its jazz swing.

When in 1982 Xalam II moved to Paris, Prosper Niang became their natural leader. He recruited keyboard player Jean-Philippe Rykiel, son of French designer Sonia Rykiel, who professed a passion for Thelonious Monk and Frank Zappa as well as for electronic, classical and African music and whose keyboard samples replicated the sounds of the kora, marimba and balafon. From Dakar, Prosper brought Souleymane Faye and Seydina Insa Wade (vocals) and Cheikh Tidiane Tall (guitar).

14. *Prosper Niang on drums.*

Xalam II took part in Mamadou Konté's first *Africa Fête* tour along with Manu Dibango (Cameroon), Ray Lema (Congo) and Ghetto Blaster from Nigeria, performing in London and Morocco and at various European festivals. In England they recorded *Gorée*, their first international album, at Ridge Farm studios in Surrey, where they were guests at the manor and played football on the lawn. The sound engineer handed a tape of their music to Mick Jagger of the Rolling Stones, who promptly invited Coundoul and Moustapha Cissé to lay down percussion lines on the Stones track 'Undercover of the Night'.

75. *Xalam II's percussionists onstage.*

Xalam II toured in Japan and Canada with their new album *Xarit*, which was produced by Jacob Desvarieux, lead guitarist with Kassav. They appeared at the Nyons and Montreux Jazz Festivals; they met Arturo Sandoval and Irakere in Guadeloupe; and they supported Crosby, Stills and Nash at the Hippodrome in Auteuil, Paris.

In 1988 tragedy struck. Prosper Niang died of cancer aged thirty-five and the group gradually disintegrated, although some of those who remained in Paris represented Xalam II at *Woodstock '94*, which marked the twenty-fifth anniversary of the original Woodstock festival.

In 2015, Xalam II released a new album, *Waxati*, which boasted a splendid cover photograph of the group by photographer Matar N'Dour. By year's end they were performing each weekend at the King Fahd Hotel in Dakar.

Gambia: Super Eagles

Back in the early 1980s, Youssou, Mbaye Dièye Faye, Ouzin Ndiaye, Marc Sambou and Balfort made their first trip beyond the borders of Senegal to Gambia, which was then at the forefront of the new popular music scene. What drew them most to Banjul was the success of the country's top group, the Super Eagles, who were pioneering their Afro-Manding jazz. The group had formed in the mid-1960s, just as the Beatles and the Rolling Stones were stirring up a musical revolution in swinging London. They too donned their Chelsea boots and took their second-hand Salvation Army uniforms, newly arrived from London, down to Leman Street in the Half-Die district of Banjul where Mamadou Diallo, otherwise known as Modou Peul, the best tailor in town, transformed them into trendy Sergeant Pepper suits complete with gold-stitched epaulettes. Living in an English-speaking state surrounded by eight francophone countries, Gambians had the advantage of being able to understand the latest British and American pop songs. Through the radio and newspapers and a growing tourist industry, they kept a hotline to London fashion and music.

Young enterprising enthusiasts like Oko Drammeh acquired copies of the London magazine *Fabulous 208*, which printed the lyrics of hits by the Beatles, the Monkees, the Rolling Stones and other top groups, then sold them at a keen price to the fans. Drammeh became the manager of the Super Eagles and their 1969 album, *Viva Super Eagles*, offered direct imitations of Western pop music sung in English, with only one or two African numbers. Keyboard player Francis Taylor, who was among the very first Africans to master the synthesiser, also played cricket for the Gambia. Paps Touray, the lead singer, was idolised then and since by the likes of Thione Seck and Youssou.

The Gambian village of Sérékunda had become a popular meeting place for musicians from Casamance (the brothers Touré of Touré Kunda), Guinea Conakry (Bembeya Jazz), Dakar (Merry Makers and Psychedelic), Mali (Salif Keita), Sierra Leone (Sabano Band) and Guinea-Bissau (Super Mama Djombo). Sustained by newly harvested palm wine, the artists exchanged ideas at Sunday afternoon jam sessions called *hawares*, which Drammeh organised in Banjul at the Swedish-owned Tropical nightclub on Clarkson Street.

Senegalese musicians Majama Fall and Cheikh Tidjiane Tall invited the Super Eagles to Dakar, where they lived in a large house in the Medina district and were joined daily by the brothers Diagne and young Omar Pene of the group Diamono. They played nightly in the Adeane Club, and by the end of their stay the Super Eagles had recorded an LP, *Saraba*, described on the album cover as 'authentic music from the Gambia'.

In 1979, inspired by the example of Xalam, who had adopted an African name, the Super Eagles changed theirs to Ifang Bondi, a Mandinka word meaning 'be yourself'. Back home in the Gambia, the group not only spent more time in the villages listening to traditional musicians like the great Jali Nyama Suso but they also began experimenting with jazz and different African rhythms.

Suddenly, with the attempted coup of July 1981, a state of emergency was declared in the Gambia. Public gatherings were prohibited and nightclubs closed. As a result, there was virtually no music for five years, and many musicians travelled abroad. Singer Moussa Ngom, like Laba Sosseh before him, moved to Dakar, where he joined the group Super Diamono, while kora player Foday Moussa Susu made for the USA to work with Bill Laswell and Herbie Hancock. Oko Drammeh was arrested by Yayeh Jammeh, the young rebel president. It is said he only survived imprisonment in a crowded cell with high windows because he was so tall; many of his fellow prisoners suffocated or died from heat exhaustion.

In 1984, Ifang Bondi travelled to Holland to record their seminal album *Mantra*, a nostalgic reference to the heady Maharishi-inspired vibes of the Sixties. This was a new Afro-Manding sound with bluesy, jazzy horns and African percussion topped by the inimitable voice of Paps Touray. *Mantra* remains a classic of the genre.

In that same year, when I returned to London from my life-changing trip to Senegal, I searched around to find someone who shared my enthusiasm for Youssou's music. I discovered just one article in the magazine *Country Life*, written by Lucy Duran, whom I tracked down to the National Sound Archive. We met for lunch in a restaurant near the Royal Albert Hall and soon became firm friends and supporters of African music. Lucy will remember the day in 1986 when she and I drove Youssou and the Super Étoile to Heathrow Airport following their concert at the Town and Country Club. Imagine the scene at the hotel in Bayswater when it was discovered that one of the musicians had allowed the bathwater to overflow, causing the ceiling to collapse in the room below. With musicians, suitcases and instruments packed tightly into the hired minibus, Lucy, who was driving, led the way while I followed behind with Youssou and Mbaye Dièye Faye on board my royal-blue Mini. Before long the back door of the bus flew open, spilling luggage into the road, and a major traffic jam ensued.

Lucy had lived in the Gambia, where she had learned to play the kora with Amadou Jobarteh and where she married Amadou Sow, with whom she had two children, Amadou and Sira. Her home at Cantelowes Road in north London was an open house for many visiting musicians, who enjoyed the delicious African dishes she cooked as well as the animated after-dinner dance parties. Lucy wrote her doctoral thesis while she was a lecturer in African music at London's School of Oriental Studies (SOAS). She also presented *World Routes* on BBC Radio 3 and has tirelessly promoted and produced the music of Mali, especially the work of Toumani Diabaté, whose composition 'Cantelowes' acknowledges her generosity and friendship. In 2017 she co-produced the album *Ladilikan*, featuring Trio Da Kali and the Kronos Quartet.

76. *Lucy Duran dancing with Balla Sidibé.*

Guinea: Bembeya Jazz National

Sékou Touré was the president of Guinea from 1958 – the year his country gained independence from France – until his death in 1984. He was the only leader in francophone West Africa to reject the terms of French president General de Gaulle's proposals for independence, which included continued French cooperation. '*Nous préferons la liberté à l'opulence dans l'esclavage*' ('We prefer to be free even if that means being less well off'), protested Touré, and his country backed him up by voting an overwhelming NO in an independence referendum.[2] While the president of the Ivory Coast, Félix Houphouët-Boigny, was inviting foreign investors into his country, and Senegal's president Léopold Senghor was defending his thesis of *negritude, enracinement et ouverture* (black pride, authenticity and openness), Sékou Touré was promoting a cultural revolution in Guinea, banning all foreign music on the airwaves, disbanding existing orchestras who played only French or Western covers and financing thirty fully equipped new bands. These included Les Amazones de Guinée, an all-female group of police officers, and Bembeya Jazz National, who were carpenters, drivers, teachers and tailors by day and musicians by night. Bembeya's epic song 'Regard sur le Passé', released in 1966 (which lasted over thirty-seven minutes, filling both sides of an LP), was regarded as a perfect synthesis of Guinea's traditional and modern music. Its subject, Guinea's national hero Almami Samori Touré, who mobilised resistance against French colonialism in the nineteenth century, was the grandfather of President Sékou Touré. This flowering of new Guinean music was recorded by the state-owned record label, Syliphone, which catalogued a staggering 800 songs, eighty-two LPs and seventy-five EPs between 1967 and 1980.

One of Sékou Touré's first foreign visits as head of state was to Cuba, where he arranged study courses for Guinean students. This Cuban connection was to prove fruitful for the band; in 1966

Bembeya Jazz National performed in Havana, and in 1972 Fidel Castro visited Guinea.

Often referred to as 'The Elephant', Touré was a radical, charismatic and strict ruler, who delivered independence to his people. He was also a generous patron of the arts. All the same, following a military coup led by Colonel Lansana Conté in 1984, accounts of Touré's time in government revealed that he was also a repressive despot who jailed his political opponents. Diapy Diawara, who for a time managed Bembeya Jazz National and subsequently distributed their discs and those of Les Amazones through his Paris-based company Bolibana, believes that Sékou Touré's tyrannical side derived from the ill treatment he received at a French-run school. Diawara also claims that Touré was albino, but this was noticeable only in the colour of his eyes. It was said a clairvoyant had told him the precise day and time of his death – he died in America in March 1984 while undergoing heart surgery in a Cleveland hospital.[3]

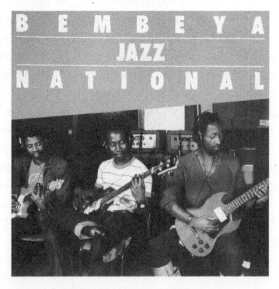

11. Bembeya Jazz National.

In 1989 Bembeya Jazz National played the Africa Centre in London. Even in that confined space they gave a spirited performance, with legendary lead guitarist Sékou Diabaté in fine form. He had acquired the moniker 'Diamond Fingers' after dazzling audiences at the 1977 Festac festival in Lagos with standout solos such as that on Bembeya's track 'Akukuwe'. When he was voted Best Artist at the festival his fans raised him aloft on their shoulders, a practice oft repeated throughout his career.

Sékou Diabaté was born into a *griot* family of famous balafon players in Kankan, 250 kilometres from Conakry, where his father bought him an acoustic guitar which Papa Diabaté, his cousin, taught him to play. When Bembeya Jazz National was formed, a car was sent to Kankan to fetch Sékou, since news of his fledgling talent had spread to the capital. A Hawaiian guitar added special character to his style, especially the melody lines, and a metallic six-string guitar gave him a powerful sound.

The day after their Africa Centre concert, I drove Sékou and Kaba to Kew Gardens, where we walked and talked and afterwards

78. *Sékou Diabaté and Kaba at Julie's Restaurant in London.*

took tea in the North African-style comfort of Julie's Restaurant in Notting Hill. In his deep bass voice, Sékou told me about the accident in Dakar in 1973 which had taken the life of Bembeya's marvellous lead singer Demba Camara, an idol of the young Youssou and so many other rising stars.

Bembeya had been invited to perform at the Sorano Theatre in Dakar on the eve of Senegal's independence celebrations on 4 April. When the band arrived at the airport in Dakar they found that the Guinean embassy had sent a car for Sékou, who asked Salifou Kaba to accompany him. Demba wanted to come too because he felt tired and wished to rest. On a bend in the coast road at Ouakam, near the spot where the Monument de la Renaissance is now, the car lost control and tumbled onto the grass verge. As it rolled over, the car door opened, Demba fell out and and was found nearby, unconscious; he died later in a Dakar hospital. Sékou survived with only a bruise on his forehead, while Salifou sprained his ankle.

Everyone was deeply shocked by Camara's unexpected death. The superstitious believed it was because the Bembeya musicians had that year omitted to sacrifice a black bull at the River Bembeya in Beyla. It took a full three months before the group felt able to perform again, though, in her book *Rockers D'Afrique* (1988), Hélène Lee contended that the group never really fully recovered from the loss of their talented friend and lead singer:

Musically they are still fantastic. But the presence of Demba, the star, was what made them exceptional, an extraordinary and bizarre phenomenon in those transitory times of new-found independence. And that is why the drama of 3 April 1973 shook all of West Africa's fans and rockers.[4]

15

ACOUSTIC MUSIC IN SENEGAL

Seydina Insa Wade, the father of Senegalese folk music

On 9 May 2012, the news of Seydina Insa Wade's death appeared
on Facebook, accompanied by nostalgic photographs and heartfelt
tributes from his many friends and fans. He had been diagnosed
with cancer in early 2012, but his death still came as a shock to the
whole of Senegal. One of the pillars of Senegalese music, Seydina
was a singer-songwriter whose texts and melodies influenced all
of Senegal's major artists, not least Youssou N'Dour, Baaba Maal,
Ismaël Lô, Les Frères Guissé, Pape and Cheikh and more recently
a new generation of rap artists, including Seydina's own nephew El
Hadji Man (ex Daara J). Youssou had in fact visited Seydina when
he was hospitalised in Dakar and made a generous contribution
towards his medical expenses.

Born in Dakar in 1948 into a Lébou fishing family, Seydina
grew up in the popular quarter of Gueule Tapée near the port of
Soumbédioune, an area he referred to as 'the Harlem of Dakar'.
Many of the musicians we know today were born and bred there,
including Charley Ndiaye and Abdoulaye Mboup, who went on
to join Orchestra Baobab but who began their musical careers
along with Seydina in the Rio Sextet, named after the nearby
Rio cinema. Son of an imam, Seydina was educated at a Koranic
school, where he learned to recite the Koran and write the Arabic
script. Although he spoke French, he did not write it; rather he
used elegantly written Arabic characters to reproduce phonetically
what he heard. He was a true artist, one for whom art is life and
life is art. Once he told me that the first time he met his friend

and fellow Lébou, the artist Issa Samb (alias Joe Ouakam), they were so fascinated by each other that they began to talk and they began to walk and they did not stop until they reached the town of Thies, some fifty miles from Dakar.

Seydina's early songs reflected the melodies of the Layenne religious community to which he belonged. He was greatly influenced not only by the Cuban music that was in vogue in Dakar during his adolescence, but also by the top groups from the entire West African region including Bembeya Jazz, Ifang Bondi and the West African Cosmos. He was especially intrigued by the flute-playing of Boncana Maïga, who had trained in Cuba.

In 1968, when a spirit of revolutionary change swept through world politics, Seydina sympathised with the intellectual left in Senegal, in particular the family of Omar Diop Blondin, who died in prison without a trial. By now Seydina had established himself as the pioneering voice of Senegalese folk music sung in Wolof and had become a well-known figure in Dakar's artistic community. His lyrics raised social issues that were controversial at the time, such as female genital mutilation and women's rights. In 1974 Seydina's composition 'Tablo Feraay' was boycotted by Senegal's state radio station, who deemed it contentious, but was chosen by film-maker Cheikh Ngaido Ba as the soundtrack for his short film of the same name. Songs like the early hit 'Khandiou', sung with style and humour, offer charming portraits of Senegalese life.

In 1975 Seydina left the original Xalam group to join the Negro Stars and then La Plantation. Later, he and Idrissa Diop were lead vocalists in Sahel, the resident band of the Sahel Club. In 1985 the pair were joined by Oumar Sow to make up an acoustic trio, Tabala, whose album *Yoff* was the talk of Dakar. When Eric Sylvestre organised a tour of France, Switzerland and Italy for Tabala, Seydina stayed on in France, where he spent six years with the group Xalam II.

It was with considerable emotion that Seydina and Oumar were reunited in Dakar in 2003 to perform together in the newly

opened Just 4 U Club, a reunion which was filmed by Ousmane
William Mbaye for a 2004 documentary entitled *Xalima: La Plume*.
When I set up the independent label Stargazer Records in Northern
Ireland, our first international release was Seydina's album *Xalima*
(*The Pen*), which features Oumar Sow on guitar, Souleymane Faye's
guest vocals and Jean-Philippe Rykiel on keyboards.

My abiding memories are from the weeks when Seydina and
Oumar, whom I married in 2002, toured in Ireland. Seydina stayed
in our home, and he liked to meet the locals over a drink at a
nearby pub, cook the evening meal and then settle in to rehearse
with Oumar. The two played well into the night, their guitars complementing each other in an original blend of African traditional
styles, blues and jazz. The audiences at their concerts from Belfast
to Derry to Dunfanaghy on the north Donegal coast responded
to a melodic acoustic repertoire similar to Irish folk music, and to
Seydina's gift for storytelling. As he introduced each song with an
anecdote in French they seemed to understand what he was saying
even before Oumar offered a translation in English.

78. *Seydina Insa Wade and Oumar Sow.*

Like all of Seydina's friends, I was deeply saddened by his passing. He was a truly gentle soul who cared about the finer things in life: good food, good wine and beautifully crafted textiles. He typically wore immaculate white plimsoles, a jaunty hat and a carefully laundered linen or cotton lawn shirt which he probably purchased in a second-hand market like the Marché aux Puces in Paris. He was laid to rest in Yoff near his spiritual guide, Mame Limamou Laye.

Pape and Cheikh

Cheikhou Coulibaly was born in Kaolack in 1961, and Papa Ahmadou Fall in Dakar in 1965, though his family also moved to Kaolack. Children of the Sixties, they were fans of Cat Stevens, Bob Dylan and Simon and Garfunkel, and theirs is a story typical of aspiring musicians, filled with struggles and moments of despair.

When he first met Cheikh, Pape was singing lead vocals in a folk choir in Kaolack. However, the weather in the town caused him to suffer with nosebleeds (Kaolack is one of the hottest places in Senegal, and the air is heavy with salt and sand) until he and Cheikh moved to Dakar. Pape spent many years working in the Colobane market in the city, sewing in a tailor's shop or sorting through the second-hand clothes that come from Europe and are then sold on stalls in the Marché des Venants street market. When he joined Cheikh at the music conservatoire in Dakar they made a special study of Serer folklore before again going their separate ways – Cheikh to play with Ouza Diallo and Pape to sing with Sampta Muna, a Serer acoustic group who performed on the hotel circuit.

In 1997 Pape and Cheikh became a performing duo, and two years later they recorded the album *Yaakar* (*Hope*) at Youssou's Xippi studio, for release on the Jololi label. They were supported by many of the leading musicians in the country including Jimi Mbaye and Oumar Sow on guitar, Mbaye Dièye Faye on *sabars*

80. *Pape and Cheikh.*

and Assane Thiam on *tama*. Canadian musician Mac Fallows, who
produced the album, played keyboards and added a refining touch
to Pape and Cheikh's song arrangements. The result is an alluring
collage of vibrant voices, acoustic guitars, staccato *sabars*, *tama* and
kora with authentic rhythms like the pulsating *ndioup*, the Serer
equivalent of the beguine, and the *ndiom* beat of a Serer wrestler's
dance. Viviane N'Dour, Youssou's sister-in-law, and Alassane Fall
sang backing vocals while Mamy Kanouté, a nineteen-year-old with
a voice as powerful as the mature Yandé Codou Sène, sang over
the opening bars of 'Mariama', setting the scene for a rustic tale
of intrigue and jealousy and securing for herself a special place in
the Pape and Cheikh repertoire. The entire album has a singular
energy and clarity.

One of the tracks on *Yaakar*, 'Yataal Geew' ('Widen the Circle'),
was taken up by Abdoulaye Wade of the Democratic Party of
Senegal, who won the presidential elections in 2000 with the slogan
Sopi, the Wolof word for 'change'. The song, which was inspired
by traditional baptisms and weddings – where the circle (*geew*)

grows around the *sabar* drummers and dancers as more and more guests arrive – recommends 'widening the circle' by standing up for universal values of democracy, tolerance and peace. In April 2001, 'Yataal Gueew' became a musical manifesto for all but a few of the twenty-five political parties contesting the Senegalese legislative elections.

The album's success didn't stop there, though. In 2002 I signed a licensing deal with Peter Gabriel's Real World Records on behalf of Jololi Productions and negotiated a publishing contract with Bug Music in London. The tracks were remixed at the Real World studios by Ben Findlay before the international release of the album, renamed *Mariama*. Tracy Chapman was so impressed by their performance on the BBC's *Later with Jools* television programme, in which she also took part, that she chose Pape and Cheikh as the support group for her 2003 European tour.

Cheikh Lô

In 1994, Cheikh Lô, a singer and songwriter whose dreads and patchwork costumes distinguish him as an artist with attitude and a Baye Fall (a follower of Cheikh Ibra Fall, Cheikh Ahmadou Bamba's right-hand man), approached Youssou with a demo tape that he had been carrying around in his bag for two years. After listening, Youssou agreed to produce the tracks in his Xippi studio for release on his Jololi label.

When it came to the recording sessions, the original ideas were so distilled and powerful and the musicians so flexible and experienced that six songs were recorded and mixed in nine days. What emerged is a beautifully understated and captivating collection of sweet melodies, seductive guitar lines and sparkling *sabar* drums.

Consummate musicianship, impeccable style and a pervasive spirituality characterise each track on *Né La Thiass*. Many of the songs are imbued with the spirit and teaching of the Mouride Islamic brotherhood. Just as the word Islam defines those who submit to the will of God, so Muslims will understand the notion of destiny which can, in an instant (*né la thiass*), change even the best-laid plans. The novelty of the album, which transcends borders and musical categories, lies in its overall concept, an acoustic/electric mix featuring double bass, acoustic guitar, *tama*, cymbals, *sabars* and brushed drums, flute and the merest hint of electric bass and keyboards. Infectious rhythms, including the rare mbalax they call *dagan* or *thieboudiene*, infuse the album with energy, but the mood is intriguingly and accessibly Latin.

Né La Thiass was instantly successful in Senegal and when, as Cheikh Lô's manager, I secured a licensing deal with World Circuit in London, it received excellent reviews; for British journalist Rose Skelton it was 'pure acoustic bliss with the rawness of reggae and the slinkiness of jazz mixed up with Cheikh Lô's cool voice full of wry humour.'[1]

81. *Mor Gueye's* suwer *painting of Senegalese singer Cheikh Lô.*

Born of Senegalese parents, Lô grew up in the late 1950s in an ethnically mixed community in Bobo Diolasso, a small town in Upper Volta (now Burkina Faso), where he showed an early passion and aptitude for music. He learned many local dialects and listened to regional styles, especially the Zairean *bolero*, which has its roots in Cuban *son*. Cuban music was all the rage at that time, and when his older brothers put their 78s on the turntable and danced with their girlfriends to hit songs by Pancho el Bravo, Cheikh could mime the Spanish lyrics exactly even though he hardly knew what they meant. Then the family moved to Senegal, where Cheikh taught himself to play guitar and drums and, once he left school, he joined Ouza Diallo's band. By the early 1980s he was entertaining tourists with cover versions of popular Western hits at the poolside bar of the Savanna Hotel in Dakar, but he soon left for Paris, spending two years as a session musician at the Bastille Studios. On his return to Dakar he composed 'Doxandeme' ('Street Hawker'), which appears on *Né La Thiass*, about the plight of his Senegalese brothers and sisters abroad.

Other tracks on the album are influenced by Cheikh's life, for example 'Guiss Guiss', a praise song written in honour of the centenarian Mame Massamba Ndiaye. Every Sunday when he lived in Dakar Cheikh would travel to Ndiguel, a village a hundred miles from Dakar, to take tea with his spiritual guide and marabout, who was an uncle of Cheikh Ibra Fall and an intimate friend of Sérigne Fallou Mbacké. Cheikh also began to refer to himself as Cheikh 'Ndiguel' Lô around this time.

The importance to Cheikh of being a Baye Fall is also reflected in the lyrics of his song 'Cheikh Ibra Fall', which suggest that there would be no waste and less poverty if everyone was as thrifty and resourceful as the Baye Fall leader. Interestingly, this song links neatly to another track on the album; while Cheikh Lô, who also believes that cleanliness is next to godliness, was completing his album there was a municipal strike in Dakar, and the subsequent accumulation of rubbish in the streets so incensed him that he

wrote 'Set' to warn of the dangers to health. Youssou's vocal inter-
ventions on this song and on 'Guis Guis' match the mood of the
album, which is warm, lyrical, passionate and entirely pleasing.

After the release of his albums *Bambay Gueej* (1999), *Lamp Fall*
(2005) and *Jamm* (2010), all on the World Circuit label, Cheikh
Lô understood that patience pays. With the release of his 2015
album *Balbalou*, produced by Swedish producer Andreas Unge for
French label Chapter Two Records, he once more gained critical
acclaim and surpassed all his previous achievements when he won
the prestigious 2015 WOMEX Artist Award. In December of the
same year he was honoured with an invitation from President
François Hollande to perform at the closing ceremony of the
historic Summit on Climate Change in Paris which hosted 40,000
delegates from 195 countries.

82. *Baye Fall followers of Cheikh Ibra Fall.*

16

SHARING THE STAGE

Telefood Concert for the UN Food and Agriculture Organization (FAO) and World Food Programme

In 1997, Henri Guillabert, former keyboard player with legendary Senegalese group Xalam and owner of the Quai des Arts complex in Saint-Louis, united the best voices in Senegal to sing on tracks that he had composed. The album *Benn*, meaning 'One' in Wolof, included performances by Youssou N'Dour, Ismaël Lô, Cheikh Lô, Pape Niang and Afsana, a singer from Rwanda.

In October the following year, Dakar was chosen to host the World Food Programme's Telefood Gala concert, which was filmed

83. Diawar, *Ismaël Lô*.

by Italian television station RAI and transmitted live by satellite on Mondovision and TV5 to more than sixty countries around the world. When I was asked to devise a programme, I felt that the tracks from *Benn* could form the centrepiece of the programme and that those who performed on the album should be joined by some special guests. Master percussionist Doudou Ndiaye Rose (1930–2015) opened the gala, accompanied by the majorettes of the Lycée Kennedy.

Coumba Gawlo Seck, whose summer single, a cover version of Miriam Makeba's 'Pata Pata', had gained one platinum and two gold discs in France, returned from Paris to perform with her team of dancers. Thione Seck, who has one of the most mellifluous voices on the continent and a firm fan base in Senegal, was also among the singers, as was Omar Pene. As lead singer of the group Super Diamono, Pene consistently produced chart hits at home and abroad with his soulful, bluesy mbalax/jazz fusion. Also present was another former lead singer with Super Diamono, Ismaël Lô,

84. *Coumba Gawlo Seck.*

who grew up listening to James Brown, Wilson Pickett and Otis Redding; his father, a civil servant, loved American soul music. When he became a solo artist, Lô, who is also an accomplished painter and actor, was dubbed 'the Bob Dylan of Senegal' because his folk style evolved from the same basic combination of acoustic guitar, voice and harmonica as his role model. A specially assembled 'Benn' band with Henri Guillabert and Jean-Philippe Rykiel on keyboards, Oumar Sow on guitar, Pathé Jassi on bass guitar, Thio Mbaye on percussion and Soriba Kouyaté on kora accompanied each of the singers.

In addition to this stellar line-up, performers like Ouza Diallo were invited to take part in the second half of the programme, but this turned out to be an error. When the credits rolled for the live TV transmission at the end of the first half of the scheduled concert, President Abdou Diouf and his party left the hall and with them the majority of the audience. As a result, these artists found themselves playing to a depleted house. When they complained bitterly to M. Jacques Diouf, president of the FAO, who was at the venue, the press had a field day.

Musicians on tour

The task of organising international music tours from Africa is often aggravated by increasingly strict rules and regulations laid down by foreign embassies, and it is true that there have been many irregularities over the years. Musicians have been known to sell passports once they obtain entry visas for Europe or the USA; there have also been cases of collusion between band managers in Africa and African promoters living in Europe who sanction work permits for those who are not musicians. Some touring musicians who have left Senegal, especially on tours destined for the UK, Italy and the USA, have remained there once their tours have finished. In the year 2000, for example, it was reported that seventeen Senegalese dancers from the Ballet d'Afrique Noire disappeared after a performance at University College in Berkeley, California, resulting in the cancellation of the remaining dates on their US tour.[1] When I was organising Cheikh Lô's first tour to the USA, the American embassy in Dakar insisted that Cheikh and each of his musicians come to the embassy with their instruments to demonstrate their skill and prove that they were indeed bona fide musicians. (Youssou and the Super Étoile, on the other hand, were so well established that they rarely experienced problems.)

In 2010, the so-called 'hostile environment' policy on illegal immigration adopted by the UK government and Home Office led to notable difficulties in musicians gaining visas. By 2018, groups who were scheduled to appear at WOMAD, including Sabry Mosbah from Tunisia, Wazimbo from Mozambique and some of the members of Niger's Tal National, were denied entry to the UK. Peter Gabriel, the festival's co-founder, called the situation 'alarming' and asked, 'Do we really want a white-breaded Brexited flatland? A country that is losing the will to welcome the world?'[2]

A World Bank music project for Africa

The music industry in Senegal remains quite underdeveloped despite the fact that there are some extremely talented, intelligent and motivated people involved in it. For example, Youssou and El Hadj Ndiaye established the first cassette duplication studios, and there are numerous recording studios, including home studios, many of them owned by Youssou's musicians. However, lighting and sound technicians are largely self-taught, and there are no trained technicians or workshops to repair the broken instruments which lie piled high in storerooms or on junk heaps.

Access to instruments is also difficult: with just one music store in Dakar, where prices are prohibitive, there is a lamentable lack of modern instruments all over Senegal. As well as this, there are few spare parts or accessories such as guitar strings, and imported instruments are subject to exorbitant import tax dues and eventually fall into disrepair.

Senegal's radio stations play wall-to-wall music, but since there are no independent publishing houses, the country's new collection society, SODAV (the Senegalese Copright and Neighbouring Rights Society), is aiming to be more proactive in collecting dues so that musicians countrywide do not miss out on the royalties they are owed. Piracy is a perennial problem, and, as elsewhere, music sales are falling in Senegal. At one time Youssou would sell 150,000 cassettes in a few days, but since the year 2000 it has been difficult to sell 25,000 copies of a new album.

In 2001, the World Bank proposed a worthy project to create a complete musical infrastructure on the Nashville model in Senegal and in four other African countries. The project promised a much-needed reform of the cultural industries, with funding and training programmes as well as an infrastructure for the music industry (including a South Africa-based electronic 'hub' for the sale of African music) suitable for the twenty-first century. Together with musicologist Aziz Dieng, I met with musicians and those working in the music industry in Senegal and then wrote some twenty proposals for submission to the World Bank. Sadly, due to administrative loopholes (World Bank rules require that monies pass through the Ministry of Finance) and the fact that the culture and finance departments in Senegal could not agree which of them should receive the funds, no money was invested and the proposed projects were never realised. On the other hand, the text of the laws governing cultural activities in Senegal was revised and republished in 2012.

In 2016, two new music schools were unveiled in Dakar. Togolese businessman Benjamin Kpeglo financed EHA (Études, Harmonie, Acoustique) while Dakar Music School, specialising in piano and music history and owned by Livia Laifrová, the Slovak wife of a Senegalese citizen, was officially opened in May by Zuzana

Ceralová Petrofová, CEO of Petrof Pianos (Czechoslovakia). Until then there was no music school apart from the Conservatoire, which caters mostly for traditional music.

Speaking in July 2018 with Khalil Gueye on the Senegalese station Box TV, Youssou lamented the continuing lack of infrastructure for the music business in Senegal as well as the difficulties experienced by so many of the country's talented musicians. He felt it was high time the government recognised the huge potential of the music industry and invested in it.

Senegal to Donegal – A musical collaboration

From the mid-1980s, when the term 'world music' was coined in London, major and independent record companies were keen to promote music from elsewhere, including African music. By the year 2000, Baaba Maal's comment, made to me in London in 1999, seemed pertinent: 'I feel now at the dawn of the new millennium, people have a need to travel somewhere, either to another country or to another music, or through the media, because everybody wants to understand what others are doing.'

85. *Senegal to Donegal.*

Irish writer and film-maker Bob Quinn's research into the roots of Celtic music leads us to believe that *sean nós*, a highly ornamental style of unaccompanied traditional Irish singing, finds echoes in the music of North Africa. In the same way that Youssou later set out to prove the links between Wolof and Egyptian music in his album *Egypt*, I arranged a unique music workshop on the peaceful island of Lusty Beg in Lough Erne, in my home county of Fermanagh, in order to test the links between Irish and Senegalese music.

'Senegal to Donegal', as I named the project, ran from 24 February to 3 March 2002. Its main aim was to prove that talented musicians from traditions as far apart as Ireland and Senegal can find common ground. It featured leading Senegalese musicians Oumar Sow on guitar, Pathé Jassi on bass, Thio Mbaye on percussion and Soriba Kouyaté on kora and their Irish counterparts, former All-Ireland Champion fiddle and banjo player Cathal Hayden, Máirtín O'Connor, a member of the original Riverdance band, on accordion, flautist Desi Wilkinson and uillean pipes player Trevor Stewart. The idea was to offer them the space and time to make music on their own terms, the only requirement being that they share their discoveries with others at a final concert performance.

It was generally agreed that the results succeeded in being organic and true to the spirit of improvisation and rhythmic energy that is so vital to Senegalese music, while at the same time emphasising the lyricism and emotional power of Irish melodies. At times the interweaving of the music from both traditions was so complete that it was no longer possible to tell which tune had begun as a Senegalese idea and which was Irish in origin.

Sadly we lost workshop participant Soriba Kouyaté, a consummate musician, in 2010. Born in 1963 into a famous *griot* family, his father Mamadou Kouyaté was President Senghor's favourite kora player. Soriba could play any style, especially jazz – he was a fan of John Coltrane, Miles Davis, Duke Ellington and Charles Mingus.

He created a truly original jazz fusion on his African kora, having devised and perfected a special tuning technique which gave him all the notes on the Western scale. Admired by the likes of Peter Gabriel, Harry Belafonte, Diana Ross and Spike Lee, his versatility knew no bounds, his sparkling improvisations were astonishing and his feeling and sensitivity profound.

17

JAZZ IN AFRICA

Saint-Louis International Jazz Festival

Over the years since its inception in 1992 in the island city often dubbed 'the Venice of Africa', the Saint-Louis International Jazz Festival has attracted Herbie Hancock, Joe Zawinul, Gilberto Gil and other leading jazz musicians. Saint-Louis du Senegal could be considered the natural home of jazz in Africa, given how author Ned Sublette traces the origins of jazz swing directly to the music brought by those slaves who left Saint-Louis and arrived in New Orleans. He writes, 'When the Company of the Indies brought their slave ships to Louisiana in the years between 1719 and 1731,

86. *The port of Saint-Louis du Senegal.*

sixteen of the twenty-two ships came from Senegal ... So what was that eighteenth-century Senegambia music like? It swung ... That swinging feel is the great-grandfather of the jazz feel.'[1]

Youssou was keen to promote contemporary African jazz and asked me to organise a Senegalese jazz band to appear at the 1988 festival. Pape Dieng (drums), Oumar Sow (guitar), Lamine Diagne (tenor saxophone), Laye Ndiaye (alto saxophone), Thio Mbaye (percussion), Habib Faye (bass) and Ibou Cissé (keyboards) made up the group we named Harmattan, after the warm Saharan wind. Their special guest was the great Aminata Fall, former vocalist with the legendary Saint-Louis band Star Jazz. Appreciative of this local addition to the programme, the audience responded enthusiastically and Aminata Fall's performance left many with tears in their eyes. Local journalist Amadou Gaye Ndiaye commented that Harmattan Jazz had generated an exquisite breeze.

African music is polyrhythmic, so you would think that jazz should come naturally to African musicians, yet not all of them understand the codes, commas and codas of jazz classics. Dieng and the other musicians in the group Harmattan did not attend a jazz school but learned all they knew by ear simply by listening to jazz standards, modern jazz, jazz rock and jazz funk. They practised twelve hours a day for years in order to gain technical dexterity; they listened to records and played along with them, to try and imitate and understand what they heard. In Dakar they jammed with American jazz musicians, but those experienced jazzmen went home and left them to decipher what they had heard.

The members of Harmattan kept asking themselves, 'What is jazz?' African rhythms turn in a loop; drummers play in phrases and uninterrupted beats, which means they can move quickly from a 6/8 rhythm to rock, reggae or zouk, but jazz leaves space for expression and dialogue with the other musicians. So the young Senegalese jazzmen had to develop and reconstitute their own jazz language without the benefit of true jazz mentors, recreating the moments of irony and humour stitch by stitch, then going beyond that to express all that they had lived, all that they had heard, their ideas and friendships.

During rehearsals, Oumar Sow, Pape Dieng and Habib Faye told me of their admiration for Chick Corea, George Benson, Stanley Clarke, Flora Purim and other jazz greats. In Dakar they had met with their heroes Stan Getz, Tommy Flanagan, Buster Williams and Ron Carter when the greats had visited the city for a jazz festival organised by Club Med in 1979. They had also jammed with Nina Simone, Archie Shepp, Bobby Few and Bobby McFerrin when they had performed in the city. As touring musicians in Youssou's band, they found opportunities to meet other leading jazz musicians.

When Pape Dieng, who claims to have 2,000 classical jazz pieces in his head, encountered Steve Gadd in New York he demonstrated, much to Gadd's astonishment, that he could reproduce many of his drum lines. Pape explained that when he plays the drums, he hears musical notes and even notes that are not there. By juxtaposition, certain notes played side by side seem to create intermediary notes, 'ghost notes', that are conjured up through the feeling and spirit of the riff. According to Pape, that is where the real magic resides. Pape's approach is similar to a tale told about Thelonious Monk in Hannah Rothschild's excellent BBC TV documentary *The Jazz Baroness*, which tells the story of her aunt Pannonica Rothschild's very close friendship with the so-called high priest of bebop and the father of modern jazz. It includes an interview with Monk's bass player, who alludes to his exceptional gifts: 'I've played with piano players who played all the white keys; I've played with piano players who've played all the black keys, but man, I've never played with one – except Monk – who played in between the cracks!'[2]

Habib Faye, whose approach to jazz was very rhythmic, was a huge fan of Weather Report, who arrived on the American jazz scene during the late 1970s with a revolutionary electric sound. In particular Habib admired the late Jaco Pastorius, whose bass guitar featured as a solo instrument. Another hero of his was Marcus Miller. Habib once told me, 'I feel as if I play the same role in Harmattan as Marcus Miller did in the Miles Davis band. Miller was younger than Miles and the others, but he came with different ideas.'

The atonal modes of John Scofield and Pat Metheny suit the 'outsider' temperament of Oumar Sow, who produces wild notes, strange notes, but notes that are often quite beautiful. As a matter of principle he will never reproduce a classic solo the same way twice. Oumar affirms that jazz is improvisation, and that is how they live in Africa: they improvise.

The newest star on the Senegalese jazz scene took his rightful place in the line-up for the twenty-sixth Saint-Louis Jazz Festival in May 2018. Ace guitarist Hervé Samb was born in Dakar to a Vietnamese mother and Senegalese father and is now based in Paris. He returned to his native city to record his third album, *Teranga*, meaning 'warm welcome'. Defined as jazz mbalax, Samb's brand of fluent, melodic jazz pulsates with polyrhythms peppered

87. Teranga, *Hervé Samb*.

by the tiny talking *tama*, Alioune Seck's sizzling *sabars*, Abdoulaye
Lo's drum patterns and Pathé Jassi's upright bass. There is humour
and romance, nostalgia, tenderness and sheer exuberance in Samb's
covers of Coltrane's 'Giant Steps', Henry Mancini's 'Days of Wine
and Roses' and Harry Warren's 'There Will Never Be Another
You'. The overall mood of the album is jovial, warmed by the sweet
voices of Adiouza and Fadda Freddy, by the gritty, gravelly tones of
Souleymane Faye and Ndouga Dieng and the rap talk of Ndongo
Lo. Samb's own compositions, 'Dem Dakar', 'Thiossane' and 'Niouk',
take us right to the heart of Senegal's capital city.

Retour à Gorée

In 2007, Swiss documentary film-maker Pierre-Yves Borgeaud
invited Youssou to retrace the routes of jazz in the company of
eminent European and American jazz musicians including pianist
Moncef Genoud, who is Tunisian by birth, Swiss by adoption and
professor of jazz improvisation at Geneva's music conservatory;
Austrian guitarist Wolfgang Muthspiel; Luxembourg-based trumpet virtuoso Ernie Hammes; and Geneva-born Grégoire Maret, a
harmonica player who has performed with Pat Metheny, Marcus
Miller and Herbie Hancock. From New York they were joined by
James Cammack, bassist and former Ahmad Jamal collaborator,
and vocalist Pyeng Threadgill.

Retour á Gorée's musical journey began in New Orleans, where
Youssou met drummer Idris Muhammad, then moved on to Atlanta
to explore gospel music. In New York, veteran African American
poet Amiri Baraka entertained the group, along with an invited
audience. Following rehearsals in Luxembourg, the musicians travelled to Dakar, where they staged a final concert on Gorée Island.
Youssou, who had never really considered himself a jazz singer,
seemed perfectly at ease, interpreting some of his own compositions such as 'Red Clay', 'Diabaram' and 'Samay Nit' in jazz mode.[3]

18

FROM EARLY RAP TO MODERN HIP-HOP

The Senegalese national language, Wolof, emerges even today in modern American street talk or rap. '*Xippi*' (pronounced '*hipi*') means a person who has opened his eyes, hence 'hip'. From '*degga*', meaning to understand, comes 'dig', while '*jiv*', which means to talk disparagingly, becomes 'jive'. The common usage of the word 'cat' to describe jazz musicians could indeed come from the '*kat*' in '*tamakat*', meaning *tama* player. In Senegal, traditional rapid singing styles like *tassou*, *taxuraan* and *bakh* anticipated modern trends in rap music. *Tassou* was developed by the Laobé, a caste of hereditary court messengers, as a fast way of talking in order to disguise their criticism. Thus young Senegalese rappers immediately found their references in modern hip-hop with its strong rhythmic pulsation.

88. Ndoumbelane, *Bideew Bou Bess.*

In the mid to late 1990s, Youssou's brother, Bouba N'Dour, who spotted the potential of many young Senegalese rap groups, produced albums by Daara J, Pee Froiss and Bideew Bou Bess for Jololi. He then licensed many of their tracks to Paris-based label Delabel.

In those years, when the role models were MC Solaar, who was born Claude M'Barali in Senegal of parents from Chad but grew up in France, and the ground-breaking Senegalese group Positive Black Soul (DJ Awadi and Doug E. Tee/Duggy-Tee), there was a burgeoning of rap groups in Senegal. Every street seemed to have its home crew, and each of them claimed to be the guardians of the real hip-hop. At one time it was said that Senegal came in at number three after the USA and France in the rap group league. Only some of them managed to record their material, however, and of those who did, only a handful made an impression on the international market.

MC Solaar applauds Africa's rappers for avoiding American stereotypes and remaining totally unconcerned about bling and designer gear – they dress in African costume.[1] The group Daara J, whose name means 'the school of life', explain that rather than become involved in the gangsta movement (hardcore hip-hop associated with American street gangs) they care about social issues and are optimistic they can lead their fans to a higher level of consciousness, hence the development of their brand of 'conscious rap'. It was touching to hear the singer Faada Freddy say, 'We try very hard to make every woman feel that she is a flower and we have to take care of them because they really deserve it. Women make men!'[2] Leading rap artist Didier Awadi claimed when I met him in Dakar in 2012 that by raising questions about current issues and demonstrating their commitment to social change, the rappers welcomed a new political regime when Abdoulaye Wade was elected on his promise of change in 2000. They were to play an even more crucial role in the run-up to the presidential elections in April 2012.

Fatou Mandiang Diatta, alias Sister Fa, proudly defends her patch in what is a predominantly male arena. Signed to the German label Piranha, who in 2010 released her first international album, *Sarabah: Tales from the Flipside of Paradise*, she speaks passionately about her crusade against the cruel practice of female genital mutilation, to which she herself was subjected.

Most successful of all has been the artist Akon, son of Senegalese parents, who was born Alioune Badara Thiam in 1973 in the US. He frequently returns to Senegal, where he has a major fan base and where he has set up the educational foundation Konfidence along with footballer El Hadji Diouf. 'Daan', his duet with Youssou N'Dour, appears on Youssou's 2016 album *Senegal Rekk*.

Wally Seck, a rising star in Senegal

Born in 1985, Wally Seck, son of Thione Seck (whose ancestors, *griots* to the Damels of Cayor, sang for Lat Dior), appeared like a meteor in the firmament of Senegal's music stars. Threatening to eclipse the success of his father and to rival Youssou as the new Prince Charming of Senegalese music, Seck seduced his audiences with his natural singing voice (uncannily similar to that of his father, though more tender and nuanced), his good looks and his glamorous lifestyle. Married to former top model Sokhna Aidara, he drives a silver Chevrolet Corvette and wears Louis Vuitton and Versace clothes, expensive perfumes and gold jewellery. His fans, the Wallyettes, the Xaley Wallys (children) and the Badiane Wallys (older women), follow him to Dakar's chic clubs like Vogue or Nirvana or the city's Grand Theatre, where they shower him liberally with banknotes. These he nonchalantly throws to the ground to be collected by a staff member who arrives on stage with a rucksack on his back.

Wally has performed in Times Square in New York; in Paris he filled the Zenith, and on 4 June 2016 he welcomed an audience of

89. *Wally Seck.*

90. *Poster for Wally Seck concert in Paris.*

13,000 to the same city's AccorHotels Arena. He has collaborated with other trending young African musicians like Magic System from the Ivory Coast, Wizkid from Nigeria, Moroccan singer Sarah Ayoub and Sidiki Diabaté, son of Toumani, Mali's foremost kora player. He also demonstrated his versatility and sensitivity in his song 'Life is Beautiful', a musical tribute to Congolese star Papa Wemba, who died in 2016.

When I met Wally in Dakar in 2017 we spoke about his sudden success and a lifestyle that prevents him from going out during the day for fear of being mobbed by zealous fans. He compared his situation to that of his *griot* parents:

> Like all *griots* I like the good life. In times gone by that meant killing a sheep and eating meat, drinking soured milk and *ataya* [sweetened Senegalese tea] and chatting into the small hours with good company. Today it's luxury cars and designer clothes.

Supported by a team of young people of his own age, his songs appear on YouTube, Facebook, WhatsApp and Twitter, accessible all around the world. This is indeed light years away from life in the courts of West Africa's great empires.

Part IV

A CONTINENT IN CONCERT

19

AFRICAN MUSIC ON BBC TV

In 1984, during the apartheid era, controversy raged around Paul Simon's visit to South Africa, as he was perceived to have broken the cultural boycott that was in place at the time. It is unquestionably true, however, that Simon's *Graceland* album introduced African music to millions of people and bolstered the confidence of Western record companies to sign up African artists who were ready to meet the rest of the world on their own terms.

Foremost among them were Youssou N'Dour (who with Mbaye Dièye Faye played percussion on the *Graceland* track 'Diamonds on the Soles of her Shoes'), Baaba Maal, Salif Keita and Ali Farka Touré from Mali, Cheb Khaled from Algeria and Angélique Kidjo from Benin.

The music of these artists did not fall into any recognised marketing category, and so the term 'world music' was coined on 29 June 1987 in an upstairs room at the Empress of Russia pub in Islington, north London, by a group of independent UK record producers keen to classify a product that was not classical, pop, reggae, jazz or folk.[1] Whilst the label applied to newly discovered music from Africa, Latin America, Asia and Central Europe, it was Africa's musicians who were gaining most attention from Western record companies and world music aficionados.

African music has been the source for many musical styles, from gospel and blues to *son* and salsa. On the continent itself there are more than fifty countries and in one of the largest, Congo, there are 450 different ethnic groups, each with its own musical repertoire. There is thus an inexhaustible supply of traditional tunes and rhythms that feed and nourish Africa's music, however it grows and develops. Cameroon's Manu Dibango made the point most succinctly when he said, 'Music is our petroleum.'[2]

Among the myriad of popular styles similar to Senegal's mbalax there is *mbaqanga* in South Africa, *gnawa* in Morocco, *rai* in Algeria, *soukous* in Zaire and *makossa* and *bikutsi* in Cameroon. Most are fusions of traditional and modern music, exotic hybrids that developed quickly to feed a massive home market. Despite the perennial problem of piracy, the African music business was itself boosted by interest from outside the continent, and an injection of revenue from Western record companies helped promote overseas record sales and tours.

We might say the world music trend began in the 1960s, when travellers on the hippy trails discovered new sounds, and musicians were already making moves to harmonise globally. Brian Jones of the Rolling Stones met with the Master Musicians of Joujuka in Morocco, Ginger Baker drummed his way to Nigeria, David Fanshawe travelled around Egypt and East Africa before writing 'African Sanctus', and Paul McCartney recorded *Band on the Run* at EMI's studios in Lagos.

As Western travellers' and musicians' interest in global music grew, African musicians also began to make an impact abroad. South Africa's Hugh Masekela, whose groundbreaking track 'Grazing in the Grass' topped the American charts for two weeks in July 1968, sneaking in ahead of the Rolling Stones, was among the first African artists to emerge on the international pop music scene.

During the 1970s, relatively soon after Hugh Masekela's success, Manu Dibango, inspired by Louis Armstrong and Charlie Parker (whom he had come to know through the jazz records brought by sailors through the port of his home town, Douala), left Cameroon to join a growing community of Francophone musicians in Brussels and in Paris. He received a Grammy nomination for his album *Soul Makossa*. Osibisa from Ghana established themselves as one of the top bands in London, while a number

81. *Les Têtes Brulées,* bikutsi *musicians from Cameroon.*

82. *Tête Brulée.*

of Zairean musicians, including Franco and his OK Jazz, based themselves in Brussels.

Despite many African musicians leaving the continent, some began to incorporate Western styles into their own music. Fela Kuti, for example, was influenced by James Brown, who was the idol of Africa's post-independence generation. When Fela visited America at the height of the civil rights campaigns, he realised just how much Africa, with its ancient yet living heritage, had to offer to the rest of the world. After his return to Nigeria, Kuti conjured up an influential new Afrobeat fusion, a jazzy, funky, stormy brew that blazed a trail for Africa's popular music.

At the same time, key African American musicians sought to realise their dream of belonging in Africa. John Coltrane in particular became increasingly Afrocentric as he wrote 'Tanganyika Strut', 'Dahomey Dance' and 'Africa', while Miles Davis was inspired by Les Ballets Africains de Guinea to write 'Kind of Blue'. Dizzy Gillespie recorded 'A Night in Tunisia', and Lamont Dozier penned 'Going Back to My Roots' with exiled South African Hugh Masekela.

And Africa welcomed its lost sons and daughters. In 1974 President Mobutu of Zaire organised a fortnight-long celebratory festival. The main attraction was the Muhammad Ali–George Foreman fight known as 'The Rumble in the Jungle', yet the boxers themselves were in the crowded stadium watching as James Brown, B. B. King and the Cubans Johnny Pacheco, Celia Cruz and Fania All-Stars took to the stage.

The African Prom

When africa95, a major festival of African music and art, took place in London in the summer of 1995, Youssou N'Dour's star was beaming so brightly outside the continent that he was the first African artist to be invited. At the BBC, I proposed an African summer season to coincide with the festival events. Programmes

93. *Programme cover for the African Prom.*

were commissioned by Michael Jackson, the controller of BBC Two, and I was asked to produce two of them, namely *Africa's Rock 'n' Roll Years* and *The African Prom*.[3] In the one hundred years of classical Promenade concerts at the Royal Albert Hall in London, African musicians had never been invited to perform during the season but then, in September 1995, as part of the africa95 festival, five of the biggest names on the continent – Youssou, Baaba Maal, Lucky Dube, Salif Keita and Khaled – were chosen to showcase their music at the first African Prom. (Sadly, South Africa's Lucky Dube was to meet with a tragic death in 2007 when he was murdered in a Johannesburg suburb. Dube, who adopted and readapted reggae so it moved with a South African swing, was influenced by township mbaqanga and the synthesised sounds of bubblegum music and was motivated by the sentiments and soul of gospel. His albums, like the hugely successful *Prisoner*, regularly sold more than 300,000 copies in South Africa alone. He signed a contract with Tabu Records, part of the Motown group, and was hoping to create closer links with African Americans and an American market that had so far proved elusive for even the bestselling African artists.)

Africa's Rock 'n' Roll Years

Following a TV format popular at the time, the hour-long documentary *Africa's Rock 'n' Roll Years*, broadcast on BBC Two on 5
August 1995, was described in the *Radio Times* of that week as 'a
survey of momentous events in postcolonial African history with
magnificent musical accompaniment.' The programme, which
did not include voice-over commentary, used subtitles to explain
images of key events in Africa from 1960 to 1995, and a mixture of
filmed music performances and appropriate African soundtracks
provided the soundtrack to these images. Key to its success was
the consummate artistry of film editor Colin Knijff.

The opening sequence featured British prime minister Harold
Macmillan, who while on a visit to South Africa in February 1960
made his famous 'wind of change' speech: 'The wind of change is
blowing through this continent. Whether we like it or not, this
growth of national consciousness is a political fact.'[4] In 1956,
when Egypt regained control of the Suez Canal from Britain, it
had given a signal to other African countries that they too could
assert themselves. Revered all over Africa for his firm stand during
the crisis, Egypt's president, Gamal Abdel Nasser, confirmed this
when he said, 'I think Suez helped many African countries to be
sure of themselves and insist about independence.'[5]

Ghana had already become independent in 1957, but in 1960
Macmillan's government granted independence to Nigeria. In that
same year and in quick succession, some fifteen African countries –
including Somalia, Kenya, Senegal, the Central African Republic,
Nigeria and Chad – became independent nations. Jubilant firework
celebrations welcomed in new African leaders all around the
continent, but the process of decolonisation and democratisation
would take many more years.

Having worked as a researcher on the 1986 BBC television
series *The Africans: A Triple Heritage*, mentioned at the beginning of Chapter 2, I was familiar with the most powerful images

in the television archive; in order to illuminate these glimpses into modern African history, I also chose relevant interviews and music sequences from the pioneering BBC series *Rhythms of the World*, which had been screened from 1988 to 1993. Thus I was able to match Papa Wemba's moving performance of 'L'Esclave' with agonising footage of Patrice Lumumba being taunted, arrested and finally executed by Mobutu's troops in 1961. Similarly, 'Land of Anaka', sung by Geoffrey Oryema (whose father, a government minister, was assassinated by order of Idi Amin), made a suitably poignant accompaniment to ominous footage of the president, formerly a sergeant in the British army and self-styled conqueror of the British Empire, who reportedly killed 250,000 of his own citizens. Paris-based musician Ray Lema described in the programme how under President Mobutu's authenticity programme no foreign music was played in Zaire from 1972 until 1980. Mobutu, who habitually wore a leopardskin hat and jacket, is the subject of Lema's satirical song 'The Leopard'.

The documentary chronicled other significant events, for example those in Ethiopia. Haile Selassie, Ethiopia's emperor – who claimed he was descended from the Queen of Sheba – had reigned for forty-five years when he was ousted by a coup in 1974. He was filmed being driven away from his palace in a Volkswagen Beetle.

Soon after Selassie was ousted, the world became aware of the plight of thousands of Ethiopians stricken by famine. Further desperate famines in the Sahel region and elsewhere meant aid agencies were providing emergency relief for 150 million people in twenty-four African countries. Viewers saw how Irish musician Bob Geldof was moved as a result to organise Live Aid, which was broadcast around the world from Wembley Stadium in London in July 1985. During a live studio interview he memorably banged the table with his fist and shouted, 'There are people dying now, so give me the money.'[6]

Postcolonial Africa was seen to be volatile; such was the political instability that some seventy military coups were mounted in just twenty-five years. Alpha Blondy's reggae track 'Coup d'État', with its lyrics 'Trop de coups d'état, ça suffit comme ça', accompanied footage of many African leaders who came and went in quick succession.

Violence was also at the fore in *Africa's Rock 'n' Roll Years* as viewers were reminded of the appalling events in Rwanda in 1994, where almost a million people were killed in a terrible genocide of Tutsis by Hutus. In the programme, Rwandan singer Cécile Kayirebwa's plaintive song 'Rubyiruko' accompanied the sad and shocking images of dead bodies strewn across churches and of mutilated children who somehow survived.

Given Africa's colonial history and the fact that so many Africans and leading African musicians live and work in Europe, it seemed fitting to include in the programme images of Senegal's master drummer, Doudou Ndiaye Rose, and his wives, the Rosettes, drumming their way down the Champs-Elysées on a red, white and blue illuminated festival float during the 1989 parade which marked the bicentenary of the French Revolution.

Footage from 10 May 1994, the day Nelson Mandela was elected president of his country, was followed by a video clip of the rap artists Prophets of Da City crying, 'Excellent, finally a black president!' Another moving sequence featured Mandela wearing the South African team's green and gold colours when he attended the final of the 1995 Rugby World Cup in Cape Town. Together with 65,000 fellow South Africans in the stadium and 43 million television viewers, he proudly watched his country's team, the Springboks, win the tournament.

Finally, as kites fashioned from fibreglass cloth by Patrick Nassagne and painted by Senegalese artist El Hadji Sy danced in a cerulean sky, Youssou ended these particular 'rock 'n' roll years' with his own version of Bob Dylan's 'Chimes of Freedom'.

The African Rock 'n' Roll Years

In 2005, I returned to the BBC in London, where I devised, researched and produced a six-part television series that followed the same format as the programme broadcast ten years earlier. This series was called *The African Rock 'n' Roll Years*. Transmitted on BBC Four, the six hour-long programmes reflected the story of modern African music in West Africa, the so-called 'Highlife Zone' (including Nigeria, Ghana, Benin and Cameroon), South Africa, Central Africa, Lusophone Africa including Portugal's ex-colonies – Cape Verde, Mozambique, Angola and Guinea-Bissau – and finally North Africa. In preparation, I trawled through hours of archive footage and filmed more than fifty interviews, mainly in London and Paris, where I was greatly helped by Fela Kuti's friend and biographer Mabinuori Kayode Idowu. When it became clear that the task of editing all six programmes myself in just four months was impossible, executive producer Mark Cooper agreed that we should invite seasoned journalist Robin Denselow to join our production team.

WEST AFRICA

Happily we completed all of the programmes in the given time frame and when the first, 'West Africa', was transmitted on 21 June 2005, Youssou N'Dour set the tone for the entire series with these opening words: 'In rich countries, developed countries, when they show Africa, they show the face of Aids, poverty, war, but Africa has another face also, a positive face, one that offers colour, joy, and wonderful music and art.' And then he sang 'New Africa', a pan-Africanist plea for unity and self reliance:

> This is Youssou N'Dour,
> Calling all Africans to share ideas,

To come together
In a meeting of minds
Let's forget about borders, let's work together
You heads of state may lead your country
But you don't own it
True leaders love their country
Though we can ask for help
Let's depend on ourselves first
We are Africans
When the sun comes up
Be on your feet
Be ready with the tools of your trade
The day passes quickly
Let's confront our problems
One at a time
United we are stronger
A long road lies ahead
We have much to do
So let's get ready
Change your thinking
Work together, keep on working
Cheikh Anta Diop, Kwame Nkrumah, Stephen Biko,
All you people,
Africa.

THE HIGHLIFE ZONE

In Sierra Leone, and all along the Gulf of Guinea coast from Nigeria and Benin to Ghana, the so-called Highlife Zone, singer-songwriters used to entertain the customers in palm wine bars with informal songs accompanied on traditional instruments like the likembe thumb piano or bottles, and, later on, guitars and banjos. Slaves who returned to Freetown from the Caribbean mixed in mento music, calypso and ragtime to create a new style called *maringa*. Such music washed all along the coast and became

84. Travel and See, *Hi-Life International*.

ashiko in Nigeria and *osibisaaba* in Ghana. Here, as the cream of society dressed in style to party in Accra's chic clubs and dance halls, onlookers named the beguiling dance music they heard within 'highlife'.[7] From Ghana, highlife moved back down the coast to Nigeria, where it developed into a whole series of new styles, including King Sunny Ade's *juju* music.

Prince Sunday Anthony Ishola Adeniyi was born in 1946 in Oshogbo, western Nigeria, into the royal family of Ondo, but he broke with family tradition to become the musician we know as King Sunny Ade. He once told me, 'I am a prince by birth but a king by my music.' His *juju* music, so named because colonial settlers once regarded the worship of the African gods of iron, thunder, fire and water as '*juju*', mixes the musical styles played at the shrines of those gods with the palm wine music the Nigerians call *ashiko*. Traditional talking drums combine with electric guitars, including the pedal steel Hawaiian guitar which Ade heard in the country-and-western music of Jim Reeves and which sounded so African to him he knew he could use it in his music. Ade's guitar technique was influenced by the way his countrymen play the *goje*, a traditional stringed instrument. Like Youssou, Ade's early career was supported by praise songs for wealthy patrons, but gradually he established his independence, and with it a new synchromatic sound, a new dance and a new beat, as showcased in his 1976 song 'Syncro System Movement'. As the name of his sixteen-piece band – the African Beats – suggests, he was more than a little influenced by Fela Kuti's Afrobeat.

In 1982, London label Island Records signed Ade on a three-album contract, believing they had found the next Bob Marley. He made his London debut with a triumphant concert at the Lyceum Ballroom in January 1983 and then recorded two albums produced by Martin Meissonnier, *Juju Music* and *Syncro System*, but when the record company revealed their plans for making his music more marketable, King Sunny refused to compromise and told them, 'Where will I say it that music came from? Where will I put my face back home?'[8] And so King Sunny parted company with Island Records, but he continued to enjoy huge popularity in Nigeria and became wealthy thanks to his music and his business interests in oil and mining.

Another Island artist, Wally Badarou, who was born in Paris to parents who were doctors from Benin, wrote a remarkable and groundbreaking album called *Echoes*, which was released in 1984 and featured heavily synthesised and innovative instrumental tracks inspired by jazz, classical music and the traditional music of Benin. Once keen to become a pilot, he was a fan of new technology and came to regard the recording studio as his cockpit where, as one fan said, he became 'chief inspector of the groove'.

According to Badarou, people did not understand his album. Island were perhaps puzzled by the range of ideas it contained, and so it proved difficult to promote. Badarou's African fans considered *Echoes* an African album, but English group Massive Attack regarded it as a hip-hop album. For this brilliant composer and musician, collaborator with the likes of Grace Jones and Mick

Jagger, jazz was not just a school, it was fundamental to his musical development. In his view, the elements of jazz which first left the shores of Africa with the slaves are now blowing back to Europe and the African continent, where jazz may be described as Africa's contemporary classical music. 'There would be no Fela Kuti, no Manu Dibango, without it,' claimed Badarou when I interviewed him in Paris in July 2005.

Emmanuel Dibango N'Djocke, another export from the Highlife Zone, arrived in Europe from Cameroon in 1949 aged just sixteen. Fellow Cameroonian writer and musician Francis Bebey introduced him to Duke Ellington and Sidney Bechet; and in jazz clubs like La Bohème, where jazz musicians met up after their shows, Manu further developed his enthusiasm for the musical style, which he described as 'the ephemeral structured around the moment'.[9]

95. *Manu Dibango.*

Once he established his own group in Paris he enlisted an array of talented young musicians from his homeland, among them bass players Étienne M'Bappé, Armand Sabal-Lecco and Richard Bona, who have a particular flair for percussive playing (who can forget Sabal-Lecco's scintillating slapping bass break on Paul Simon's track 'You Can Call Me Al'?), inspired by the techniques of traditional balafon musicians back home.

In 1972, as Cameroon was due to host the eighth African Cup of Nations, Dibango was commissioned to write the football anthem for it. On the B-side of the single was 'Soul Makossa' (soul for soul music and makossa meaning 'dance'), which was to become an instant hit. Dibango explained the reason for this choice to journalist Katharina Lobeck: '[Soul music] ... corresponded more to the African temperament than jazz. It was more danceable, and Africans tend to hear music with their feet.'[10]

Twelve years later, in December 1984, Manu Dibango organised and produced the recording in Paris of the double-sided single 'Tam Tam Pour L'Éthiopie' in aid of Ethiopia's famine victims. The African musicians who took part included Youssou, Salif Keita, Mory Kanté, Touré Kunda, Souzy Kasseya, Ray Lema, Hugh Masekela and King Sunny Ade. The single sold over 80,000 copies, and the proceeds were given to international humanitarian agency Médecins Sans Frontières.

Olufela Olusegun Oludotun Ransome-Kuti (1938–97), son of the Reverend Israel Ransome-Kuti, headmaster of Abeokuta Grammar School and his wife Funmilayo, a feminist activist and militant communist sympathiser, gained worldwide fame as Fela Kuti. He studied at Trinity College of Music in London and in 1969 travelled to America at the height of the civil rights movement, where Malcolm X in particular made a deep and lasting impression on him. When he returned to Nigeria the following year, fired with new insights into politics and music, the Biafran war had just ended but federal soldiers were still patrolling the streets of Lagos and chiefs and former generals were sharing the profits from oil revenues.

Fela's fight against the military, corruption and injustice brought retribution upon him and his family. He was beaten, imprisoned and exiled. In 1977, the year he married his 27 decorous singers and dancers, the Queens, in a traditional Yoruba ceremony, the family compound he called the Kalakuta Republic was besieged by a thousand soldiers who raped the women, threw his mother and brother from a balcony and burned the property. Fela was such a thorn in the side of the authorities that when he decided to run for president as leader of the MOP (Movement of the People) party in the 1983 elections his candidacy was overruled.

Fela's innovative musical style combined West African highlife, which first evolved in the coastal towns of Ghana and was popularised by E. T. Mensah and others with James Brown-style American funk (the singer had visited Lagos in 1970) and jazz. The talented drummer Tony Allen, who was so technically accomplished that

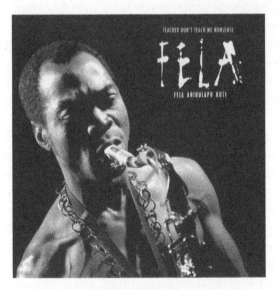

86. Teacher Don't Teach Me Nonsense.

he sounded more like four drummers than one, was acknowledged by Fela to have put the 'beat' in Afrobeat. The songs, delivered in pidgin or broken English, offered lengthy and piquant commentaries on the times, and Fela was a prolific writer and composer. At his club, the Shrine (which incorporated an actual shrine to the Yoruba gods), Fela and his band Africa '70 (later Egypt '80) put on nightly shows that could last for up to six hours.

Fela's long-time manager and friend Rikki Stein described him as a giant of a man whose music was 'the rumble of thunder and the crack of lightning – layer upon layer of sublimely interwoven rhythm and melody, tangled in a delicious knot of divine inspiration.'[11] As for Fela's stage shows, Stein appreciated their sheer spectacle:

> The icing on the cake of a Fela performance was his singers and dancers, fabulous glittering unreal creatures from another world who would exude waves of sensuality and downright sexiness that you could cut with a knife … In the center of this audio-visual feast for the senses, Fela reigned supreme. He was everywhere at once, playing keyboards, soprano or alto sax, the occasional drum solo, a sinuous dance from one side of the stage to the other and then it was time to sing, the ever-present spliff held in his elegant fingers.[12]

Such was Fela's fame when he died aged 58, reportedly of an Aids-related disease, that many thousands of people gathered in Tafawa Balewa Square in Lagos to file past his glass coffin and pay their last respects. The funeral cortege continued to the Shrine in Pepple Street, Ikeja, where his family and friends conducted a private ceremony. Next morning, as Fela Kuti was buried in front of his Kalakuta house, his son Femi said farewell with a plaintive saxophone solo. Fela's legacy was celebrated in the award-winning stage musical *Fela!*, which premiered at the Eugene O'Neill Theatre in New York in 2009 before moving to

Broadway, and was later programmed at the National Theatre in London.

The Shrine has been refurbished and is now run by Femi Kuti and his sister, Yeni. Both Femi and his brother Seun have their own bands, Positive Force and Egypt '80 respectively, and neither is afraid to speak his mind on social issues. Femi, in particular, is known for speaking out against the corruption that has now filtered from the top down through Nigerian society. In his view, the leaders are so corrupt that they make the people corrupt.

Born in Nigeria in 1968, Olufemi Sanyaolu, aka Keziah Jones, broke free from the conservative Yoruba society in which he grew up and perfected a funky, percussive beat called Blufunk that brought him success in Paris and in London. He told me of his admiration for Fela Kuti, whom he interviewed a year before he died in 1997: 'He covered all bases, politics, religion, culture, fashion, and did it in a very stylish way.'

97. *Keziah Jones.*

According to Ghanaian journalist and presenter Rita Ray, Jones provides the musical bridge between Fela and today's increasingly popular and global Afrobeats.[13]

Angélique Kpasseloko Hinto Hounsinou Kandjo Manta Zogbin Kidjo, better known by Westerners as Angélique Kidjo, was born in 1960 in Cotonou, Benin, where her father was head of the Post Office. As a young woman and aspiring musician Angélique found the atmosphere in her country stifling. It was ruled by a Marxist–Leninist president, Mathieu Kérékou, who had seized power in a military coup in 1972 and who expected musicians to write songs in support of his regime. In 1983 she moved to Paris to study at the CIM jazz school, and here she met her husband, musician and producer Jean Hébrail. With him by her side in Paris and later in New York, Angélique forged a brilliant career, collaborating with the likes of Dianne Reeves and Alicia Keys. But there was one woman in particular who gave her the confidence to pursue her dream of becoming a famous singer: Miriam Makeba. Angélique told me in 2005,

> It's hard in Africa to be a woman and a singer. It's a macho society. But when I heard Miriam Makeba it completely changed my life. This was an African woman singing on the same level as the men and I said to myself if she can do it so can I!

Ever curious and inventive, Kidjo is blessed with a remarkably powerful and versatile voice; she is energetic and ambitious and has known how to exploit modern marketing tools, including promotional videos such as the brilliant gold-burnished, glitzy images conjured up in 'Agolo'. On her album *Black Ivory Soul* she explored the links between her music and that of the black diaspora in Bahia, Brazil, while *Oyaya!* reflects her interest in calypso, steel drums and Cuban *son*. She has earned many accolades, including three Grammy awards – in 2008 for her album *Djin Djin*, in 2015

98. *Angélique Kidjo with her 2015 Grammy award for* Eve.

for *Eve*, and in 2016 for *Sings*, a groundbreaking fusion of classical and African music which she recorded with the Orchestre Philharmonique du Luxembourg.

In 2017, Kidjo featured on 'Dombolo', a standout track on the album *République Amazone*. Interviewed for *Rolling Stone*, she explained, 'I sing about the beauty and strength of women, and about how women together can help everybody see a different perspective on society.'[14] The CD showcases the work of Les Amazones d'Afrique, an all-female collective of West African musicians – including Kandia Kouyaté, Mamani Keita, Mariam Doumbia, Mariam Koné, Massan Coulibaly, Nneka, Pamela Badjogo, Rokia Koné and Mali's only eminent female drummer, Mouneissa Tandia – who came together in Bamako in 2014 to help victims of violence against women. Charlie Brinkhurst-Cuff describes in the sleeve notes how the music produced by Liam Farrell, aka Doctor L, gives a fresh twist to traditional African instruments like the *tama*, and sounds like 'an aural actuation of the new melting pot cities of the African continent.' For her part, Kidjo said it made her aware of 'a new generation of producers

99. *République Amazone.*

and artists in Africa tweaking our rhythms and sounds in a way that's never been done before.'[15]

SOUTH AFRICA

One cannot tell the story of modern music in South Africa without describing the immense contribution of four of its most iconic figures, Dollar Brand, Miriam Makeba, Hugh Masekela and Thomas Mapfumo.

Adolph Johannes Brand, aka Dollar Brand, was born in Cape Town in 1934, where he began taking piano lessons at the age of seven. He grew up in a multicultural environment listening to traditional songs, gospel music and Indian ragas, but it was his discovery of American jazz through records brought into the country by sailors which sparked his lifelong love of that music. His pianistic career began with Alfred Herbert's African Jazz and Variety Show at the Windmill Theatre in Johannesburg, where

Miriam Makeba was one of the singers, and then he founded the Jazz Epistles with Hugh Masekela. In 1962 he formed his own trio and set off for Europe, where he persuaded none other than Duke Ellington to attend his concert in Zurich. Ellington introduced him to Paris-based label Reprise Records, and soon the Dollar Brand trio was appearing at major jazz festivals in Europe and was invited to perform at the Newport Jazz Festival in 1965. In New York, Dollar Brand studied at the Juilliard school and collaborated with progressive jazz musicians such as Don Cherry, John Coltrane, Ornette Coleman and Archie Shepp. In 1968 he converted to Islam and changed his name to Abdullah Ibrahim. In 1987 he was the subject of an excellent documentary film, *A Brother with Perfect Timing*, directed by Chris Austin.[16] Here he gives a marvellous and memorable rendition of his piece 'Mannenberg', inspired by the Cape Flats Township which housed many of those who were forcibly removed from District Six, near the centre of Cape Town, during the apartheid regime.

Miriam Makeba (1932–2008) sang in school and church choirs in Johannesburg, and at the age of twenty became female vocalist in one of South Africa's top touring bands, The Manhattan Brothers. In 1959, she was the female lead in *King Kong*, a jazz opera based on the life of a murdered black boxer. When she appeared in the documentary *Come Back Africa* (1959), she was invited to the Venice Film Festival and to London, where she sang on the BBC's flagship current affairs programme *Tonight*. Another guest on that show was Harry Belafonte, who was so impressed by Makeba's voice and talent that he became her mentor, collaborator and 'big brother'.

When Makeba moved to the USA, Belafonte supported her opposition to apartheid, and she was received by world leaders including John F. Kennedy and Fidel Castro. But when she tried to return home in 1960 for her mother's funeral, the South African government annulled her passport, forcing her for the next thirty years to live in exile. She said of this,

100. Sing Me a Song.

I am a singer, not a politician, but since I was exiled from my
home, every song I sing becomes a political statement that
echoes the hopes and aspirations of my people. I'm not a political
singer. I don't know what the word means. People think I con-
sciously decided to tell the world what was happening in South
Africa. No! I was singing about my life, and in South Africa we
always sang about what was happening to us – especially the
things that hurt us.[17]

In 1962 Makeba and Belafonte performed at President John F.
Kennedy's birthday celebration at Madison Square Garden, the
same night Marilyn Monroe sang her famous birthday salute to the
president. Their anti-apartheid album *An Evening with Belafonte/
Makeba* was released in 1965 and won a Grammy award.

Although Miriam Makeba married Hugh Masekela in 1964,
the couple divorced two years later, and in 1968, following her
marriage to black activist Stokely Carmichael, she began to meet
with discrimination in America, her adopted country. After her

shows were cancelled and record companies reneged on recording contracts, she moved to Conakry in Guinea, where President Sékou Touré asked her to represent Guinea at the UN; continuing to oppose apartheid, she addressed the UN Assembly on the subject in 1975 and 1976.

Miriam Makeba and her fellow South Africans, guitarist Ray Phiri, award-winning a cappella group Ladysmith Black Mambazo and Hugh Masekela, joined Paul Simon on his worldwide *Graceland* tour in 1987. The lady who has been called 'The Empress of African Music' and 'Mama Africa' died aged seventy-six of a heart attack following a concert in Italy.

Hugh Ramopolo Masekela (1939–2018) was born in Witbank near Johannesburg. When he was ten his parents moved to the black township Alexandra, where he became a pupil at St Peter's secondary school, run by Father Trevor Huddleston. When he

101. *Hugh Masekela.*

was fourteen, Hugh went to a local cinema to watch the Michael Curtiz film *Young Man with a Horn* (1950), about the trumpeter Bix Beiderbecke, and decided there and then that he was going to play jazz. He began to learn the trumpet, and Father Huddleston bought him his first instrument from a local music shop. Shortly after this, he and some of his schoolmates formed the Huddleston Jazz Band, the first youth orchestra in South Africa, which played a mix of local marabi music and jazz. When Father Huddleston met Louis Armstrong in New York and told him about his young protégé, Armstrong promptly sent him one of his own trumpets.[18]

Masekela's first professional break came when he joined the musical *King Kong* in 1959, along with the Manhattan Brothers and Miriam Makeba. A year after that he went to London to study at the Guildhall School of Music, but just five months later he left to join Miriam Makeba in New York, where he continued his studies at the Manhattan School of Music.

His music studies paid off; when his single 'Grazing in the Grass' hit number one in the Billboard Hot 100, Masekela played a sold-out concert on 15 June 1968 at Carnegie Hall in New York. However, something was obviously missing for him, and by 1972, he was anxious to reconnect with African music and travelled to West Africa, where he spent time working with like-minded musicians including the group Xalam in Dakar and Fela Kuti in Lagos. In 1980, while still in exile, he set up a mobile studio in Gabarone, Botswana, just across the border with South Africa. Here he recorded the album *Technobush*, which included the bestselling single 'Don't Go Lose It Baby'. Perhaps Masekela's best-loved tracks are 'Stimela', which describes the hard life of South Africa's migrant workers, and 'Bring Him Back Home', his song about Nelson Mandela.

When the exiled Hugh Masekela, Miriam Makeba and Abdullah Ibrahim eventually returned to South Africa at the end of the apartheid era they found an emerging network of chirpy, confident singer-songwriters with modern hip-hop, jazz and new styles such as kwaito music, among them Thandiswa Mazwai, Simphiwe Dana and Skwatta Kamp. Given the demise of many international record labels and the global fall in album sales, these young stars understand that they will probably never attain the international acclaim enjoyed by Masekela, Makeba or Abdullah Ibrahim, yet they are happy to accept their considerable success at home and in neighbouring African countries.

In Zimbabwe the political and social situation began to deteriorate dramatically in early 2000. Thomas Mapfumo, the so-called 'Lion of Zimbabwe' – who had played such an engaged and pivotal role in the years before independence, inspiring ZANLA (Zimbabwe African National Liberation Army) guerrilla fighters with his *chimurenga* music, who was imprisoned for ninety days by the government of Ian Smith and who appeared alongside Bob Marley at the Independence Day concert in Harare – found the Mugabe regime increasingly iniquitous and decided to move to the state of Oregon in the USA, the land of his early musical heroes Elvis Presley, Otis Redding and Sam Cooke.

A shy, reserved and very gentle man, Mapfumo deplores injustice and is sensitive to innocent people dying of hunger and children sleeping in the street. For him, music is the voice of those who cannot speak for themselves. In a BBC interview in 1991 he told me, 'We speak for the poor people when we write these songs, so in that sense I still consider myself a freedom fighter.'[19] Just as Youssou integrated Wolof *sabar* drums into his mbalax music, Mapfumo and his band, the Blacks Unlimited, took inspiration from the mbira thumb piano and sang in Shona so everyone could understand. When Robert Mugabe, who had been president of Zimbabwe for thirty-seven years, was forced from power in November 2017, Mapfumo decided to return to Harare for the first time in fourteen years; with his seventeen-strong band of musicians and dancers he played to 20,000 exultant fans, both old and new, in the Glamis open-air arena. On that occasion, he told journalist Banning Eyre,

'My message is still the same, it hasn't changed. I want to stand with the poor people, that's where I belong.'[20]

CENTRAL AFRICA

François Luamo 'Franco' Makiadi (1938–89), possibly the greatest African guitarist of them all, the one they called the 'sorcerer' and grand master of big band soukous music, was born at Sona-Bata in the Belgian Congo. When he was ten years old his father died and he helped his mother sell doughnuts in the street by singing *kebos*, popular songs of the time, accompanying himself on a makeshift guitar.

In Kinshasa, where he formed Tout Puissant OK Jazz, a group of up to twenty musicians, he perfected a guitar technique similar to that used by players of the traditional likembe thumb piano and developed the *sebene*, a style of rumba powered by layer upon layer of repetitive accompanying guitar loops that gave his big band music

102. *Le Grand Maître Franco.*

its unique vitality and power. As fellow Zairean musician Ray Lema explained to me in Paris in July 2005, 'To create the *sebene*, you take a phrase and you repeat it until it becomes hypnotic, till you get dizzy.'

Franco set up a base in Brussels, where he showed himself to be a canny businessman (and a role model for the likes of King Sunny Ade and Youssou), founding the record labels Visa 80, Edipop and Choc as well as a publishing company, African Sun Music, that collected royalties from the lucrative sales of a prolific music catalogue that included some 3,000 tracks and 150 albums.

Poignantly, one of the last and most impressive tracks in Franco's repertoire was 'Attention Na Sida' ('Beware of Sida'), released in 1987. It lasted a full twenty minutes and sent out a powerful message to his fans:

> Protect your own bodies against this disease which spares no one:
> Students beware of unknown partners;
> Ladies avoid getting pregnant if you know you have the virus;
> Teachers, priests and pastors spread the message;
> Doctors be careful with needles and always wear gloves when you touch blood.

Franco died in Brussels in October 1989 of what was thought to be an Aids-related disease. Just three weeks beforehand, his biographer Graeme Ewens, author of *Congo Colossus: The Life and Legacy of Franco and OK Jazz* (1994), introduced me to him in a hotel in King's Cross, London. Franco was plainly exhausted and a shadow of his former imposing self. Upon his death, his body lay in state for three days at the Palais du Peuple in Kinshasa and the Zairean government declared four days of national mourning. In an obituary, UK journalist Philip Sweeney wrote:

> Franco was a performer of great magnetism and of striking stature. Those who attended his only British performance at the Hammersmith Palais in 1984 recall the instant energy boost to the

music when the massive blazer-draped bulk of Franco joined the
band on stage, having spent the warm-up numbers being photographed upstairs with a succession of London African notables.[21]

Franco's contemporary and great rival was Tabu Ley Rochereau
(*c.*1940–2013), who took his stage name 'Seigneur Rochereau'
from the French general Pierre Denfert-Rochereau, whom he
knew from school history lessons. He changed his birth name,
Pascal-Emmanuel Sinamoyi Tabu, to Tabu Ley in 1971 in line
with President Mobutu Sese Seko's *authenticité* (sometimes called
Zairianisation) programme. Like Franco, Tabu Ley composed thousands of songs, headed up a hugely successful big band, Orchestre
Afrisa International, and travelled widely from his base in Brussels
promoting his brand of soukous music. He married his one-time
singer Mbilia Bel, with whom he had a child, but is said to have
fathered sixty-eight children with different women.[22]

Tabu Ley lived in exile during most of the Mobutu era – he
boasted of having played alongside the Beatles in Hamburg, where
he taught them how to sing in unison – and only returned to
Kinshasa in 1997 when he was given a ministerial post in President
Laurent Kabila's government. Continuing his career in politics, he
also became vice-governor of Kinshasa in 2005. Unfortunately,
he suffered a stroke in 2008 and died in Brussels five years later.

One of the singers in Rochereau's big band was Papa Wemba
(1949–2016), born Jules Shungu Wembadio Pene Kikumba in the
Kasai region of the country. When he was six years old his family
moved to Kinshasa, where his mother worked as a *pleureuse*, a
professional female mourner at funerals. His future career was
moulded by these early ceremonies, by church music, and by
American R & B, particularly that of Otis Redding.

In 1974 during the 'Zaire 74' festivities, Papa Wemba heard the
Fania All-Stars from New York use the phrase 'Viva La Musica' on
stage in Kinshasa and chose that name for the band he formed in

1977. They adopted the village of Molokai in the heart of Kinshasa's Matonga district as their base (a charming film, *La vie est belle* (1987), documents those early days).

Five years later, following a tour in Europe and a growing fascination with designer clothes, Wemba began promoting the Sapeurs (members of the Société des Ambianceurs et Personnes Elegantes). In his view a Sapeur should be 'well groomed, well shaven, well perfumed'.[23] Sapeurs spend small fortunes on clothes; they stage their own events and adhere to a published manifesto and codes – such as the ten ways of walking – in order to best show off their designer gear.

As well as his promotion of the Sapeurs, Wemba's international career flourished, with the help of promotion by his record companies in the UK, France and Japan, but in 2005 he was imprisoned in France for smuggling 200 illegal Congolese immigrants into the country, claiming they were band members.[24] Following his release, he continued to perform until his sudden and dramatic death (some said he was the victim of poison applied to his microphone) after collapsing onstage in Abidjan on 23 April 2016.[25]

In 2004, French film-makers Renaud Barret and Florent de la Tullaye slept rough on cardboard boxes in the streets of Kinshasa as they searched for contemporary Congolese music. Then they stumbled upon a group of paraplegic buskers named Staff Benda Bilili and recorded a complete album with them entitled *Très Très Fort*. The pair filmed images of the group for marketing purposes and they supplied me with some footage for the Central African edition of *The African Rock 'n' Roll Years*. Little did I suspect that they were hatching an award-winning documentary. Their film *Benda Bilili!* (2010), starring band members Coco Ngambali, Ricky Likabu and Roger Landu (who makes exquisite music on his makeshift violin, the *satongé*, fashioned from a milk powder tin and electrical wire), received a five-minute ovation following its world premiere at the Cannes Film Festival.

In nearby Rwanda, a young musician, Corneille Nyungura, miraculously survived the genocide massacres but his Tutsi father, his Hutu mother and his brothers and sisters were all killed. He managed to hide from the attackers and then fled to Zaire and on to Europe. His album *Parce qu'on vient de loin* was highly acclaimed in France.

LUSOPHONE AFRICA

The Portuguese colonisers who ruled over Angola, Mozambique, Guinea-Bissau and Cape Verde left behind a group of countries cut off from neighbouring states for the simple reason that their common language was Portuguese and not French or English. The struggle for freedom was bitter and bloody, and it was not until 1975 that most gained their independence.

The Lusophone countries have developed their own distinctive music, from the high-energy styles of Angola to the sad-edged blues and minor key morna ballads of the Cape Verde islands that made Cesária Évora (1941–2011) an international diva. Born in Mindelo on the island of São Vicente, her father died young, leaving his albino wife to raise seven children. Cesária sang in bayside bars such as the Calypso or the Café Royal on Lisbon Street, but she remained completely unknown outside of Cape Verde until 1988 when a fan, producer José Da Silva, arranged for her to record her first album in Paris, *La diva aux pieds nus* (*The Barefoot Diva*), a title derived from Cesária's penchant for appearing barefoot on stage. Three years later when her third album, titled simply *Cesária*, was released, the news was well and truly out that an incredible voice had been discovered. Appearances at the New Morning club in Paris, and articles in *Le Monde*, *Libération* and other influential journals confirmed her talent, comparing her simple and authentic singing style to that of Piaf, Bessie Smith or

103. *Cesária Évora.*

Billie Holiday. By 1994 Cesária was touring the world, thrilling audiences with the beauty of her mellow voice and the mournful tones of her morna, a mix of Argentinian tango and Portuguese fado. Cesária Évora was awarded the ultimate prize, a Grammy, for her album *Voz d'Amor* in 2004.

A group of windswept islands, Cape Verde, named after the Cap Vert peninsula at Dakar, is just forty minutes by plane from the Senegalese capital. So numerous were the Cape Verdeans who emigrated in the past, unable to eke out a living on this mostly barren and rocky terrain, that there are now more of them living outside the country than in it.

In Paris I spoke with Lura (Maria de Lurdes Assunção Pina), an emerging talent who, though she lives in Europe, is keen to

explore the musical traditions of her Cap Verdean parents, notably the accordion-based *funaná* or the cavaquinho-cadenced
coladeira. Here too I met the very courteous Angolan musician
Bonga (Barcelo de Varvhalo), who moved to Lisbon and became
an athlete, winning the national 400 metres and playing football
for Benfica. Obliged to flee Lisbon for a time because of his support for Angolan independence, he is today a successful musician
whose *semba* music has clear links with the Brazilian samba. In his
unusually deep and slightly gravelly voice, he sings in Kangolais,
a mixture of Portuguese and Angolan slang; his touching compositions, which often take the form of a lullaby, paint nostalgic and
touching scenes of daily life in his homeland.

In Gateshead, at the 2003 BBC Radio 3 World Music Awards, where
she won the prize for Best European Artist, I caught up with the
supremely elegant, poised and talented contemporary fado singer,
Mariza. Born Marisa dos Reis Nunes in 1973 in Mozambique,
the land of her mother, Mariza came to Lisbon, the home of her
Portuguese father, when she was three years old.

104. *Mariza*.

The family owned a restaurant in the suburb of Mouraria, which is said to be the home of fado. Like the morna of Cape Verde, fado blends African rhythms and Portuguese melody and verse. The word means fate, but Mariza describes it as a feeling: 'To sing fado is to express the intensity of the Portuguese soul, and very often that means expressing saudade, a bittersweet yearning for something indefinable and impossibly beautiful.'[26] Mariza's deeply emotive voice is matched by the plangent tones of the steel-string Spanish guitar, while her dramatic stage presence is enhanced by her tall bearing, her braided, sculpted blonde hair and her wardrobe of fashionable designer gowns. She took her rightful place on stage in Lisbon at the Grand Final of the Eurovision Song Contest in May 2018 singing 'Barco Negro', her clear, limpid voice unaccompanied save for a battery of drummers. Once again she proved that her music, like that of many so-called 'world music' artists, has now become mainstream.

NORTH AFRICA

Arriving at the airport in Algiers in the mid-1980s, I felt a distinct sense of foreboding. In the city, the frustrated gazes of men in the street and the austerity of the women's dress denoted a general atmosphere of repression. The university-educated schoolteacher would ask her husband's permission before she left her house and would never sit alone in a street cafe. At the elegant St George Hotel, its sunlit gardens perfumed with jasmine and tiled with mosaics moistened by the spray of sparkling fountains, I remember lying in my bedroom, listless, as though overcome by some deep and inexplicable sorrow. It occurred to me that the ghosts of that most bloody of wars, Algeria's struggle for independence from its French colonisers, might still be stalking the land. Or perhaps it was a premonition of the bloodshed to come, the horrible, hopeless carnage of innocent civilians killed by fundamentalist terrorists in the name of Allah during the 1990s.

Khaled Hadj Ibrahim, a policeman's son, was born in the Algerian port of Oran in 1960 and was a key figure in the development of the musical form *rai* (which means 'opinion'). A sensuous hypnotic dance music, *rai* was originally sung by women, but the Chebs, the young male singers who modernised it with the help of electric guitars, saxophones and synthesisers, represented youthful rebellion in Algeria during the 1970s and early 1980s just as rock 'n' roll was the voice of Western youth in the 1960s. Dubbed 'The King of Rai', Cheb Khaled was the most notable and the most notorious of the *rai* artists, so winsome and charismatic that his one-time producer Don Was remarked upon how, when he entered a room, his spirit lit up the entire space. He was also the first to bring *rai* to an international audience, making his debut in France in 1986 to rapturous reviews. His music is an amalgam of Algerian traditional songs and rhythms, French accordion, Arab oud and Gypsy violin music with hints of Spanish flamenco, funk and rock 'n' roll. His early songs called for religious and cultural tolerance,

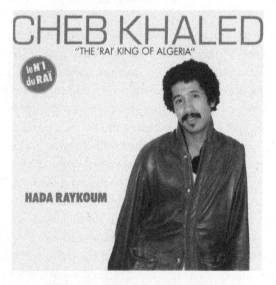

105. Hada Raykoum, *Cheb Khaled*.

and for women's liberation in a one-party state where fundamentalist Islam threatened social freedoms. When several *rai* artists and producers, including singer Cheb Hasni and producer Rachid Baba Ahmed, were murdered by Islamic militants, Cheb Khaled became more and more nervous about the political situation in Algeria and, fearing for his own safety, moved to France in 1990. Then thirty years old, Khaled dropped the prefix Cheb, signed a recording contract with Barclay and, under the influence of top producers like Don Was, Clive Hunt and Michael Brook, his music began to incorporate jazz, hip-hop and reggae.

One of the female stars who featured in the North African edition of *The African Rock 'n' Roll Years* was Amina Annabi from Tunisia, who represented France, her current home, in the final of the 1991 Eurovision Song Contest, with 'C'est le dernier qui a parlé qui a raison'. The song, for which she wrote the lyrics, was composed by Senegalese musician Wasis Diop, who accompanied her on guitar, and was produced by her then husband, Martin Meissonnier. Amina came second in the competition.

106. *Amina Annabi.*

Annabi is one of a group of talented and articulate North African women who grew up in a society that repressed them but who have found their own way to freedom. When I met her in London in 2005, she told me,

> To feel free is to know yourself. The more you know yourself the more you can choose for yourself. We women have a big responsibility. We have to teach men, with a softness and determination, how to respect us, and when we are respected we can respect them.

Singer and activist Rachid Taha (1958–2018), whose music was influenced by many different styles including *rai*, rock, electronic and punk, was born in Algeria but grew up in France. He did not blame Islam for inequalities between Algerian men and women; rather he pointed to the *Code de la Famille* introduced by Algeria's President Bendjedid during the 1980s and 1990s as the chief reason for women becoming submissive and obedient.

Singer, songwriter and guitarist Souad Massi, who grew up in the ancient labyrinthine Bab El Oued quarter of Algiers, explained the difficulties of wearing jeans and playing guitar in the early 1990s when Islamist rebel groups waged war on the Algerian government and a 7 p.m. curfew was imposed. The civilian population was also targeted and thousands were killed, but among those who escaped with serious gunshot injuries was popular radio and TV presenter Aziz Smati, who subsequently fled to France. In 1999, when Smati and Mohamed Allalou organised the Femmes d'Alger festival at the Cabaret Sauvage in Paris they invited Massi to take part. She then remained in France, where she signed a deal with Island Records and blossomed as a performer. Known best for her acoustic folk style, she sings to her own guitar accompaniment in Arabic, French and English, but many of her compositions, including nostalgic tracks like 'Mesk Elil' (sweet-smelling honeysuckle), are inspired by the gardens of Algiers and the Kabyle homeland of her Berber parents. (It is worth noting that it was Idir, a singer from that region of Algeria, who first introduced the music of his country to Western audiences as far back as 1976 with 'A Vava Inouva', surely an early example of world music.)

Malika Zarra's creative journey took her from Morocco to Paris and then New York, where she was signed to the label Motema (home of Grammy award-winner Gregory Porter). Malika's music is inspired by the rhythms of her native land, but her collaborations have taken her in new and exciting directions, and her versatile vocal style is well suited to improvisation and jazz.

I befriended Malika when she performed at FESMAN in Dakar in 2010. She told me of her firm belief that African artists will come into their own in the twenty-first century, saying simply, 'A huge well of talent will spring forth.'

My good friend Izza Genini produced a series of important films in the 1980s entitled *Maroc corps et âme*. In 2007, one of them, *Transes Marocaines*, which features Nass El Ghiwane, a group of musicians from Casablanca, was chosen by Martin Scorsese to inaugurate the World Cinema Project, a non-profit organisation he founded to preserve and restore neglected world cinema. He writes,

> In 1981, I was working at night to edit *The King of Comedy*. The television was always playing. One evening about two or three in the morning, a film entitled *Transes* came on. I was immediately fascinated by the music and by the way the documentary was made. The mix of poetry, music and theatre goes right back to the origins of Moroccan culture. The musicians sing about their country, its people, their suffering. Since then, I have been obsessed by this film.[27]

'Women are the backbone of Tuareg society,' boasted one of the female vocalists from the Malian group Tartit (meaning 'union'), who came together in a refugee camp in Mauritania in 1992. Coloured by the sound of traditional instruments such as the *ngoni* or the *imzad* and animated by call-and-response refrains and vigorous clapping, their desert blues songs often carry a message of solidarity for their fellow women. They will, for example, sing for a new divorcee to console her, lift her spirits and help her forget her sorrow.

The Grammy award-winning Tuareg band Tinariwen, formed in a refugee camp in Libya, includes lead singer Ibrahim Ag Alhabib, whose father was killed in the first Tuareg uprising in 1963. These accomplished and hugely successful musicians come from a line of independent-minded, nomadic Tuaregs who have long been at odds with Malian governments. In 2012, using arms they acquired in Libya, Tuareg rebels mounted a coup which ousted Mali's president, Amadou Toumani Touré, who fled to Dakar with his family.

107. *Tinariwen.*

The six programmes in our television series earned good reviews, beginning with this description of the first in the series:

> If you've never heard the glorious sounds of West African music you're in for a revelation. If you have, this superb documentary will introduce you to more irresistible music. Stuffed with strong interviews it could be the documentary of the year but ... there are five more films to come. Can't wait.[28]

The series as a whole received reviews such as: 'Watching this you'd be pretty cynical to still claim that music cannot affect [sic] change,'[29] and

> As well as being a well-stocked video jukebox, *The African Rock 'n' Roll Years* was also a stealthy lesson in modern history, repeating a familiar pattern of post-colonial collapse and corruption which enrages, inflames and inspires the musicians (most of them exiles) to this day.[30]

108. *Youssou N'Dour in concert, Dakar.*

CODA

In his book *My Festival Romance* (2017), Thomas Brooman, co-founder of the WOMAD festival, includes a chapter titled 'An Albatross called World Music'. He describes the unfortunate elision which occurred between the term world music as it was conceived by himself and other UK promoters and labels to market music other than reggae, blues, jazz, folk or classical, and its subsequent interpretation as a musical genre that caused its artists to feel alienated from the mainstream. As Brooman puts it,

> Intellectually it was deeply frustrating and many artists felt uncomfortably caught up in the whole thing. Youssou N'Dour, a world music artist? Well, no thank you very much. How about an artist from Senegal? What's so wrong with that? And while we're at it, how about a great artist from Senegal?[1]

Back in 1993 Youssou's compatriot, Baaba Maal, had already expressed his concerns to UK journalist Chris Salewicz: 'World music has become the refugee camp of the record business: only a handful have succeeded in escaping its confines and getting permanent residence in the West.'[2]

In 2015, British journalist Anita Awbi noted how African music continues to conquer the world: 'African music has burst its banks, spilling out from its "world music" categorisation and its concert hall programming to flood the mainstream, the underground and beyond.'[3]

In 2018 Nigerian German musician, producer and social activist Ade Bantu explains how, in the twenty-first century, perceptions have changed:

African music is now generally considered to be hip, cool and
sexy. At one time, all you had was world music to gain access to
an audience in Europe or America. Now you don't have to take
that route. In an R & B club in Berlin they are playing Nigerian
music and second- and third-generation Africans are walking
with pride because of that.[4]

All the same, the 'world music' tag allowed many artists to achieve
worldwide fame, and though the number of record labels marketing this music is in decline, the world's musicians are listening to
each other from the four corners of the earth and many are on the
move. There has been a marked increase in collaborations between
African musicians and those from outside the continent, a trend
set by Youssou N'Dour and Neneh Cherry, Ali Farka Touré and
Ry Cooder, Taj Mahal and Toumani Diabaté (to name just a few).
In 2006, British pop star Damon Albarn and journalist Ian Birrell
established the Africa Express collective, which offers African
musicians and their collaborators a platform for musical meetings
and experimentation. Juldeh Camara, the remarkable *ritti* player
from Gambia, teamed up with UK guitarist Justin Adams as part
of this collective.

One of the most successful so-called fusion albums, *Clychau
Dibon*, released in 2013, features Welsh harpist Catrin Finch and
Senegalese kora player Seckou Keita, now based in England. This
deft duetting between harps from two different continents has been
described as 'intricate, ethereal and entrancing, an elaborate pas
de deux'.[5] The album *Ladilikan* by Trio Da Kali and the Kronos
Quartet, recorded in just four days in a studio in Switzerland,
features traditional musicians from Mali: the rich and ravishing
voice of Hawa Kassé Mady Diabaté, daughter of singer Kassé Mady
Diabaté; the ngoni of Mamadou Kouyaté, son of *xalam* player
Bassekou Kouyaté; and the virtuoso balafon of Lassana Diabaté.
David Harrington, founder and artistic director of the Kronos
Quartet, who are famous for their musical adventures outside of

the Western classical tradition, has described this album as one of the most beautiful the quartet has ever made.

Youssou's 2016 album *Africa Rekk* was classified, tellingly, as pop music and not as world music, and it is resolutely pan-African in style and tone. In an interview with Ibrahima Khalil Wade of Dakar magazine *l'Enquête* Youssou said this:

> *Africa Rekk* is a cry of hope, a pan-African message for everyone and especially for Africa's young people, who need to take responsibility for their continent. Given the mixed achievements of the last fifty years, it is they who must now work peacefully and resolutely towards sustained success in every domain. As well as the talents of a new generation of poised and promising artists, *Africa Rekk* also showcases the beauty of African sounds and rhythms. This album points to a positive future for Africa.[6]

Youssou's guests on *Africa Rekk* include Nigerian guitarist Femi Leye ('Bull Ko Door') and his compatriot Spotless ('Dawal'), Congolese singer Fally Ipupa ('Ban La') and Senegalese American superstar Akon ('Conquer the World'). In what is undoubtedly the most powerful song on the album, two strong voices express their admiration for each other's talent. 'If you open my heart, you'll find You there', sings Akon before affirming triumphantly, 'As long as I have you in my soul I will conquer, conquer the world.'

By 2050 it is estimated that around 2.2 billion people could be added to the global population, and more than half of that growth will occur in Africa. Nigeria alone is projected to have over 300 million inhabitants.[7] Following years of poverty and war, Africa, the second largest and second most populated continent on earth, is developing at a dizzying pace, and six of the world's ten fastest-growing economies are now African. This burgeoning prosperity is reflected in a similar surge in creativity in the arts, fashion, music and sport. Africa is set to reveal its twenty-first-century face to the world.

It was in Lagos, a town of 30 million inhabitants in the most populous country on the African continent (one in seven Africans is Nigerian) that Sony Music set up its African head office in January 2016. Interviewed for the French newspaper *Le Monde* by Joan Tilouine, Sony Africa CEO Michael Ugwu said, 'We believe that the moment has come for our artists to take their place on the international stage and we see this as the beginning of a cultural revolution in Africa.' For Tilouine, young artists like Tiwa Savage, Wizkid aka Ayodeji Ibrahim Balogun and Davido aka David Adeleke are now able to negotiate important contracts while preserving their artistic freedom. They are key players in a new generation of confident, enterprising young artists who know what they want and are proud to be African.[8]

In the BBC TV series *Africa: A Journey into Music*, transmitted on BBC Four in 2018, Ghanaian-born presenter Rita Ray visited three countries – Nigeria, South Africa and Mali – and noted how in Nigeria in particular a space has opened up for women artists like Tiwa Savage, often dubbed the Beyoncé of Nigeria, who have moved into the mainstream. Today's Afrobeats have become a global phenomenon and, as Rita Ray observed in the series, 'Africa is owning her culture and identity in a thrilling way.' You might say that, thanks to the struggles of a Fela Kuti or a Youssou N'Dour, these rising stars have the talent, the imagination, the momentum and the media tools to finally break free of the confines of the 'world music' label and take their place alongside Jay-Z or will.i.am. In short, they have the ambition to conquer the world.

ACKNOWLEDGEMENTS

I am most grateful to all those who helped and encouraged me in this project, beginning with Youssou N'Dour himself and the musicians from the Super Étoile de Dakar as well as the late Joe Ouakam, Nicholas Cissé, Babacar Ndaak Mbaye, Massamba Mbaye, Fadel Diagne, Pierre Hamet Ba, Bara Diokhane, Yousseynou Wade, Souleymane and Arame Diakhaté, Alassane and Clarice Mbodj, M. Racine Senghor, Dr Abdoulaye Diallo, Dudu Sarr and the Cama and Sow families.

Jane Sparrow and Anne Marie Villeneuve read early versions of the manuscript and were generous with their suggestions. Dr William Vaughan offered invaluable support and advice about format, footnotes and layout. My nephew, Dr Robbie Maxwell, read the proofs and made further useful comments.

I am indebted to all those who made subscriptions in advance for copies of *Notes from Africa*. To Xander Cansell, Georgia Odd, Sara Magness and all the team at Unbound who so courteously and efficiently guided me through to final publication, I say a special thank you.

NOTES

1. DAKAR, SENEGAL

1 Ryszard Kapuściński, *The Shadow of the Sun: My African Life*, Penguin, 2001, p. 271.
2 Population figures taken from worldometers.info, accessed 1 March 2019.
3 Maya Angelou, *All God's Children Need Travelling Shoes*, Virago, 1986, p. 109.
4 Michael Jackson, *Moonwalk*, William Heinemann, 2009, p. 108.

2. A NEW DAWN

1 Dr Ali Mazrui, *The Africans: A Triple Heritage*, BBC/PBS WETA Washington, 1986.
2 'Soros among those viewing Africa as a strong growth opportunity', *Asia Asset Management*, 26 March 2012. Also available at https://www.asiaasset. com/news/afric_soros.aspx, accessed 1 March 2019.
3 Speaking on BBC Two's *Newsnight* on 3 February 2017, the British-Senegalese businesswoman Mariéme Jamme said the middle class now represents 34 per cent of the population.
4 Tony Blair, 'Get wise to the good news coming from Africa', *The Times*, 19 March 2012.
5 The full interview was screened on 8 May 2004 and can be viewed on the Channel 4 website at https://www.channel4.com/news/bob-geldof-nigeria-africa-progress-panel-video, accessed 1 March 2019.
6 'Youssou N'Dour: Open N'Dour', *Independent*, 13 December 2002. Available at www.independent.co.uk/arts-entertainment/music/features/youssou-ndour-open-ndour-135888.html, accessed 1 April 2019.
7 Drew Hinshaw, 'Senegal to build "Seven Wonders" complex in capital', *Bloomberg*, 29 March 2011. Available to subscribers at https://www.bloomberg. com/news/articles/2011-03-29/senegal-to-build-seven-wonders-complex-in-capital-soleil-says, accessed 1 March 2019.
8 David Murphy, 'The performance of pan-Africanism: staging the African Renaissance at the First World Festival of Negro Arts', in David Murphy (ed.), *The First World Festival of Negro Arts, Dakar 1966: Contexts and Legacies*, Liverpool University Press, 2016, pp. 1–52.

9   Randy Weston and Willard Jenkins, *Randy Weston: African Rhythms*, Présence Africaine, 2016, p. 161. Author's translation.

10   Richard Bona, Facebook, 24 November 2015.

11   Diadie Ba, 'Senegal braces for "Tahrir Square" protest day', *Reuters*, 18 March 2011. The real Tahrir Square (also known as 'Martyr Square') is in the centre of Cairo and has been the location of many political demonstrations, including those which led to the resignation of President Hosni Mubarak.

12   Sophie Eastaugh, 'From sand, to grass, to Europe? Senegal's football dream house', CNN, 8 June 2016. Available at https://edition.cnn.com/2016/06/07/football/senegal-football-school-diambars/index.html, accessed 1 March 2019.

4. THE BEAT ON THE STREET

1   Grabación Victor (GV) records were launched in Britain in 1933 by EMI (His Master's Voice) and released in America on the Victor label.

2   Jim Washburn, 'Pop music review: Senegalese sensation N'Dour rivets audience with rhythms', *Los Angeles Times*, 24 July 1990.

3   Lucy Duran, 'Key to N'Dour', *Folk Roots* 64, October 1988, p. 34.

5. LORDS AND LADIES OF THE DANCE

1   A *taneber* party is a *sabar* dance party which is held at night.

2   Conversation with the author, October 2006.

3   Lucy Duran, 'Key to N'Dour', *Folk Roots* 64, October 1988, p. 34.

6. SONGS FOR THE PEOPLE

1   More information about the Great Green Wall movement can be found at https://www.greatgreenwall.org/about-great-green-wall, accessed 1 March 2019.

2   'Two jailed over Ivorian pollution', BBC News, 23 October 2008. Available at http://news.bbc.co.uk/1/hi/world/africa/7685561.stm, accessed 1 March 2019.

3   *Banc Jaaxle*, Massamba Ndiaye, 2002.

4   Fatou Diome, *Le Ventre de L'Atlantique*, Éditions Anne Carrière, 2003. Author's translation.

7. INSPIRATIONAL FEMALE SPONSORS

1   El Hadj Amadou Mbaye, 'Marieme Dieng Salla Une fée qui passait', *Icône* 9, May 2006. Author's translation.

2　Jean-Luc Angrand, *Céleste ou le temps des Signares*, Édition Anne Pépin, 2006. Author's translation.

8. EMPERORS AND KINGS

1　The Ceddos were animists, believers in a supernatural power that organises the universe.
2　Youssou performed 'Birima' in front of French president Emmanuel Macron, his own president Macky Sall, the American star Rihanna and delegates assembled for the Global Partnership in Education conference which took place in Dakar in February 2018.
3　As told to the author by Babacar Ndaak Mbaye, Dakar, June 2006.

9. ALL THE WORLD'S A STAGE

1　James Fox, *White Mischief*, Jonathan Cape, 1982; Vintage 1998.
2　*Melody Maker*, 13 December 1986.
3　Bruce Springsteen, *Born to Run*, Simon & Schuster, 2016, p. 353.
4　Don Snowden, 'Youssou N'Dour pulls it all together', *Los Angeles Times*, 5 July 1994.
5　Nigel Williamson, 'First rays of a new African star', *The Times*, 13 November 1996.
6　Zycopolis TV, 'Youssou N'Dour – Bercy Paris – LIVE HD', YouTube (uploaded 24 June 2014), https://www.youtube.com/watch?v=qOdim5d61a4, accessed 1 March 2019.

10. THERE'S NO PLEASING ALL OF THE PEOPLE ALL OF THE TIME

1　Rick Glanvill, 'Get set go', *World Beat*, December 1990.
2　Jon Pareles, 'Making African pop safe for Western ears', *New York Times*, 5 July 1998. Available at https://www.nytimes.com/1998/07/05/arts/pop-jazz-making-african-pop-safe-for-western-ears.html, accessed 1 March 2019.
3　Mark Hudson, 'Supernatural superstar', *Telegraph*, 12 December 2002. Available at https://www.telegraph.co.uk/culture/music/rockandjazzmusic/3587019/Supernatural-superstar.html, accessed 1 March 2019.
4　Ibid.
5　Nigel Williamson, 'Songs of praise', *Songlines* 24, 2004, p.22.
6　Matt Pascarella, 'A voice from Senegal: Youssou N'Dour', *The Progressive*, 26 February 2010. Available at https://progressive.org/dispatches/voice-senegal-youssou-n-dour, accessed 1 March 2019.
7　Sylvie Clerfeuille and E. Nago Seck, *L'Afrique de Toutes les Musiques*, Paris, pre-publication copy sent to the author. Author's translation.

8   Harry Belafonte with Michael Schnayerson, *My Song: A Memoir of Art, Race and Defiance*, Canongate, 2012, p. 408.

11. THERE IS BUT ONE GOD

1   Sidi Lamine Niasse, 'Dabakh Pleuré par la Nature', *Walfadjiri*, 16 September 1977. Author's translation.
2   Carlou D, liner notes, *Muzikr*, World Village, CD450013, 2010.

12. ROLE MODEL AND ICON

1   Mark Hudson, 'A song and a prayer', *Observer Music Monthly* 33, 23 May 2004, p. 31. Available at https://www.theguardian.com/music/2004/may/23/worldmusic.islam, accessed 1 March 2019.
2   *Le Quotidien*, 19 August 2004. Author's translation.
3   Ibid.
4   www.buzzsenegal.com, 1 March 2016.
5   'Richest musician: who is the richest musician in Africa?', Constative (website), www.constative.com/celebrity/who-is-the-richest-musician-in-africa, accessed 1 March 2019.
6   'Africa works', Benetton press release, undated. Available at http://www.benettongroup.com/media-press/press-releases-and-statements/africa-works/, accessed 1 March 2019.
7   *Le Pays au Quotidien*, Dakar, 2013. Author's translation.
8   Ibid.
9   www.lapresse.ca, 10 November 2015. Author's translation.
10   Mark Hudson, 'Womad 2014: Youssou N'Dour – Senegal's minister of sound', *Daily Telegraph*, 24 July 2014. Available at https://www.telegraph.co.uk/culture/music/worldfolkandjazz/10986092/Womad-2014-Youssou-NDour-Senegals-minister-of-sound.html, accessed 1 March 2019.
11   Geldof made this statement in his interview for Channel 4 on 8 May 2004. Available at https://www.channel4.com/news/bob-geldof-nigeria-africa-progress-panel-video, accessed 1 March 2019.
12   Martin Fletcher, 'Mutant mosquitoes: Can gene editing kill off malaria?', *Telegraph*, 11 August 2018. Available at https://www.telegraph.co.uk/news/0/mutant-mosquitoes-can-gene-editing-kill-malaria/, accessed 1 March 2019.
13   Oumar Sankhare, *Youssou N'Dour: Le Poète*, Les Nouvelles Éditions Africaines du Sénégal, 1997, blurb on back cover. Author's translation.
14   Jon Pareles, 'Review/Pop; a singer from Senegal by way of the world', *New York Times*, 9 November 1992. Available at https://www.nytimes.com/1992/11/09/arts/review-pop-a-singer-from-senegal-by-way-of-the-world.html, accessed 1 March 2019.

15 Gérald Arnaud, *Youssou N'Dour: le griot planétaire*, Collection Voix du Monde, Éditions Demi-Lune, 2008, p. 113.
16 Citations for recipients of honorary degrees at Yale University 2011, Yale University. Available at https://news.yale.edu/citations-recipients-honorary-degrees-yale-university-2011, accessed 1 March 2019.
17 The Polar Music Prize website has a page dedicated to former winners of the prize. Youssou's page can be found at https://www.polarmusicprize.org/laureates/youssou-ndour/, accessed 1 March 2019.
18 Rick Glanvill, 'Get set go', *World Beat*, December 1990.

13. THE SOURCE

1 This information can be found on Salif Keita's own website, www.salifkeita.us, accessed 1 March 2019.
2 *Review: Paris, Africa*, BBC, broadcast 6 May 1988.
3 *Arena: Destiny of a Noble Outcast*, BBC Two, 1990.
4 Robert K. G. Temple, *The Sirius Mystery*, St Martin's Press, 1976.
5 Miriam Makeba and James Hall, *My Story*, Bloomsbury, 1987, p. 2.
6 Interview by the author for 'Viva Zimbabwe', *Rhythms of the World*, BBC Two, broadcast 2 March 1991.
7 Bonnie Greer, *Obama Music: Some Notes from a South Sider*, Legend Press, 2009, p. 83.
8 Ryszard Kapuściński, *Travels with Herodotus*, Penguin, 2007, p. 100.
9 Doris Lessing, *Collected African Stories, Vol 2: The Sun Between Their Feet*, Michael Joseph Ltd, 1973; Triad Panther, 1979, cover note.
10 Interview with the author for 'Africa meets the blues', *Rhythms of the World*, BBC Two, broadcast 18 September 1988.
11 Daniel Brown, 'Building bridges', *Songlines* 114, January/February 2016.
12 Janet H. Gritzner, *Senegal*, Infobase Publishing, 2005, p. 97.
13 Interview with the author for 'Acoustic sounds from Africa', *Rhythms of the World*, BBC Two, broadcast 25 February 1989.
14 The concert was screened as part of the programme 'Acoustic sounds from Africa'.
15 Hélène Lee, *Rockers D'Afrique*, Éditions Albin Michel, 1988, p. 145.
16 Chris Hawkins, 'Alpha Blondy, African reggae star', *Africa Beat* 8, Summer 1988.

14. THE GREAT WEST AFRICAN ORCHESTRAS

1 Robin Denselow, 'An emotional return for Senegal's superstars', *Guardian*, 7 May 2001. Available at https://www.theguardian.com/culture/2001/may/07/artsfeatures4, accessed 1 March 2019.

2 Francis Akhalbey, 'The speech by Sekou Toure that angered colonial France to pack out of Guinea [Video]', Face 2 Face Africa, https://face2faceafrica.com/article/the-speech-by-sekou-toure-that-angered-colonial-france-to-pack-out-of-guinea-video

3 Conversation with the author, Paris, 2002.

4 Hélène Lee, *Rockers D'Afrique*, Éditions Albin Michel, 1988, p. 72.

15. ACOUSTIC MUSIC IN SENEGAL

1 Rose Skelton, 'Dedicated followers', *Songlines* 70, 2010.

16. SHARING THE STAGE

1 'Senegalese dancers go missing in US', BBC News, 13 April 2000. Available at http://news.bbc.co.uk/1/hi/world/africa/712068.stm, accessed 1 March 2019.

2 Laura Snapes, '"A Brexited flatland": Peter Gabriel hits out after Womad stars refused entry to UK', *Guardian*, 31 July 2018. Available at https://www.theguardian.com/culture/2018/jul/31/brexited-flatland-peter-gabriel-womad-stars-refused-entry-uk-visa, accessed 1 March 2019.

17. JAZZ IN AFRICA

1 Ned Sublette, *Cuba and its Music: From the First Drums to the Mambo*, Chicago Review Press, 2004, pp. 162, 165.

2 *Storyville*: *The Jazz Baroness*, BBC Four, broadcast 18 February 2012.

3 The results of this can be seen in *Retour à Gorée* (*Return to Gorée*), CAB Productions, 2007.

18. FROM EARLY RAP TO MODERN HIP-HOP

1 Speaking on 'West Africa', *The African Rock 'n' Roll Years*, BBC Four, broadcast 21 June 2005.

2 Ibid.

19. AFRICAN MUSIC ON BBC TV

1 Philip Sweeney, *The Virgin Directory of World Music*, Henry Holt & Co, 1992, p. ix.

2 Frank Tenaille, *Music is the Weapon of the Future: Fifty Years of African Popular Music*, Lawrence Hill Books, 2002, p. 229.

3 *Africa's Rock 'n' Roll Years*, BBC Two, broadcast 5 August 1995, and

The African Prom: The Gala Concert for Africa '95, BBC Two, broadcast 22 September 1995.

4   The full speech can be heard in 'Pointing the way', part of the BBC's *Tuesday Documentary* series, broadcast 6 June 1972.

5   Nasser stated this in an interview about the Suez crisis for *British Empire*, BBC One, broadcast 4 April 1972.

6   The clip in question can be seen in various places online, including Francis Perraudin, 'Bob Geldof cut off by Sky News for saying "bollocks" – twice', *Guardian*, 17 November 2014. Available at https://www.theguardian.com/media/mediamonkeyblog/2014/nov/17/bob-geldof-cut-off-by-sky-news-for-saying-bollocks-twice, accessed 1 March 2019.

7   According to Chris Stapleton and Chris May, authors of *African All Stars: The Pop Music of a Continent*, Quartet Books, 1987, p. 37, 'The people outside clubs like the Roger Club called it highlife as they did not reach the class of the couples going inside, paying high entrance tickets and wearing full evening dress including top hats if they could afford it.'

8   Interview with the author, London, July 2005.

9   Interview with Beatrice Soulé for her film *Silences*, *Rhythms of the World*, BBC Two, broadcast 7 August 1993.

10   Katharina Lobeck, 'Soul Manu', *Folk Roots* 249, March 2004, p. 40.

11   Rikki Stein, 'A giant of a man, 1938–1997', liner notes to double CD/DVD box set *The Best of Fela Kuti: Music is the Weapon*, Wrasse Records, WRASS 132, 2004.

12   Ibid.

13   *Africa: A Journey into Music*, BBC Four, broadcast May 2018.

14   Richard Gehr, 'Les Amazones d'Afrique: hear the debut LP from West African supergroup', *Rolling Stone*, 24 March 2017. Available at https://www.rollingstone.com/music/music-news/les-amazones-dafrique-hear-the-debut-lp-from-west-african-supergroup-110206/, accessed 1 March 2019.

15   Ibid.

16   *Arena: A Brother with Perfect Timing*, BBC Two, broadcast 27 February 1987.

17   Alan Cowell, 'Miriam Makeba, South African songstress, dies at 76', *New York Times*, 10 November 2008. Available at https://www.nytimes.com/2008/11/10/world/africa/10iht-obits.1.17682273.html, accessed 1 March 2019.

18   Sue Lawley, 'Hugh Masekela', *Desert Island Discs*, BBC Radio 4, broadcast 16 July 2004. Available at https://www.bbc.co.uk/programmes/p00938bc, accessed 1 March 2019.

19   'Viva Zimbabwe', *Rhythms of the World*, BBC Two, broadcast 2 March 1991.

20   Banning Eyre, 'Thomas Mapfumo, "Lion of Zimbabwe", returns from exile with triumphant homecoming', NPR, 7 May 2018. Available at https://www.npr.org/sections/therecord/2018/05/07/609046651/thomas-mapfumo-lion-of-zimbabwe-returns-from-exile-with-triumphant-homecoming?t=1552493170720, accessed 1 March 2019.

21   Philip Sweeney, 'Obituary: Franco', *The Independent*, 16 October 1989.

22   'Le chanteur Tabu Ley est mort', BBC News Afrique, 30 November 2013.

23   'Groove Zaire', *Rhythms of the World*, BBC Two, broadcast 24 February 1990.

24   'Guilty verdict for Congolese star', BBC News, 16 November 2004. Available at http://news.bbc.co.uk/1/hi/world/europe/4015473.stm, accessed 1 March 2019.

25   'Papa Wemba, Congo music star, dies after stage collapse', BBC News, 24 April 2016. Available at https://www.bbc.co.uk/news/entertainment-arts-36123214, accessed 1 March 2019.

26   Isabel de Lucena, 'A guide to fado', *Songlines* 27, November/December 2004.

27   Quoted in the sleeve notes to the DVD *Martin Scorsese présente Transes, Un film de Ahmed El Maanouni*, released 18 January 1985 and restored in 2007. Author's translation.

28   Geoff Ellis, 'The African rock 'n' roll years', *Radio Times*, 18–24 June 2005.

29   Phelim O'Neill, 'The African rock 'n' roll years', *Guardian*, 28 June 2005. Available at https://www.theguardian.com/media/2005/jun/28/tvandradio.television, accessed 1 May 2019.

30   Rupert Smith, 'The cradle will rock', *Guardian*, 3 August 2005. Available at https://www.theguardian.com/media/2005/aug/03/tvandradio.television3, accessed 1 March 2019.

CODA

1   Thomas Brooman, *My Festival Romance*, Tangent Books and Bristol Archive Records, 2017, p. 247.

2   Chris Salewicz, 'Going the extra Maal', *Independent*, 12 May 1993. Available at https://www.independent.co.uk/arts-entertainment/art-going-the-extra-maal-baaba-maal-has-cracked-the-big-entrance-on-the-live-stage-now-hes-set-on-2322381.html, accessed 1 March 2019.

3   Anita Awbi, 'Awesome Africa', *M Magazine* 57, September 2015. Available at https://www.m-magazine.co.uk/features/awesome-africa/, accessed 1 March 2019.

4   Interview with Rita Ray on *Africa: A Journey Into Music*, BBC Four, broadcast 2 June 2018.

5   Neil Spencer, *Uncut*, November 2013.

6   Ibrahim Khalil Wade, 'Mon secret', *l'Enquete*, Dakar, 9 December 2016. Author's translation.

7   Joel E. Cohen, *Asia-Pacific Review* 7/2, 2000; the issue is discussed in 'Nigeria to pass U.S. as world's 3rd most populous country by 2050, UN says', *NBC News*, 22 June 2017. Available at https://www.nbcnews.com/news/world/nigeria-pass-u-s-world-s-3rd-most-populous-country-n775371, accessed 1 March 2019.

8   Joan Tilouine, 'Le boss de l'afropop Davido, l'autre sale gosse de Lagos', *Le Monde Afrique*, 5 November 2017. Available at https://www.lemonde.fr/afrique/article/2017/11/05/le-boss-de-l-afropop-davido-l-autre-sale-gosse-de-lagos_5210487_3212.html, accessed 1 March 2019.

BIBLIOGRAPHY

Angelou, Maya, *All God's Children Need Travelling Shoes*, Virago, 1986

Arnaud, Gérald, *Youssou N'Dour: Le griot planétaire*, Éditions Demi-Lune Collection, Voix du Monde, 2008

Ba, Mariama, *Une si longue letter*, Les Nouvelles Éditions Africaines du Sénégal, 1979; Le Serpent à Plumes, 2001; *So Long a Letter*, Heinemann, 1981; Serpent's Tale, 2011

Belafonte, Harry with Michael Schnayerson, *My Song: A Memoir of Art, Race and Defiance*, Canongate, 2011

Benaiche, Marc, *Great Black Music*, Actes Sud/Cité de la Musique, 2014

Brooman, Thomas, *My Festival Romance*, Tangent Books and Bristol Archive Records, 2017

Cathcart, Jenny, *Hey You! A Portrait of Youssou N'Dour*, Fine Line Books, 1989

Cruise O'Brien, Donal, *The Mourides of Senegal: The Political and Economic Organization of an Islamic Brotherhood*, Clarendon Press, 1971

Diome, Fatou, *Le ventre de L'Atlantique*, Éditions Anne Carrière, 2003

Fox, James, *White Mischief*, Jonathan Cape, 1982; Vintage, 1998

Greer, Bonnie, *Obama Music: Some Notes from a South Sider Abroad*, Legend Press, 2009

Idowu, Mabinuori Kayode, *Fela le combattant*, Le Castor Astral, 2002

Jackson, Michael, *Moonwalk*, William Heinemann, 1998, 2009

Kapuściński, Ryszard, *The Shadow of the Sun: My African Life*, Penguin, 2001

——, *Travels with Herodotus*, Penguin, 2007

Kidjo, Angélique with Rachel Wenrick, *Spirit Rising: My Life, My Music*, Harper Design, 2014

Lahana, Michelle, *Youssou N'Dour: La voix de la Médina*, Telemaque, Patrick Robin editions, 2005

Lee, Hélène, *Rockers D'Afrique: Stars et legends du rock mandingue*, Editions Albin Michel S.A., 1988

Lessing, Doris, *Collected African Stories, Vol. 2: The Sun Between Their Feet*, Michael Joseph, 1973; Triad Panther, 1979

Leymarie, Isabelle, *Les griots wolof du Sénégal*, Maisonneuve and Larose, 1999

Makeba, Miriam and James Hall, *Makeba: My Story*, Bloomsbury Publishing, 1988

N'Dour, Youssou with Eric Chenebier, Caroline Fait, Isabelle Rozenbaum and Laurence Touitou, *Sénégal: La cuisine de ma mère*, Minerva, 2004

Samba, Papis, *Musique Sénégalaise*, Vives Voix, 2014

Sankhare, Oumar, *Youssou N'Dour: le poète*, Les Nouvelles Éditions Africaines du Sénégal, 1998

Springsteen, Bruce, *Born to Run*, Simon & Schuster, 2016

Stapleton, Chris and Chris May, *African All Stars: The Pop Music of a Continent*, Quartet Books, 1987

Sting, *Broken Music*, Simon & Schuster, 2003

Sublette, Ned, *Cuba and its Music: From the First Drums to the Mambo*, Chicago Review Press, 2004

Tolle, Ekhart, *The Power of Now: A Guide to Spiritual Enlightenment*, Hodder & Stoughton, 1999

YOUSSOU N'DOUR DISCOGRAPHY

Diongoma (Mandingo, MP122, 1983)

"*Djamil*": *inédits 84–85* (Celluloid, CEL6809, France, 1985)

Nelson Mandela (Magnetic, 2404461, France, 1985; Earthworks/
Rough Trade, ERT1009, UK, 1986; Earthworks/Rough Trade,
ET004, UK, 1986; Polydor, 831 294-2, USA, 1986)

Immigrés/Bitim Rew (Celluloid, CEL66709-1, France, 1988;
Earthworks, STEW10CD, UK, 2002)

The Lion (Virgin, V2584, UK, 1989)

Set (Virgin, V2634, UK, 1990)

Eyes Open (Columbia, 40 Acres and a Mule Musicworks, CD album,
471186 2 COL, 1992)

The Best of Youssou N'Dour (Virgin, CDV2773, UK, 1994)

The Guide (Wommatt) (Chaos/Columbia, 4765089, Europe, 1994)

Joko: From Village to Town (Sony/Columbia, 489718-2, France,
2000)

Birth of a Star: 11 Giant Dakar Hits (Manteca, MACICD025, UK,
2001)

Nothing's In Vain (Coono Du Réér) (Nonesuch, 7559-79654-2,
Europe, 2002)

Egypt (Nonesuch, 7559-79694-2, UK, 2004)

Hey You! The Best of Youssou N'Dour (Nascente, NSCD111, UK,
2005)

Rokku Mi Rokka (Nonesuch/Warner Music, 7559799745, UK,
2007)

Alsaama Day (Global Voice Syndicate, Senegal, 2007)

Dakar–Kingston (Decca/Universal, 06007 5325472 1, France,
2010)

I Bring What I Love (From the Film) (Nonesuch, 7559-79802-1, Europe, 2010)

(with the Super Etoile de Dakar) *Live Fatelliku* (Real World Records, CDRW210, UK, 2013)

Africa Rekk (Sony Music, Jive/Epic, France, 2016)

History (Naïve Records/Believe NJ7026, France, 2019)

100 CLASSIC AFRICAN TRACKS

ALGERIA

Khaled, 'Aïcha (Mixed Version)', *The Best of Khaled* (Wrasse Records, WRASS214, 2007)

Rachid Taha, 'Valencia', *Made in Medina/Olé Olé* (Wrasse Records, WRASSE150, 2003)

Souad Massi, 'Ech Edani', *Deb* (Wrasse Records, WRASSE096x, 2004)

ANGOLA

Bonga, 'Olhos Molhados', *Swinga Swinga* (Piranha, CD-PIR1040, 1996)

Waldemar Bastos, 'Sofrimento', *Pretaluz* (Luaka Bop, LBCD20, 1998)

BENIN

Angélique Kidjo, 'Agolo', *Ayé* (Island/Mango, IMCD244, 1994)

Gangbé Brass Band, 'Remember Fela', *Whendo* (World Village, 468050, 2004)

Wally Badarou, 'Hi-Life', *Echoes* (Island Records, ILPS9822, 1984)

CAMEROON

Manu Dibango, 'Soul Makossa', *Soul Makossa* (Musidisc, CO1506, 1979)

Richard Bona, 'Dina Lam' (Incantation), *Munia: The Tale* (Universal, 980 109-3, 2003)

Sam Fan Thomas, 'African Typic Collection', *The African Typic Collection* (Earthworks, EWV12, 1989)

CAPE VERDE

Cesária Évora, 'Sodade', *Miss Perfumado* (Lusafrica/BMG, 74321188212, 1992)

Lura, 'Marinhero', *Eclipse* (Lusafrica, 562222, 2009)

Tam Tam 2000, 'Ti Chérie', *Symbiose* (Syllart Records, 8227, 1987)

CONGO

Bisso Na Bisso, 'Bisso Na Bisso', *Racines* (V2 Records, VVR1005632, 2005)

Franco and Le TPOK Jazz, 'Bolingo Ya Bougie', *Francophonic, Vol. 1* (Sterns, STCDE3041-42, 2008)

Konono N°1, 'Lufuala Ndonga', *Congotronics* (Crammed Discs, CRAW27, 2004)

Papa Wemba, 'Esclave', *Molokai* (Real World Records, CDRW71, 1998)

Ray Lema, 'Af Coeur', *Nangadeef* (Mango, CIDM1000, 1989)

EGYPT

Ali Hassan Kuban, 'Bettitogor Agil', *Walk Like a Nubian* (Piranha, PIR 43-2, 1991)

Musicians of the Nile, 'Al Bahr Al Gharam Wasah' (Love is as Vast as a River), *Luxor to Isna* (Real World Records, CDRW8, 1989)

ETHOPIA

Mahmoud Ahmed, 'Ere Mela Mela', *Ere Mela Mela* (Crammed Discs, CRAMCD047, 1986)

GABON

Pierre Akendengué, 'Ntin'oba', *Owende* (Le Chant du Monde, LDX74677, 1978)

GAMBIA

Ifang Bondi, 'Mantra', *Mantra-Afro Manding Sound* (Interstate Records, LPH2366, 1983)

Juldeh Camara and Justin Adams, 'Sahara', *Tell No Lies*, (Real World Records, CDRW170, 2009)

GHANA

A. B. Crentsil, 'I Go Pay You Tomorrow', *Toronto By Night* (Wazuri Productions, WAZ101, 1985)

George Darko, 'Hi Life Time', *Hi Life Time* (Oval Records, OVLP509, 1984)

Osibisa, 'Sunshine Day', *Best of Osibisa* (Prestige Elite Records, BBCCD2009, 1990)

GUINEA

Bembeya Jazz National, 'Telegramme', *Bembeya Jazz National* (Disques Espérance, Sono Disc ESP8418, 1985)

Jali Musa Diawara, 'Fote Mogoban', *Direct From West Africa* (Oval Records, OVLP511, 1988; Go! Global, GGLP1, 1988)

Mory Kanté, 'Yé Ké Yé Ké', *Mory Kanté à Paris* (Barclay, 829690-1, 1984)

——, 'Kouma', *10 Cola Nuts* (Barclay, 837 614-1, 1986)

Sékou Bembeya Diabaté, 'Diamond Fingers', *Guitar Fö* (Discorama, WVF479016, 2004)

GUINEA-BISSAU

Manecas Costa, 'Pertu Di Bo', *Paraiso Di Gumbe* (BBCLJ3007-2, BBC Worldwide Ltd, 2003)

Zé Manel, 'African Citizen', *African Citizen* (M10 Records, 323222; Modjo Music, M659, 2003)

IVORY COAST

Alpha Blondy and the Wailers, 'Jérusalem', *Jérusalem* (Stern's Africa, Sterns1019, 1986)

Reine Pelagie, 'Biande', *Reine de Feu* (DEG Music, DM025, date unknown)

Tiken Jah Fakoly featuring Didier Awadi, 'Quitte Le Pouvoir', *Coup de Guele* (Barclay, 9823320, 2004)

KENYA

Ayub Ogada, 'Kothbiro', *En Mana Kuoyo* (Real World Records, CDRW42, 1993)

MALI

Ali Farka Touré, 'Goye Kur', *The Source* (World Circuit Records, WCD030, 1992; Hannibal Records, HNCD1375, 1992)

Bassekou Kouyaté and Ngoni Ba, 'I Speak Fula', *I Speak Fula* (Out Here Records, OH013, 2009)

Fanta Damba, 'Djadjiri', *Fanta Damba* (Celluloid, CEL6637, 1982)

Fatoumata Diawara, 'Bakonoba', *Fatou* (World Circuit Records, WCD086, 2011)

Oumou Sangaré, 'Djôrôlen', *Worotan* (World Circuit Records, WCD045, 1996)

Rokia Traoré, 'Tounka', *Tchamantché* (Nonesuch, 7559-79934-5, 2008)

Sali Sidibé, 'Djen Magni', *The Wassoulou Sound: Women of Wassoulou* (Syllart/Sterns, STCD1035)

Salif Keita, 'Mandjou', *Salif Keita Ambassadeur International* (Celluloid Tangent, CEL6721, 1984); also *The Mansa of Mali… A Retrospective* (Mango, 74321 20849 2, 1994)

——, 'Sina (Soumbouva)', *Soro* (Sterns, STCD1020, 1987)

Salif Keita and Steve Hillage, 'Chérie', *L'Enfant Lion (Bande Originale du film)* (Mango, 578 084-2, 1993)

Songhoy Blues, 'Soubour', *Music in Exile* (Transgressive Records, TRANS192, 2015)

Tinariwen, 'Aldhechen Manin', *Amassakoul* (Wrasse Records, WRASS125, 2004)

MAURITANIA

Khalifa Ould Eide and Dimi Mint Abba, 'Hassaniya Song for Dancing (Lebleyda Wigsar)', *Moorish Music from Mauritania* (World Circuit Records, WCD019, 1990)

MOROCCO

Aziz Sahmaoui and University of Gnawa, 'Inchallah', *Mazal* (World Village, WVF479099, 2014)

Malika Zarra, 'Prelude to Mossameeha', *Berber Taxi* (Motéma, MTM-60, 2011)

MOZAMBIQUE

Eyuphuro, 'Mwanuni (The Bird)', *Mama Mosambiki* (Real World Records, CDRW10, 1990)

Mariza, 'Há Uma Música do Povo', *Concerto em Lisboa* (World Connection, 0946 3 77886 22, 2006)

——, 'Quando Me Sinto Só', *Transparente* (EMI, 7243 47 76462 2, 2005)

NIGERIA

Fela Kuti, 'Lady', *Music is the Weapon: The Best of Fela Kuti* (Wrasse Records, WRASS132, 2004)

Keziah Jones, 'Rhythm is Love', *Best of Keziah Jones* (Virgin 875251, 2004)

King Sunny Ade, 'Synchro System', *Best of the Classic Years* (Shanachie, SH66034, 2003)

Tony Allen, 'Secret Agent', *Secret Agent* (World Circuit Records, WCD082, 2009)

RWANDA

Cécile Kayirebwa, 'Rubijizuko', *Rwanda* (GlobeStyle, CDORBD083, 1994)

Stromae, 'Carmen', *Racine Carrée* (Universal, 3751449, 2013)

Somi, 'Ingele', *Red Soil in My Eyes* (Harmonia Mundi/World Village, 468068, 2007)

SENEGAL

Africando All Stars featuring Thione Seck, 'Sey', *The Rough Guide to the Music of Senegal* (World Music Network, RGNET1284CD, 2013)

Baaba Maal, 'Baayo', *Baayo* (Mango, CIDM1061, 1991)

———, 'African Woman', *Firin' in Fouta* (Mango, CIDM1109, 1994)

Carlou D, 'Namenala', *Muzikr* (World Village, CD450013, 2010)

Cheikh Lô, 'Doxandeme', *Né La Thiass* (World Circuit Records, WCD046, 1996)

Coumba Gawlo, 'Djessy', *African Garden: The World of African Grooves* (Lola's World Records, CLS0000642, 2006)

Daara J Family, 'Temps Boy', *School of Life* (Wrasse Records, WRASS262, 2010)

Ismaël Lô, 'Tadieu Bone', *Tadieu Bone* (Sono Sylla, CDS7053, 2000)

Orchestra Baobab, 'Ndongoy Daara', *Specialist in All Styles* (World Circuit Records, WCD064, 2002)

Pape and Cheikh, 'Mariama', *Mariama* (Real World Records, CDRW108, 2002)

Positive Black Soul, 'Ataya', *Salaam* (Mango, CIDMX1114; Island Records, 524 185-2, 1995)

Thione Seck, 'Yeen', *Le Pouvoir d'un Coeur Pur* (Sterns Africa, STERNS1023, 1988)

Touré Kunda, 'Natalia', *Natalia* (Celluloid, CEL6740, 1985)

Xalam, 'Kaniane', *Apartheid* (Encore, ENC134C, 1986)

Youssou N'Dour, 'Immigrés', *Immigrés/Bitim Rew* (Celluloid, CEL66709-1, France, 1988; Earthworks, STEW10CD, 2002)

SIERRA LEONE

S. E. Rogie, 'Please Go Easy With Me', *The 60s Sounds of S. E. Rogie, Vol. 1* (Cooking Vinyl, COOK010, 1988)

Sierra Leone's Refugee All Stars, 'Manjalagi', *Libation* (Cumbancha, CMB-CD-30, 2014)

SOMALIA

Maryam Mursal, 'Qax (Refugee)', *The Journey* (Real World Records, CDRW70, 1998)

SOUTH AFRICA

Abdullah Ibrahim (Dollar Brand), 'Mannenberg', *Mannenberg 'Is Where It's Happening'* (The Sun, SRK786134, 1974)

Hugh Masekela, 'Grazing in the Grass', *The Best of Hugh Masekela* (Colombia-498266 2, SONY JAZZ-498266 2, 2000)

Johnny Clegg and Savuka, 'Asimbonanga', *The Best of Johnny Clegg and Savuka: In My African Dream* (EMI, 830073 2, 1994)

Lucky Dube, 'Respect', *Respect* (Gallo, CDLUCKY15, 2006)

Mahotella Queens, 'O Boshako', *Khwatha O Mone* (Hit Special, IAL4005, 1984)

Miriam Makeba, 'Pata Pata 2000', *Homeland* (Putumayo, PUTU 164-2, 2000)

Soul Brothers, 'Inhlalayenza (Usual Thing)', *Jive Explosion* (Earthworks, EWV8, 1988)

Thandiswa, 'Ntyilo Ntyilo', *Zabalaza* (Gallo, ESC6525-2, 2004)

Yvonne Chaka Chaka, 'Motherland', *Princess of Africa: The Best of* (Teal Records CDRBL190, 1992)

SUDAN

Abdel Aziz El Mubarak, 'Na-Nu Na-Nu', *The Rough Guide to the Music of Sudan* (World Music Network, RGNET 1152 CD, 2005)

Emmanuel Jal and Abdel Gadir Salim, 'Gua', *Ceasefire* (Riverboat Records/World Music Network, TUGCD1038, 2005)

TANZANIA

Bagamoyo College of Arts, 'Tanzania Yetu', 'Mateso', *Our Tanzania* (Triple Earth Records, Terra 101, 1985)

Remmy Ongala and Orchestre Super Matimila, 'Muziki Asili Yake Wapi', *Songs For The Poor Man* (Real World Records, CDRW6, 1989)

TUNISIA

Amina, 'Dis-Moi Pourquoi', *Nomad: The Best of Amina* (Mercury, 548 935-2, 2003)

UGANDA

Geoffrey Oryema, 'Land of Anaka', *Exile* (Real World Records, CDRW14, 1990)

ZIMBABWE

Machanic Manyeruke and the Puritans, 'Ndofara (I Am Happy)', *Machanic Manyeruke and the Puritans* (Cooking Vinyl, 025, 1989)

Stella Chiweshe, 'Chachimurenga', *Talking Mbira* (Piranha, CD-PIR1681, 2002)

Thomas Mapfumo and The Blacks Unlimited, 'Chigwindiri', *Corruption* (Mango, CIDM 1019, 1989)

LIST OF IMAGES

All images courtesy of the author unless otherwise stated.

INDEX

References to images are in *italics*.

Unbound is the world's first crowdfunding publisher, established in 2011.

We believe that wonderful things can happen when you clear a path for people who share a passion. That's why we've built a platform that brings together readers and authors to crowdfund books they believe in – and give fresh ideas that don't fit the traditional mould the chance they deserve.

This book is in your hands because readers made it possible. Everyone who pledged their support is listed at the front of the book and below. Join them by visiting unbound.com and supporting a book today.